Knit and Crochet Your Own Designs

Diamond Classic with Jewel skirt (page 197)

Knit and Crochet Your Own Designs

Francesca Parkinson

ARCO PUBLISHING, INC.
NEW YORK

Published by Arco Publishing, Inc.
219 Park Avenue South, New York, N.Y. 10003

Copyright © 1979 by Francesca Parkinson

Library of Congress Cataloging in Publication Data

Parkinson, Francesca.
   Knit and crochet your own designs.

   1. Knitting. 2. Crocheting. I. Title.
TT825.P37   746.4'3   76–41163
ISBN 0–668–04126–9

Printed in the United States of America

To my dear husband, ROBERT

Acknowledgments

I am grateful for the understanding and help of Susan Osberg and my son, Robert Philip Porter, in the editing of this book. For the encouragement of Mildred Mowll, Reya Dreben, Medea Cosgrave and David Sofro, I say "Thank you." Special mention to the many new friends who also encouraged me along the way.

My sincere appreciation to Margaret C. Manley, Jacqueline M. Flynn and Sandra Lee Halady for the modeling.

CREDITS

Drawing of figure for measuring: Claude Croney
Diagrams: Francesca Parkinson
Photography:
  Stitch Patterns: Charles E. Spooner, Jr.
  Director of Model Photography: Jeanne Dickson
  Model Photography: Dale Wickberg and Charles E. Spooner, Jr.
  Automobile: Courtesy of John Austin

Special thanks to the following yarn companies:

Emile Bernat & Sons Co.
Reynold's Yarns Inc.
Takhi Imports
Berga Ullman
Stanley Berroco

William Unger & Co.
Yarn Shops
Coulter Studios, Inc., New York City
Yarn Bouquet, Boston, Mass.

Preface

This book explains the utter simplicity of knitting and crocheting your own original designs. All that you have to know is how to knit and purl and how to crochet the single and double crochet.

If you can count from one to twenty, the Visual Pattern approach explained in this book will be simple to learn. You will no longer be dependent on a particular yarn, stitch, or needles. One Visual Pattern may be used for many different results. Varied yarns, combinations of yarns, and stitches create individual designs, and each design or pattern is adaptable for either knitting or crocheting.

Separate chapters describe equipment, measuring, sewing, pressing, and care of fine handmade garments.

Anything hand knitted or crocheted with proper thought and direction will last for years and always be in style. The Visual Patterns, design, stitches, and ease of construction are your guarantee of success. Good techniques, designs, and accessories plus the Visual Patterns will open the door to your most creative dreams.

Francesca Parkinson

Tupelo Hollow
North Falmouth, Massachusetts

Contents

	PREFACE	ix
1.	CREATE YOUR OWN LOOK	1
2.	EQUIPMENT	7
3.	MEASURING	10
4.	VISUAL PATTERNS	23
5.	SEWING	64
6.	PRESSING	69
7.	TENDER LOVING CARE	73
8.	TECHNIQUES	76
9.	STITCHES	97
10.	DESIGN	138
11.	ACCESSORIES	210
	INDEX OF DESIGNS	221

Knit and Crochet Your Own Designs

Rosy Glow A skirt with Delight variation (page 182)

CHAPTER ONE

Create Your Own Look

Do you become enthusiastic when you see a picture of a beautiful hand knitted or crocheted dress or coat? Do you imagine wearing it? Have you ever asked yourself, "How do I make something as elegant as that for myself? How do I go about it? What do I do?"

You may know how to knit and purl, but do you know how to make a garment that is individually yours? You may know how to single or double crochet, but do you know how to shape a skirt and a stunning sweater? Most important of all, do you know the challenge of yarns and needles?

Knitting and crocheting are for dreams and dreamers. From your first encounter with needles and yarn there is involvement and a challenge to create. There is great satisfaction in exploring colors and textures, and in knowing that you are making a sweater, dress, or coat that is going to be just "you."

Imagination is the most stimulating quality in all of us. Simply trying will open your mind to many combinations of yarns, colors, and stitch patterns.

Thinking about what you want to make is the first step toward developing your own style; style which expresses you, and how you choose to feel and look. Style is *not* which skirt length is being worn today, style is understanding one's life, one's activities, and one's desires. Style is timeless. Fashion is temporary.

The youth of today, with their love of the casual and their desire to feel free and comfortable, are picking up needles and yarn and working away to have clothes that give them ease and individuality. They use colors as if they were painting. They wear what becomes them, expressing their moods, reflecting the spirit of the times we live in. It is infectious!

The resurgence of interest in knitting and crocheting clothes is also based on their lasting qualities and the simplicity of line that makes them stand out anywhere, anytime.

My purpose in writing this book is to share my experiences with you, step by step, and to encourage you to feel the joy of creating. When I started to knit and crochet I found the instructions difficult to follow, and I would often lose my place. I started to think of my designs as shapes, just as if I were working with fabric. I would picture the shape, lay it out on paper, and calculate. As time went on, I developed the idea of doing my calculations on an actual-size pattern. This also became my method for recording my directions.

I would familiarize myself with the stitch

pattern while making my gauge sample. I would work on this until I had the stitch pattern firmly in mind and was satisfied with the evenness and uniformity of the gauge sample. I would rely on this sample for the correct gauge; the exact number of stitches to the inch. I then had all that I needed to know.

The Visual Pattern method will enable you to enjoy learning to knit or crochet while making a garment that will fit properly, that you will wear, and that you will cherish. This is made possible simply by knowing your own measurements, working your gauge sample, and being able to multiply 5 by 10! Visual Patterns are your designs drawn on brown wrapping paper using your measurements. Once you make and use your first Visual Pattern you will understand how this method will change knitting and crocheting for you. *You* will become the designer.

The designs in this book have been created with you in mind. They are adaptable to different yarns and stitch patterns, while versatility is achieved through the variety of yarns available. The most important fact to remember about any yarn is that you are going to put your time into making your design and that you will be living with it for a long time.

Knitting or crocheting your gauge sample is a must, not only to know how the yarn looks and the number of stitches to 1″ or 2″, but also to help you to make up your mind as to whether you even like the yarn. Many times a yarn that was purchased for a dress is more desirable for a sweater or coat. Each yarn has its own character, and when you are making this judgment you are doing what the best designers do. They also make a sample, look at it, and feel it. They study the color in various kinds of light, drape it, knit or crochet it in different stitch patterns and with differently sized needles. Then, and only then, do they decide how to use the yarn.

Many read about making the gauge sample and think that it is not necessary or, even worse, follow the specified gauge on the yarn wrapper (label). They immediately proceed to buy all the yarn called for and start to work without calculating or considering the elements involved. Gauge specifications on labels are based on the company's knitters. It is not *your* gauge, even though you may be using the same yarn with the same size needles. Your hands, your tension, and your expertise control the needles.

Gauge samples, knitted or crocheted, should be about 6″ to 8″ square, although I suggest wider samples for cable or lace stitch patterns. Knitting and crocheting are thoroughly detailed in the Techniques chapter. Always work with a range of needles and hooks at your side. Look closely at your work to determine if the stitches are loose, tight, or uneven. (Poor quality yarns do not work evenly as they do not have the needed elasticity.) Assuming that you have worked with a good yarn but have not achieved an even result, it is quite possible that there is a difference between your knit and purl rows. You may have to use a smaller needle on the purl rows. A way to overcome this is to make a scarf and concentrate on the tension of the yarn when purling. Your future work will benefit, and you will have a decorative and useful scarf.

Look again. Your work may be even but too loose or too tight. If it is too loose, it will look sleazy and limp. If it is too tight, it will feel hard. A simple change in needle size will remedy this. Learn to make this judgment since you are the one who has to be satisfied. Always make your decision on needle size at this stage. Experienced knitters always use smaller needles since they know that firm knitting is less apt to sag or "sit out" and will retain its shape and hang evenly.

You now know the first reason for knitting a sample: to see the result, the look, and to know if you are working with a quality yarn.

Working my gauge samples has taught me *awareness*. I have learned to pay attention to myself, to listen to the slightest doubt, and to know when I feel dissatisfied. Listen to your-

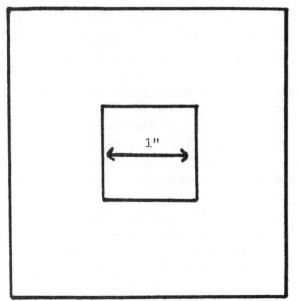

Figure 1. Be accurate! Do not take measuring lightly.

as if spun with gold; the shadings of color and the texture were exquisite. The yarn shop owner had suggested using a #15 wooden hook. I bought sizes #10 to #15. I double crocheted my sample, my fingers flying with eagerness and anticipation, until I suddenly realized that my fingers had slowed down! I looked at the sample: it was limp, the stitches were large, and the beauty of the combined yarns was gone. I ripped it out and crocheted, still using the combination of yarns. It was not until I crocheted with the #10 hook that I had the look, the feeling I was striving for.

The next reason for making a gauge sample is to determine your *own* knitting gauge. The success of your future designs depends on this. Take your square sample and mark off the center inch using common pins. (Refer to Figure 1.) Measure across with a wooden ruler. Count the exact number of stitches within the inch. Be accurate! Do not take measuring lightly! Do not ignore an extra one-eighth of an inch. Measure two inches exactly in the middle of

self and pay heed. Do not ignore your doubts. This is sensitivity. Be aware—your fingers are talking to you.

I recently worked with four strands of yarn at once. I loved the entwined colors, glistening

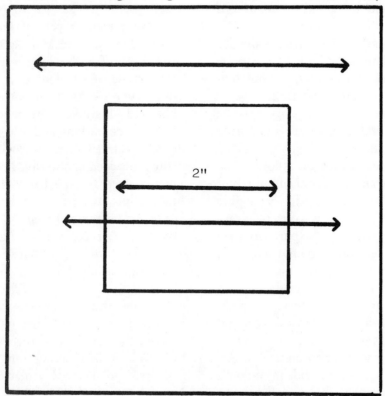

Figure 2. From the start have a notebook to record your findings.

your sample and count the stitches. The exact count is most important when working with bulky yarn or a combination of yarns, as the slightest deviation may add an inch every few inches. The full width should also be measured and counted so that you have the average for an exact count.

Note: The exact count may be within 2″, and all calculations would therefore be based on the stitches for 2″. Rule: Divide the measurement (width of your exact count) into the desired width, then multiply the answer by the exact count (gauge). For instance, if you are knitting 7 stitches to 2″ and desire a width of 14″ you would multiply 7 x 7 for the result. (Figure 2.)

The gauge sample for your design must be in the *color, yarn, stitch pattern*, and *needles* that you intend to use. Keeping this sample is a must. It will be with you for the life of your garment. You will use it to test pressing, spotting, and washing. Pin it in your notebook, along with the yarn label, and record what you made, the size needles used, and the amount of yarn purchased.

Note: Gauge samples should be made for each garment, even though you may be repeating the yarn, stitch, and needles, as your tension and work may change with time.

Measuring and recording the gauge must be done both before *and* after pressing. Pressing is done as detailed in Chapter Six.

Buying yarn is an adventure. Allow yourself time to browse and to investigate different resources. Learn to write away for catalogues or color cards, to visit factory stores or weaving shops where yarn may be purchased by the pound, or to telephone a knowledgeable yarn shop. Do not accept yarns that will not do what you desire. Fight for individuality and do not be forced into a mold through expediency. Buy a ball of this and a skein of that and learn the differences in texture. Learn to combine two or three shades for an unusual affect. Make your sample, and then decide if you wish to use it and how much yarn you will need.

Be absolutely certain that you buy more than the amount that you think you will need —ALL IN THE SAME DYE LOT. Understand the differences between the color number and the dye lot number. Pay attention to the weight and the yardage. Whether the yarn is in a skein or ball is immaterial; what counts is the yardage. This is the determining factor when deciding how much yarn to purchase. ALWAYS RESERVE EXTRA YARN. Immediately work up one ball to aid you in calculating the needed amount then add an extra ball or two. You will appreciate extra yarn when you mend a tear, repair a burn, or decide to lengthen a skirt or coat.

If you do run out of yarn and the same dye lot is not available, do not add the different lot in the middle of your work, as there will be a line of demarcation. Think out the problem. Use the different dye lot in the sleeves, collar, or ribbing, or use a contrasting color, placing stripes through the body or the sleeves. Be imaginative and turn your problem to advantage.

I once made a pair of knickers in apricot ombred yarn. After knitting them I decided to top them off with a long sweater, and had the misfortune of needing additional yarn. It was only two weeks later but the dye lot had changed. I studied the wool under various lighting conditions and was unable to distinguish between one dye lot and the other. I still proceeded cautiously. I decided to use the newer yarn for the back; the yarns blended perfectly.

Many years ago I yearned for a black cashmere scarf, three yards long, no less and no more. Even then, over ten years ago, the price was frightening. The yarn shop had many odd balls and skeins which varied in dye lot, texture, and price. As no one thought that they were of any value I made a terrific buy! I solved the problem of this random collection by sorting and laying out a plan for odd stripes. This created a black-on-black design with luxurious fringe—elegant beyond belief!

If you have the opportunity to make a good buy, do so. Apply a little ingenuity and save money. However, remember that a good buy is only a good buy if you use it and enjoy it.

The decision to use synthetic yarns versus natural-fiber yarns should be based on desirability, not availability. I use various types of yarns, depending on the result I am striving for. I find that there may be a color or texture in one and not the other. I constantly combine yarns, searching for depth and character in the blend. Yarns are my palette.

Try various colors, hues, and intensities; hold them to your face and see what they do. Allow yourself to feel their excitement, the vibrance of color and texture. Have fun with yarn and create!

Now there is nothing that will hold you back. Your fingers will fly in anticipation of wearing something that you designed and that you will be proud of.

Make your gauge sample in the *color, yarn, stitch pattern,* and *needles* you will be using; do not be lazy. Creativity does not come easily. Work, think, and do not resent having to plan or rip. The challenge is to express your latent talent. Do not neglect your gauge samples. This is when you really grow—when *you* recognize what you *want.*

Think about this: since the beginning of time, men and women have found satisfaction in working with their hands. Yarn and dreams were linked together, fingers flying, colors creating patterns like the rainbow. Knitted or crocheted clothes were worn as far back as the 4th and 5th centuries. Remnants of these garments have been found in tombs. Early paintings depict men, women, and children knitting.

You may ask, "How did the people learn to knit; who taught them?" It is thought that the Arabs, while traveling far and wide with their beautiful carpets and wall hangings, spread this craft. Picture the bazaars with colorful displays spread out before the eager eyes of people who had never seen patterns and colors so vividly executed!

Think of these people awkwardly using the single stick with the hook at the end, yarn clutched in their hands, but with determination to learn in their hearts and minds. They may not have had colorful threads, but they learned. From the lordliest to the lowest, knitting became an art and an industry.

Men and women adorned themselves; garments were a panorama, much like paintings on their backs. The purl stitch was used to create lifelike raised flowers, birds, and trees. Men studied this art and were required to create masterpieces before they were accepted into the guild. Women and children walked the lanes to market knitting away. Clothes, from that day to this, were not only to keep people warm, but also for personal expression.

English noblemen spent small fortunes for Italian silk hose, for elegantly knit suits, and hand-made objects of art. Knitting needles were intricately carved, and bejeweled silver tips were used to keep stitches from falling off the needles. These were worn dangling from heavy chain belts.

History is again repeating itself. Men and women are now crocheting and knitting as never before. Museums are exhibiting crocheted wall hangings and other hand-made objects of art. There is no limit for the creative mind. Hooks, needles, and yarns have traveled with us through the centuries. Patterns were recorded on samplers and preserved through generations.

The 16th century saw the birth of the stocking-frame, which was the forerunner of the modern knitting machine and the printing press.

The 19th century saw patterns being published in books and journals which reached more and more people.

The 20th century has seen a resurgence of interest in hand-knitting and crocheting. Its elegance is still considered the height of luxury. The difference is that this beauty is now available to anyone who desires it and wants it!

Designers from all over the world are featur-

Jewel short (page 24)

ing knitted and crocheted clothes. They are listening to the public and concentrating on giving them what they want.

Think about this: if you wish to buy a hand-knitted or crocheted coat your purchase will cost you hundreds, just as in the days of Charles II of England. Now think about how you are able to make your own clothes in the yarn, color, and style that you prefer and only have them cost a nominal amount.

The designs, ideas, and methods in this book are here for you to use. The cost of each garment is only determined by the cost of the yarns you select. Quality, style, and originality are yours.

CHAPTER TWO

Equipment

Knitting and crocheting have been favorite activities of mine since childhood. I was always thinking of designs, colors, and yarns. Through the years I collected yarn, needles, and hooks. The boxes accumulated and served as reminders for the design in mind. I would draw lines, write notes, and tuck them into my treasure chest. I guard my knitting needles and steel crochet hooks as zealously as I do my books, jewelry, and garden tools. I know that if they are lost and replaced they may not have the familiar feeling that I love.

Sculptors, artists, gardeners, knitters, and crocheters have one thing in common: tools or equipment.

Proper equipment is vital: even as a child, I knew instinctively that a bent needle would create an uneven row of stitches and that a poor point would fray my work.

I cannot emphasize strongly enough the importance of having a full assortment of sizes, lengths, and types of needles and hooks. This will prevent you from compromising and making an incorrect size do. Collect your needles and hooks carefully. Take the time to feel them, since they must be smooth. Try a few pairs in the same size; do not just buy. Feel the points, as you do not want them too sharp. Run your fingers over the wooden crochet hooks, as they should be hand-rubbed.

Take pride in your collection and designate a definite drawer or chest for it as there is nothing more frustrating than looking all over the house for a lost needle!

I am going to list my collection as this will enable you to know what you have and what you will want to buy. After this list I am going to tell you why each item is necessary.

1. Straight knitting needles, all sizes, different lengths.
2. Round needles, 16"—24"—29", all sizes.
3. Double-pointed needles, all sizes.
4. Crochet hooks, all sizes. Hooks may be aluminum, steel, plastic or wood. Steel hooks are numbered in reverse. Aluminum and plastic hooks are designated by alphabet plus the number. American and English sizing may differ. Wooden hooks range from #10 to #15.
5. Wooden ruler, 12" or 15".
6. Wooden yardstick.
7. Linen tapemeasure.
8. Scissors.
9. Emery boards.
10. Steam iron.

11. Ironing cloth.
12. Ironing board.
13. Common pins.
14. Small safety pins.
15. Mercerized cotton thread, #50, assorted colors.
16. Notebook.
17. Black fiber pens.
18. Large roll, 30″ width, brown wrapping paper. (Width is optional.)
19. Brown sealing tape.
20. Heavy brown envelope or folder.
21. Metal gauge.
22. Knitting bag or case.
23. White pillowcase.

Owning different sizes of needles is a must since it enables you to experiment in order to obtain the best result. Straight needles come in different lengths and are used accordingly. Less stitches may be cast onto a shorter or longer needle, but many stitches on a short needle will create havoc!

The 16″ round needle is used for sleeves, collars, neckbands, or turtlenecks. The 24″ round needle is for skirts, dresses, sweaters, and cardigans. The 29″ round needle is for fuller garments. Round needles are an aid in measuring and pressing (this is discussed in later chapters).

You may not use double-pointed needles often if you have the 16″ round needle, but as you become more proficient and make various stitch patterns and garments there will be a definite need for them.

Crochet hooks are a must for edgings, in addition to their use for magnificent designs.

Next in importance is your measuring equipment. A linen tapemeasure is specified because linen does *not* stretch. Do not use a metal tapemeasure.

The wooden ruler and yardstick are used when making your Visual Pattern.

Scissors should be small and fine for your knots, and heavier for cutting your Visual Patterns.

Emery boards must always be by your side to aid in avoiding snags. File hangnails or rough spots immediately and protect your work.

Your ironing board should be the proper height, thickly padded, and with a clean surface. This is a must!

Always work with an iron that you understand. Your ironing cloth must be of proper texture and flawless.

Common pins, safety pins, and mercerized cotton thread are discussed in the Sewing chapter. Always have them available.

Brown wrapping paper, sealing tape, ruler, yardstick and fiber pens are the tools for making your Visual Pattern.

Record all details in your notebook, pin gauge samples and yarn labels to a page, write the amount of yarn used, stitch patterns, and ideas. Learn to record your thoughts.

The large envelope or folder is for keeping your Visual Patterns together.

A metal gauge card has the United States Standard and millimeter sizes for sizing needles. When you are testing the size of your needle it should slip easily into the hole. If it doesn't, put it into the next larger hole. Round needles often slip off their cards, so always test the size before starting any project. Straight needles may easily get mixed up, so test them and avoid mistakes.

Take your knitting or crocheting with you wherever you go. Knitting or crocheting does not confine you, and people love to see what you are making. Allow them to admire you and your work. It inspires them! Use something lovely, something unique to carry your work. I adore baskets and vary them constantly.

The pillowcase is last, but far from least. Keep your yarn and work inside. *Do not* leave yarn exposed. If necessary, use two cases, one for extra yarn and the other for your work. Take you work out, rest the pillowcase on your lap, and you will be amazed at how this helps your vision, especially when you are

Spiced Apricot (page 192)

working on dark colors. Every stitch, every mistake will stand out.

Remember! Towel and soap. Never approach your work without washing your hands. Do not use hand lotion prior to picking up your work as it will make your needles or hook sticky, soil your yarn, and create stains. There should be no need to wash or dry clean your garment when you are finished working on it.

CHAPTER THREE

Measuring

How many times have you walked into a store, browsed, and found that the dress or pants you selected did not fit? You looked at the tag, read the size, and your first thought was, "Oh dear, no eating today or tomorrow!" How many of you have walked out of the shop in disgust? How many of you nonchalantly go through the racks, find the next size, try it on, and buy it?

Your first mistake was to have a preconceived idea about your size in relation to the garment. Garments vary in size according to manufacturer and price. A size six in a fifteen dollar dress is not the same as a size six in a two hundred dollar dress.

After going through a stage of thinking I was malformed, I finally became wiser. I tried on clothes regardless of size and only bought what fitted me.

For years women had the feeling of being misfits. The price tag on a dress was not the amount that had to be paid. The alteration bill had to be added, or hours spent at home fitting, adjusting, and sewing.

The popularity of sportswear is not surprising. Every sportswear department carries skirts, pants, sweaters, blouses, and shirts in different sizes. You can walk in and buy a shirt in your bust size and a skirt or pants in your hip or waist size and very little altering is involved.

If you sew and have bought patterns, you know that there are misses, juniors, and womens' sizes. Size ten does not have the same measurements in these different categories.

Age has nothing to do with what size we are. We must know our own measurements and then see which category we are in. Fortunately, with knitting and crocheting there are no categories, just *correct measurements*.

If you are wondering what all this has to do with knitting and crocheting, I will now tell you.

First, have you ever opened a magazine or a knitting book, looked through the pictures, decided on a sweater, skirt, or coat, read the directions for a size ten or twelve or a specified bust or hip measurement, and proceeded to knit away? You may have taken great pains to buy the yarn and needles suggested, yet when you completed your project the result was sheer disaster because it did not fit.

I have had very upset friends visit me and I have always tried to salvage something from the disaster, but so many times I have asked "Why didn't you call me before you started?

This is just like locking the barn door after the horse has been stolen!" After calming them down I look at their directions and then ask for their knitting sample. They usually look at me as if I had spoken in a foreign language or made some ridiculous request, and answer that they know how to knit. I then ask if they have measured themselves. Pandora's box has now been opened! I heard about the latest fashionable diet, how much they weigh and, of course, that they are a size six or eight!

If you read size charts, you will find that a thirty-four inch bust, twenty-six inch waist, and thirty-four inch hip are put into different sizes—anywhere from size eight to size twelve! Naturally, you know what size you are and what size bra you buy, but what happens when you buy a sweater in the same measurement? Nine times out of ten it is too tight!

Knitting or crocheting directions can only work if you know your own measurements, if your gauge is the same as that stated in the instructions, and if the directions *you* use are calculated with your measurements and your gauge.

My success in knitting and crocheting started when I learned how to measure myself, to make an adequate sample for gauge and stitch, and to plan my own directions, always considering *ease* and *drape*. I give much thought to the look that I desire—how I want the dress to fit through the bust and how tight I want the dress in the seat. This statement sums up quite a bit! There are many people who love a tight look, and that is their perogative. Decide now whether you are one of them; know your preferences.

With each design I will explain what determines its uniqueness, its look, and what measurements you will need.

The first thing I want you to do is to be true to yourself. You may have avoided measuring yourself because you may not want to know if you have gained or lost weight, but what better way is there to keep you on your toes?

This chapter has a body chart which I want you to copy in your notebook, placing your measurements on it as depicted. (Figure 3.) Note the date when you measured your body and constantly refer to it. Do not just write it down and forget about it. Measure yourself accurately, holding the tape measure *loosely*.

Stand straight but comfortably, with your shoes and proper underwear on. Remember, never wear a tight bra or girdle. You can ruin a good figure with poor undergarments. Do not create bulges. Rolls and bulges are not the sole property of heavier people, and thin women often ruin their appearance with a tight panty girdle or by wearing underwear with tight elastic or lumpy seams. If you normally wear a padded bra, wear it. Try a body stocking or a one-piece foundation: you may be treating yourself to a beautiful surprise! Help yourself, experiment.

After you have your shoes and proper undergarments on, put on a slip. This should be one piece and supple in material, for you do not want to wear anything that will detract from the beauty and flexibility of knitted clothes. Make certain that the slip is made of a static-free material because otherwise it may affect your silhouette.

Measure your bust by putting your linen tapemeasure loosely around you, high in back, under your arms, and over the fullest part of your bust. (Older women usually measure the same, front and back.)

Measure for underarm width by placing the tapemeasure high in back and around *up* over your bust, as pictured in the body diagram. Leave this tape around you, pinning it carefully together.

Use another tape to measure vertically for armhole length and length from tape to collarbone (upper shoulder neck edge). Add allowance of one-quarter to one-half inch for your shoulder seam. Measure exactly where pictured, in the body diagram.

Using the horizontal tapemeasure as a guide, measure vertically for front and back necklines, as pictured. This measurement will re-

Figure 3. Measuring your body.

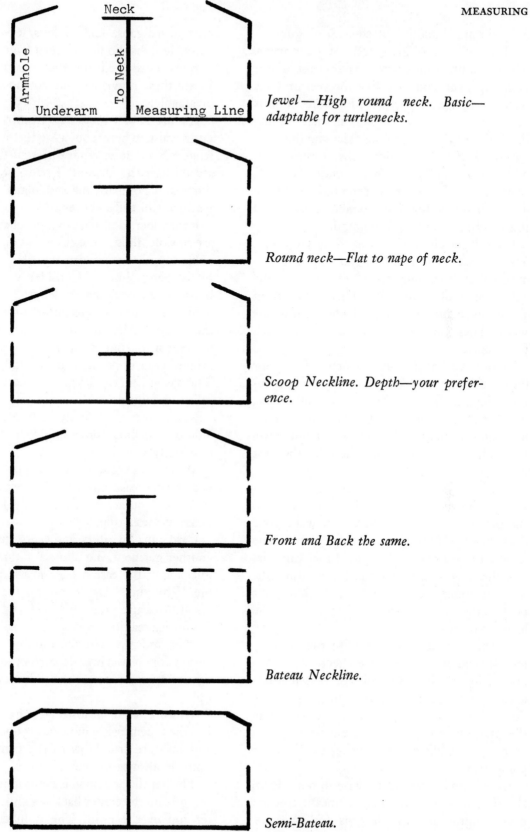

Jewel — High round neck. Basic—adaptable for turtlenecks.

Round neck—Flat to nape of neck.

Scoop Neckline. Depth—your preference.

Front and Back the same.

Bateau Neckline.

Semi-Bateau.

Figure 4. Neck Measuring.
These are also detailed in Chapter Ten.

13

quire the aid of another person. (See Figure 4.)

Measure your waist, exactly at your waist. Then measure a little below your waist, above your hips, for you may like the feel of your skirt resting there, over your hip bone. This is the measurement to consider in determining the width of the top of your skirt and the belting inside. If you use your waist measurement, which may easily be two inches less, you would be making your skirt too tight and have many an uncomfortable moment. Please read this carefully and keep it in mind.

Consult the chart when measuring your hips. You will see horizontal lines showing where to measure. Also measure from your waist to the fullest area of your hips. This varies from about seven inches to nine inches below the waist. These measurements are a must for a fitted skirt.

You have taken measurements for your bust, underarm, back-neck, front-neck, armhole, length from underarm to collarbone, waist, and hips and noted them down. Now look at the chart and look at the underarm line. This is the *horizontal* line *over* the bust line.

The length of your dress is derived by measuring from the underarm (this line) down to the place on your leg where you want your dress to hit. Various popular lengths are: ankle length (above the ankle bone), mid-calf, below the knee, and above the knee. Also, take the measurement from the center back of your neck to the length desired. Only you know the length you want.

Have someone help you with this measuring. If you wish to double-check, put on a dress you like the length of and have it measured on you. Also measure it off, *flat* on the floor, using a wooden yardstick. Measure from the armhole down. Never hesitate to use a garment you like as a measuring guide or for comparison.

At this time it would be wise to note down all of your different length measurements: dress lengths and top lengths for sweaters, vests, cardigans, and jackets long or short. These lengths should be taken from the underarm as illustrated on the measuring chart. Write these down in your notebook; they are invaluable.

A skirt is best measured from the point on your waist, where you wear it, to the desired length. Note down your different skirt lengths as you did with dresses. Try on your favorite skirts and compare measurements. Develop a wardrobe of different lengths.

Remember, knitted and crocheted clothes are flexible, fluid; they react to your body. An ankle length dress worn with boots will definitely hang shorter. Consider your shoes or boots when deciding on length.

Sleeve length is determined by you and by the design. Measure this length from your underarm to your wrist. Also measure loosely around your upper arm and around your wrist. The sleeves that I design eliminate any possibility of failure.

Remember, your body is under the dress! You are making something that should skim gracefully over it.

When you are satisfied that you have all the necessary measurements and are certain that they are accurate, you are ready for the next phase of measuring.

Cardigans, sweaters, and coats are worn over another garment. To allow for this simply by guessing at the ease needed is asking for trouble. Why guess? Dress yourself for the desired result. Measure yourself loosely while dressed. If you are making an ensemble, make the dress or skirt and top first, and use this as the foundation for measuring. Be certain to note these figures on a separate chart—do not mix them up.

Measure your headsize for hats or berets. Pin the tapemeasure in place around your head and measure from this to the center top for your depth measurement.

The depth for a hood is determined by measuring from the center back neckline to the center top of the head. The number of inches added to this measurement controls the length. The width for a hood is measured from the sides of the head around the widest part of the head (ear to ear), with sufficient ease added.

Measure your hands at the wrist, palm, and length of fingers for making gloves and mittens. Measure your ankle, calf, and length to the knee for socks.

Body measurements must be taken periodically. This is a must, because although we may weigh the same our bodies change. I weigh exactly the same as I did twenty years ago but I do not have the same figure; weight shifts. Each age has its attractiveness, its beauty, its compensations.

If you feel that you are too large for knitted clothes you are wrong; all of the designs in this book are utterly simple and flattering to everyone—young, middle-aged, or older. There is not a person in this world who cannot wear knits and crochets if they understand the secrets of proper undergarments and fit, know where the clothes should touch the body, and use proper construction and design.

Posture, carriage, and demeanor are vitally important. Who is attractive? Is it perfection of face and figure? Rarely! Beauty is often an illusion. Create it for yourself. Hold your head high, take pride, think beauty. Allow the design that you have created to express you.

Measuring your Work

Never use your tapemeasure. Always use your ruler or yardstick. Consult your Visual Pattern. Always keep your work *flat*, and do *not* stretch or pull on it. Your knitting or crocheting should measure exactly as specified; *do not skimp*. Do not expect pressing to release it more than one inch. Your work should be exact. Strive for this. There is no mystery to good fit: it depends on accurate measurements, both of yourself and of your work, and sufficient ease.

You will be able to achieve accuracy when measuring by referring to your Visual Pattern constantly, since each design specifies where to place your pins and where to measure your garment. Your body measurements are the foundation on which you base your Visual Pattern and your Visual Pattern becomes the foundation for making your design and measuring. This is detailed in the next chapter.

Figures 5, 6 and 7 show you where to measure your work and the importance of proper measuring.

When you are knitting, measure from where you start with a ruler in order to determine hem or border depth. The use of your wooden ruler also applies to crocheting. Your Visual Pattern details the placement of pins to aid you in future measuring. As your work progresses, refer to your Visual Pattern and measure your gauge at the designated point, and the complete width, as there may be a slight difference in your stitch count. This rule is most important, especially when working on round needles as there is a difference between knitting on straight needles with a small number of stitches and knitting on round needles with the full number. Also, the change from Stockinette Stitch to plain knitting can affect the measurement as there will be a definite difference if the tension of your knitting and purling are not the same.

Using a yardstick, measure as shown on the Visual Pattern, always in the center of your work and never along the edge. Remember to always have your work flat, and to use your yardstick and your Visual Pattern.

Your Visual Pattern shows you where to try your work on. You can never do this too much. This is done by knitting half-way around and then adding another round needle of the same size, and knitting the remaining stitches. This allows you to drop the garment over your body and see exactly how it fits. If any adjustments are needed place them as detailed on your Visual Pattern.

Garments with seams may be tried on and fitted accurately by using two round needles and pinning the sides together.

Re-check the length at this time. Place a pin

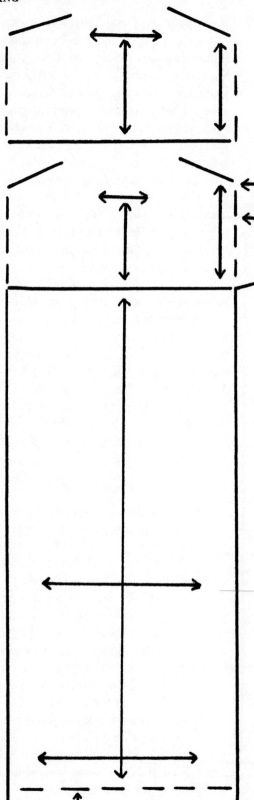

Figure 5. Measuring your work. Arrows designate direction and place.

on the last row of work and measure for the additional length that is needed. Write this down, work accurately, and do not skimp, stretch, or pull!

Each design has details for accurate measuring. These principles should be applied when making similar garments.

Never measure an armhole around the edge or curve. Your Visual Pattern shows you exactly where to measure: in from the outer edge at least two inches and straight up to the shoulder line, as illustrated. This measurement is taken from the underarm line. Do not skimp! Allow at least one-half inch for shoulder seams, and allow for ease in the armhole.

The underarm line is also the measuring point for the front and back necklines. When measuring your work, first place pins on this line of your garment to help maintain accuracy in measuring. Center the pins, front and back, and at each armhole. (Armhole pins in at least 2″ from the edge.) Avoid any errors.

The neckline of your garment should be completed before you make sleeves, as the neckline finish affects the shoulder line and armhole, which then affect the length of the sleeve. The garment must be tried on for accurate measuring.

Sleeves should be measured *flat* and down

the center, never along the edge. Try your sleeve on more than once. Judge the additional length needed, mark with a pin, and measure. Be accurate.

Necklines, hems, and ribbing edges should be measured with a ruler. If the work is double, allow for turning.

Ease is the essential in design. Allow ease for fit and comfort. Each design will tell you how much ease should be added to your body measurements when drawing your Visual Pattern. Ease allowance is the secret of good design. You should be just as comfortable in your knits or crochets as you are in your favorite pair of blue jeans! Knitted or crocheted clothes blend with the body, and quality yarns have a resilience that nothing else equals. Your ease is built in.

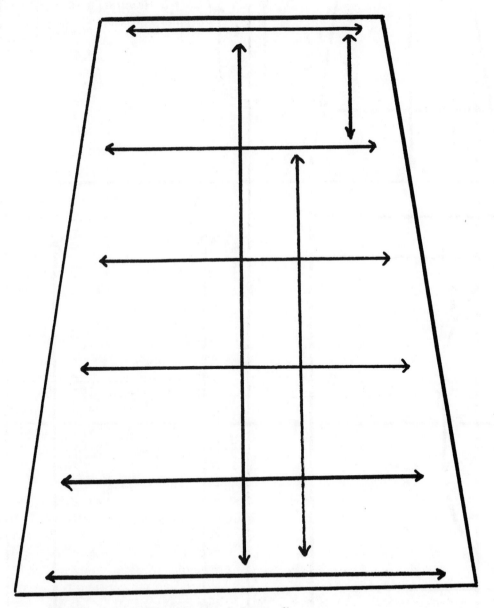

Figure 6. Measuring a Skirt. Arrows designate direction and place.

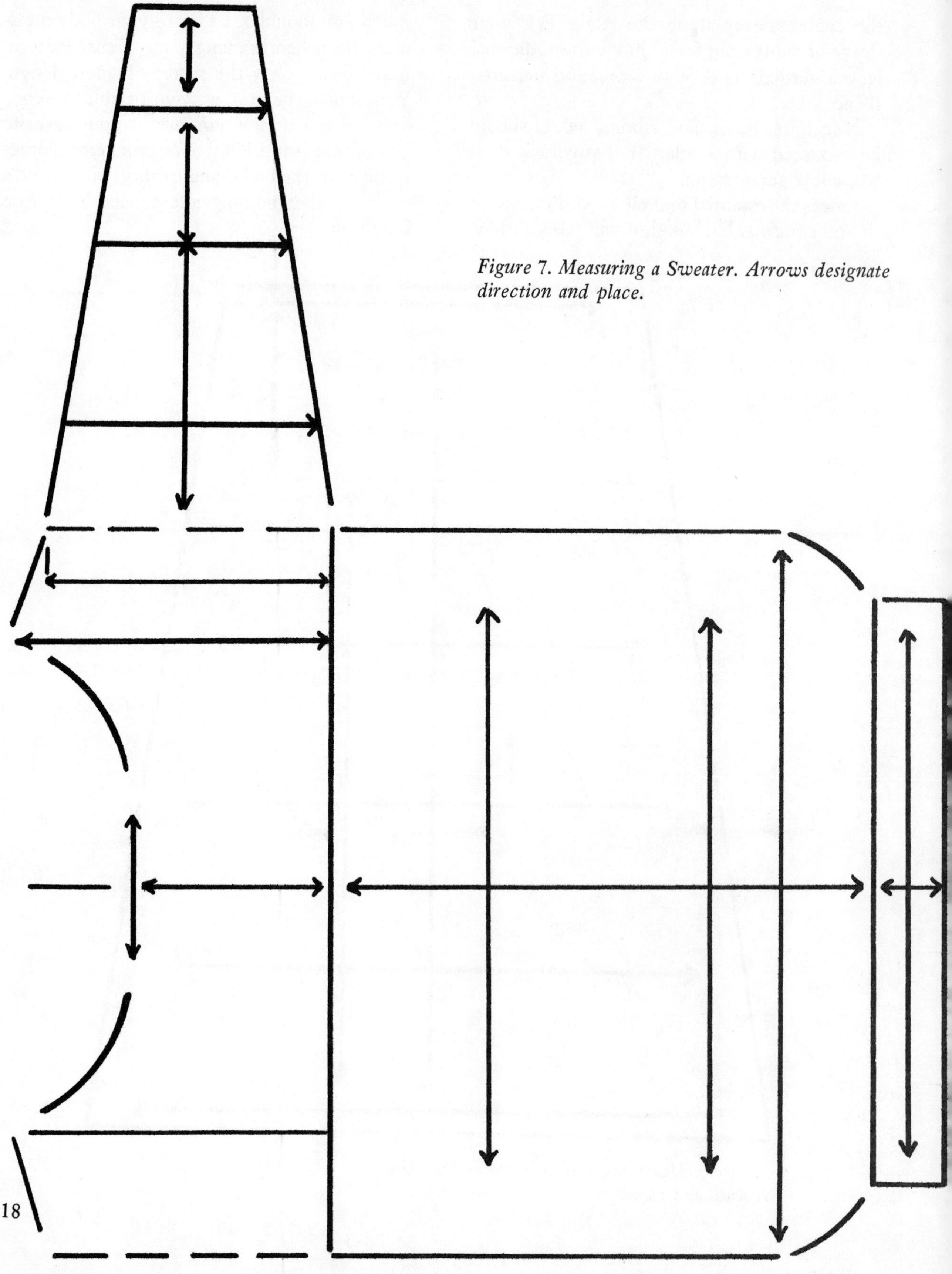

Figure 7. Measuring a Sweater. Arrows designate
direction and place.

Hot Chocolate Sweater (page 169)

*Tiger Eye Skirt, a variation of Cape Cod Minx
    (page 192)*

Amethyst Tweed (page 200)

Amethyst Delight Sweater (page 203)

Amethyst Delight Sweater (page 203)

Amethyst Short Pants (page 203)

Tiger Eye Skirt, a variation of Cape Cod Minx (page 192)

Tiger Eye Jewel Sweater with scooped neckline and puffed sleeves (page 192)

Jewel long (page 24)

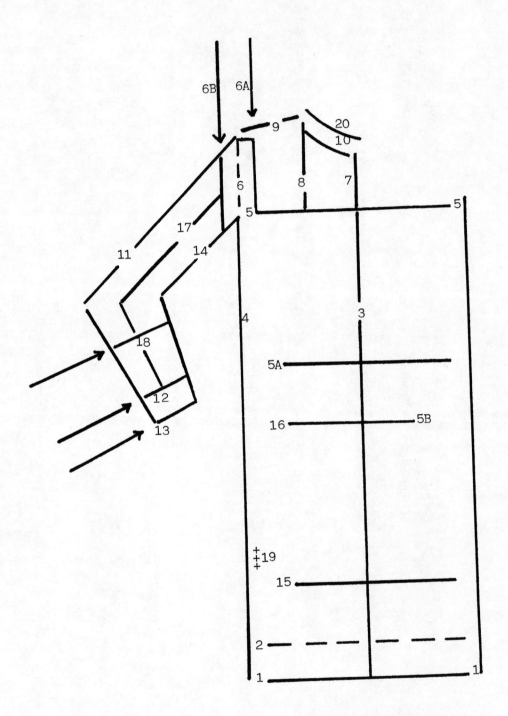

Figure 8. Visual Pattern Key.

VISUAL PATTERN KEY

1. Beginning Hem or Border.
2. End of Hem or Border—change needles.
2A. Bust Measurement plus Ease.
2B. Horizontal line pointing to lines 4 for joinings.
3. Measuring—Center line from Hem to Underarm.
3A. Measuring—Center line.
4. Side Folds or Seams.
5. Underarm—Horizontal line. Measuring point for Armhole, Upper Front, Upper Back Necklines.
5A. Waistline.
5B. Hipline.
5C. Mid-hipline.
6. Armhole line plus seam allowance.
6A. Armhole measuring line plus seam allowance.
6B. Upper Arm measuring line.
7. Length from Underarm to Neckline —Front or Back.
7A. Neckline measuring line.
8. Length from Underarm to Upper Shoulder at neck edge.
9. Shoulder line—binding off.
10. Basic Neck edge—picking-up stitches.
11. Sleeve Center Fold—Measuring line for complete length.
12. Wrist Width—changing needles.
12A. Hem edge of Sleeve.
13. Finished Wrist Width and Length— binding off.
14. Sleeve Seam—open seam and shaping.
15. Horizontal Measuring Line—check gauge.
16. Horizontal Measuring Line—reminder to TRY ON.
17. Measuring Line—center of sleeve— length.
18. Measuring Line—Try Sleeve on—decrease to wrist.
19. + + + + Denotes where to add increases or decreases.
20. Neckline finishing.

ABBREVIATIONS AND SYMBOLS— VISUAL PATTERNS

Arm	Armhole	M	Measure
AH	Additional Hem Allowance	MG	Measure Gauge
Beg	Beginning	PP	Place Pin
Bdy	Body	Pat	Pattern
BG	Body Gauge	S	Sleeve
BM	Bust Measurement	T	Tie Another Strand In
BNk	Back-neck	Try	Try On
Bs	Backstitch	VP	Visual Pattern
Ct	Count Stitches	Z	Zipper
Cont	Continue		
Ctr	Center		*Symbols*
E	Ease	x	Decrease
FNk	Front-neck	+	Increase
G	Gauge	*	Repeat
H	Hem		
HM	Hip Measurement		

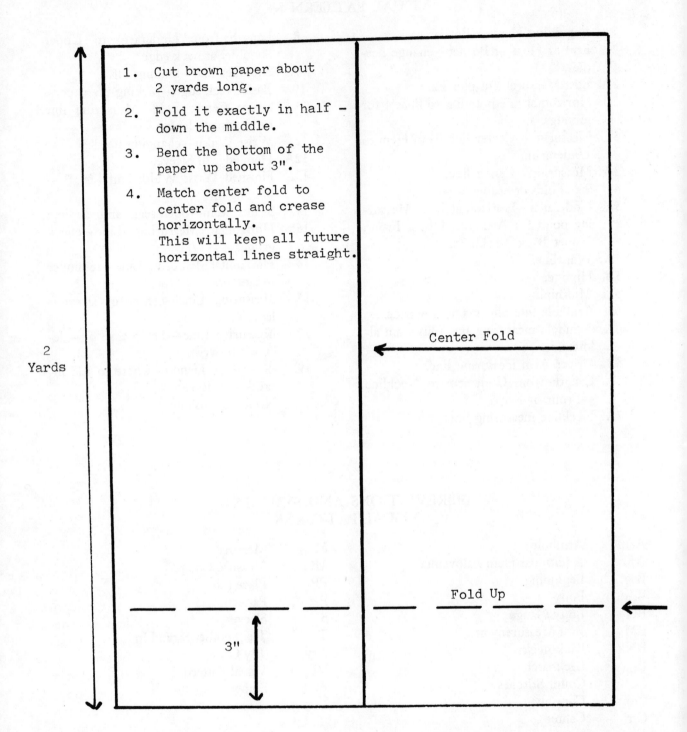

Figure 9. Preparation of paper for Visual Pattern.

CHAPTER FOUR

Visual Patterns

Wouldn't it be wonderful if you could walk into a store, browse through a catalogue and find that special pattern for the suit, dress, or sweater that you would like to knit or crochet—in *your proportions*. This pattern would suggest the yarns that you could use, what colors you would consider combining, stitch patterns, and show exactly where to make adjustments if there is the slightest variation in measurements. Suggestions would be made so that you could wear your outfit in many different ways, day or night.

Close your eyes and imagine that you are in a store. Now picture an envelope, look inside, and take out the paper dress, the pattern. Perhaps it looks like one you used when sewing with fabric, but this one is marked with knitting or crocheting instructions. This is your Visual Pattern.

Pattern making is not the difficult art that many people think it is. Think of yourself as a paper doll and that you are making a paper dress.

Designers make patterns: paper patterns and muslin patterns. They know that it is impossible to produce a garment that fits properly without a pattern. This has been standard practice since the early days of couture.

Women would industriously knit or crochet in their little cottages in the country, or deep in the hills, for exclusive couture houses. They worked with utter confidence because their muslin patterns were their guides. Thus the "cottage industry" was born. This method of producing finely made hand-knitted or crocheted clothes continues to this day.

You will accomplish the identical results by making *your* pattern, in your *measurements*, for the designs in this book. How you could be expected to knit or crochet, sew, and press a perfect design, without any of this help is a complete mystery to me!

These patterns are your key to adventure, since by making the basic patterns you will gradually see the other designs emerge. Glance through the patterns and pictures of my designs. You will notice that they are in sequence: the basic set, variations of the basic set, and then various outfits. Look at Midnight Jewel. This pattern has lines creating the shape of the finished dress (Figure 11). Within this shape there are lines designating where to measure (Figure 10) and written instructions placed as you will use them (Figures 15, 16, and 17).

Many of you start to read written instructions in books, magazines and leaflets, try to comprehend them, get frustrated, and become completely discouraged.

Visual Patterns are designed to help you to knit or crochet with minimum strain. They show you exactly where to measure, where to increase or decrease, and anything else pertaining to the garment. *You will never lose your place.*

Visual Patterns constantly remind you of the exact size of your finished garment. Constant comparison is available at your fingertips, simply by placing your work against your pattern.

DRAWING YOUR VISUAL PATTERN

You will need a roll of 30″ brown wrapping paper, a package of brown sealing tape (optional: Scotch tape), yardstick, ruler, black fiber pen, and scissors.

Allow yourself plenty of room; preferably on the floor. Roll out the paper and open the book to Figure 11, Midnight Jewel, the basic dress pattern. You are going to enlarge it to actual size, *your* size, by drawing lines in your dimensions, plus ease, as numbered. Do not worry about perfection in drawing. Your yardstick will do most of the work.

Roll out about two yards of your brown paper and cut. Refer to Figure 9. Fold your paper evenly in half lengthwise, and then open it flat. This center fold is the middle of your pattern. Bend the bottom of your paper up about 3″. Match center fold to center fold and crease horizontally. This is to aid you in keeping all future horizontal lines straight. Try this on a small piece of paper. You will be amazed at how easy and accurate it is. Open your paper flat.

Look at Figure 11, Midnight Jewel, from the *bottom up*. You are going to use your measurements, follow the number sequence, and draw your pattern.

Measurements Needed: Refer to Figure 10. Remember, all measurements are to be taken

loosely. Allow for ease through the body and sleeves. This allowance is optional.

VISUAL PATTERN FOR MIDNIGHT JEWEL

Line 1. Starting 3″ from the bottom, draw a horizontal line, using the *center crease* as the middle of your pattern. This line measures *one-half* of your hip or bust measurement (use the larger dimension) plus 1″ ease. For instance, 36″ hip plus 1″ for ease equals 37″. Dividing this in half equals 18½″. Your pattern is a flat view of exactly one-half of the dress. This pattern has an allowance of 1″ for ease. For larger sizes, ease may be 2″ or more. (Figures 11 and 12.)

As you draw, *number* your lines. Line 1 is the beginning of your dress.

Line 2. The second line is drawn dashed, two inches over the first line. It is the same width.

Line 3. You are going to draw a vertical line, using the center crease and starting from line 2, of the length to your underarm. Refer to your measurements, as this length is determined by your desire.

Note: Midnight Jewel is designed ankle-length. This is my preference as it is so adaptable. It becomes slightly shorter when worn with boots, mid-calf if worn with a belt, and if you wish you may make it shorter by blousing it fully over your belt. Knitting or crocheting Midnight Jewel shorter does not diminish its beauty.

Lines. 4. At each end of line 1 you will draw vertical lines the same length as line 3, plus the 2″ hem allowance. Refer to Figure 12.

Line 5. Draw a horizontal line from line 4, across the top of line 3, to line 4. This line is the same width as line 1. Refer to Figure 11.

Line 6. Using your armhole measurement plus ease and seam allowance (for shoulder seams), draw dashed lines at each side above lines 4. Seam allowance should be a minimum of ½″.

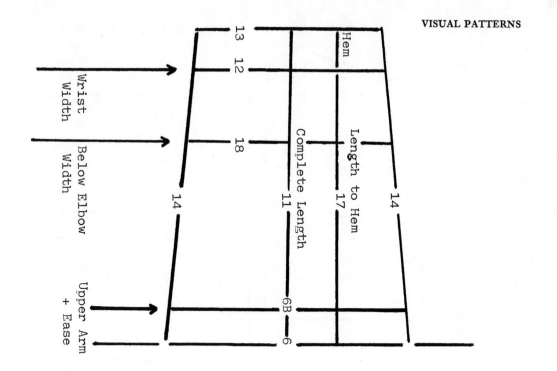

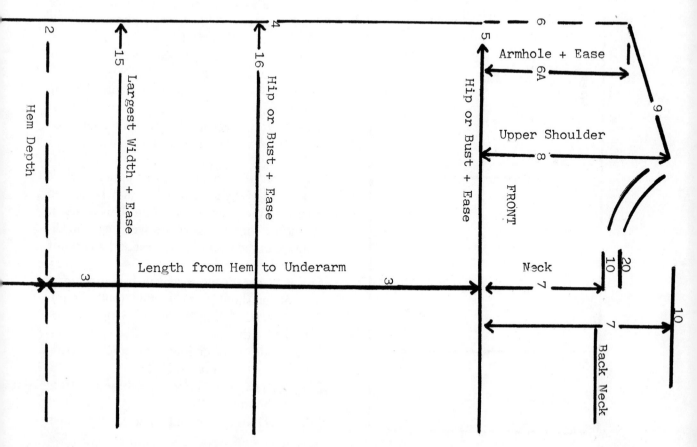

Figure 10. Body Measurements needed for Mid-night Jewel.

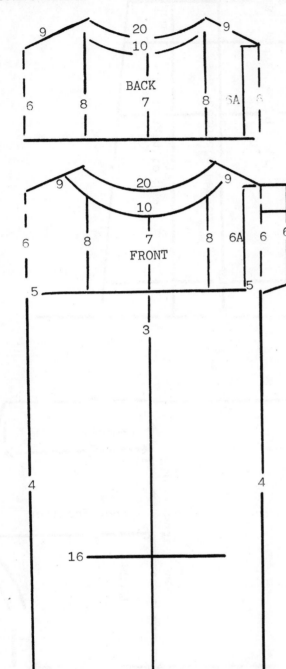

Figure 11. Midnight Jewel Visual Pattern plan. Lines are drawn in number sequence from the bottom up.

Line 6A. Draw a vertical line, the same length as line 6, 2″ in from the right of line 6.

Line 7. Refer to your measurements for the length from the underarm to front center neckline. Draw a vertical line directly above line 3. Draw a 3″ horizontal line over line 7 as shown in Figure 13.

Line 7B. Make a separate pattern for the upper back section as there is a difference in the length of line 7: the measurement from the underarm to the center back neckline is used. Draw a vertical line directly above line 3. Draw a 5″ horizontal line at the end of line 7B.

Note: A pattern for the upper back is optional as the back neckline may be shaped exactly the same as the front. This makes it possible for you to rotate wearings and diminishes the strain on the seat and elbows of your dress.

Line 8. Using the measurement from underarm to upper shoulder neck-edge (collarbone), draw vertical lines from line 5 up, in one-fourth of the total width between lines 6, on each side, thus dividing the upper section into quarters. Refer to Figure 13.

Line 9. Draw slanted lines across the top from lines 6 to lines 8.

Line 10. Draw curved lines and x's from each

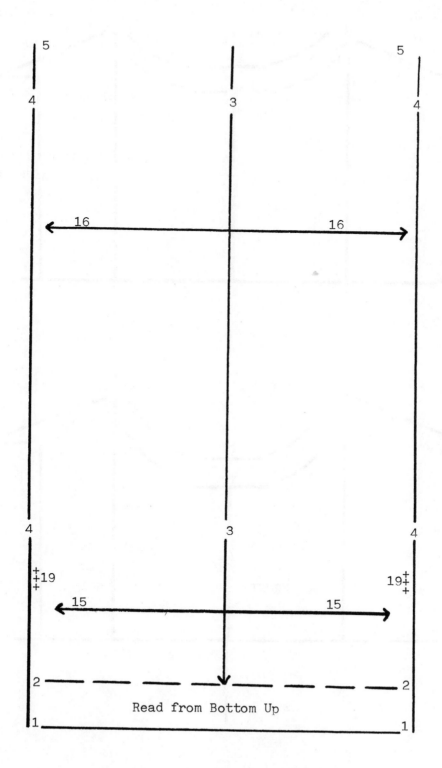

Figure 12. Partial view of Midnight Jewel.

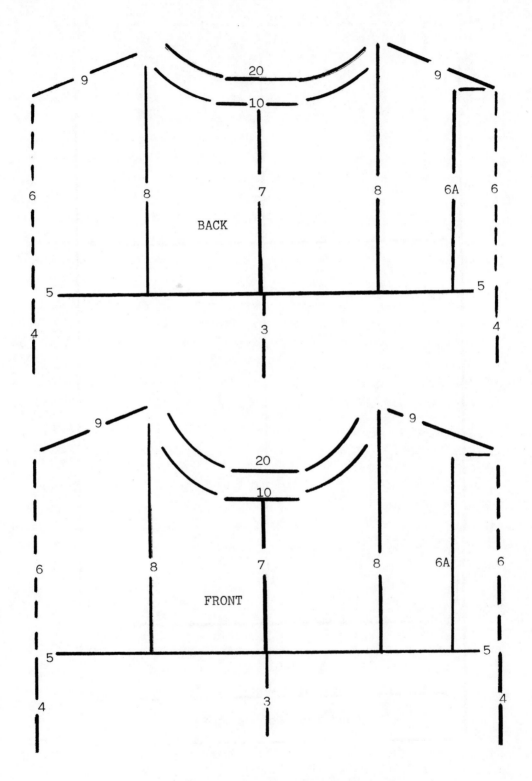

Figure 13. Upper sections of Midnight Jewel.

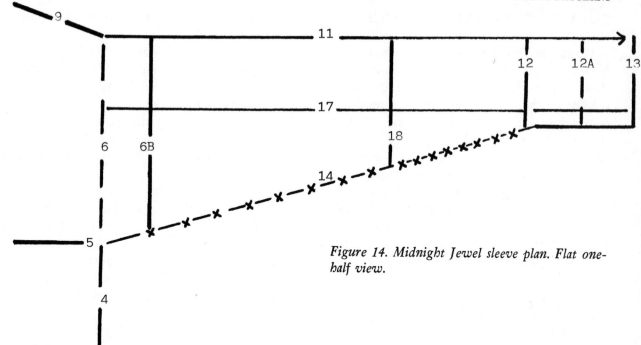

Figure 14. Midnight Jewel sleeve plan. Flat one-half view.

end of the horizontal line on line 7 to the top of lines 8. Do not worry about your drawing; it will improve with time. The shape of the dress is what counts! Look at Figure 11, look at your pattern, isn't it great! All that you have to do now is prepare your pattern for drawing the sleeves. It is now necessary to add pieces of brown paper approximately where the sleeves will be drawn. Fasten this additional paper to your pattern with tape.

Line 11. Refer to Figure 14. The length of line 11 is from the underarm to the wrist, plus 2″ for a hem. Draw a horizontal line from line 6 where it meets line 9. The diagram and pattern represent a one-half view. Continue to number your lines; this will help you when writing in your instructions.

Line 12. Draw a vertical line, using one-half the wrist measurement, 4″ from the lower end of line 11.

Line 12A. Draw a vertical line, the same length, 2″ to the right of line 12. Use dashes.

Line 13. This line is the same length as lines 12 and 12A. It is drawn at the end of line 11.

Line 14. Draw a slanted line and x's from line

5 (at meeting point of lines 4 and 6) to line 12. Continue in a straight line to line 13. Refer to Figure 14.

Line 15. Draw a horizontal line 3″ above line 2.

Line 16. Refer to your measurements for the length from hem to 9″ below your hips. Place a horizontal line at this point on your pattern.

Line 17. Draw a line down the center of your sleeve pattern. Refer to Figure 14.

Line 18. Refer to Figure 14 and draw a vertical line 10″ from line 6.

Line 6B. Refer to Figure 14 and draw a vertical line 2″ from line 6.

Line 19. Refer to Figure 15. + + + + + Denotes increases and shows placement. Mark above line 15. The same principle would apply for decreasing.

Line 20. Follow the curve of the neckline (line 10), 2″ above line 10.

The basic pattern that you have made is going to make each successive pattern easier for you. The same numbers will be used to define lines on different designs wherever possible.

29

VISUAL PATTERN DETAILS

Write the following instructions onto your Visual Pattern. Place them *within the pattern.* Prominently place your gauge, needle sizes, pattern stitch, and the type of yarn used for future reference. Abbreviations are used on diagrams; refer to Visual Pattern Key.

Line 1. Cast on hip measurement or bust measurement, *using the larger measurement*, plus 1″ ease X gauge on 24″ round needle, one size smaller than gauge needle. Join. Knit 2″. (Ease allowance is optional.) (Figure 15.)

Line 2. Change to 24″ round gauge needle. Measure. Place Pins (use PP) on lines 4 and line 3 where it meets line 2.

Line 3. Measure.

Line 4. By Count Divide Stitches in half. PP on each side.

　Important Note: This represents the side folds (no seams) of your dress. Place all joinings of yarn at the side folds.

Below Line 5. By Count Divide Stitches in Half. PP at lines 4, 6, 6A and 3. T on line 5, left side (where lines 4 and 5 meet). Refer to Figure 16, Front Upper Section.

Above Line 5. STOCKINETTE STITCH. Work front and back separately. Work front and back at the same time. (Method is detailed in Section Three.)

Line 6. Pick up stitches front and back plus ease and seam allowance X gauge on 16″ round gauge needle. Purl a row, knit a row. (Detailed in Section Three.)

Line 6A. Measure.

Line 6B. Measure.

Line 7 at line 10, Front. Bind off 3″. T on right of horizontal line. Make arrows at each side of horizontal line, refer to Figure 16. Count stitches. Divide evenly.

Line 7B at Line 10, Back. Bind off. Refer to Figure 16.

　A. Count total stitches on the back needle.

　B. Count stitches on front sides.

　C. Subtract B from A. Remainder is the number of stitches to bind off from the center back.

T right corner of horizontal line 7.

　Note: The front and back may be made the same. Refer to your Visual Pattern.

Line 8 at line 9. Fasten or End.

Line 9. Bind off 1″ at the beginning of each row, front and back, armhole side. Sew shoulders together on the wrong side. Refer to Sewing Chapter.

Line 10. Decrease every other row, each side of neck edge. Pick up stitches on 16″ round needle, two sizes smaller than gauge needle. Knit 2″.

Line 11. Measure. Refer to Figure 17.

Line 12. Change needles, two sizes smaller than gauge needles. Knit a row, purl a row for 4″.

Line 12A. Measure.

Line 13. Measure. Bind off. Sew. 2″ hem.

Line 14. Decrease at beginning and end of a row as calculated. Sew seam.

Line 15. Measure for Width and Gauge.

Line 16. TRY ON. LAY WORK AGAINST VISUAL PATTERN.

Line 17. Measure.

Line 18 to line 12. Decrease more often.

Line 19. Measure. Increases or decreases one inch apart; refer to gauge.

Line 20. Bind off. Sew. 1″ Hem.

Review: Make certain that each number and instruction is written on your pattern. Look at your pattern and compare it to Figures 15, 16, and 17. Re-check the instructions and your work will then go smoothly.

Carefully cut your pattern along the outer lines. Use this pattern *constantly.* Lay your work against it and only measure on a flat surface, not on your lap.

I have used numbers, step by step, to guide you to draw the lines for *your pattern* with *your measurements.* The numbers were next used to designate the *instructions* that you were to write on your pattern exactly where needed. Your Visual Pattern Key will now be used to detail the *reasons* and *techniques.*

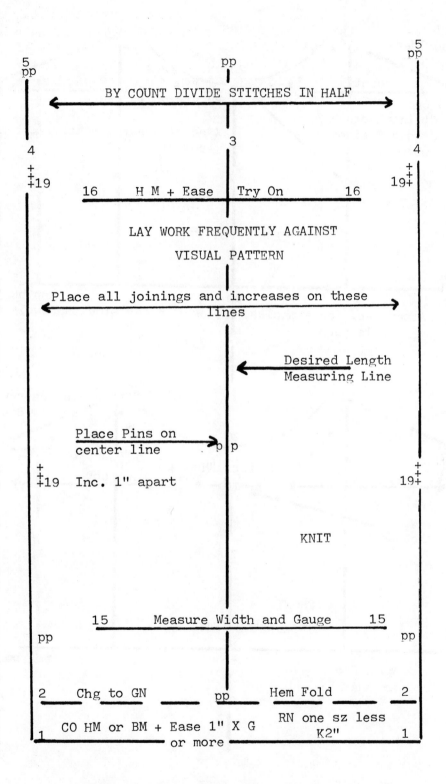

Figure 15. Partial view of Midnight Jewel. Read from the bottom.

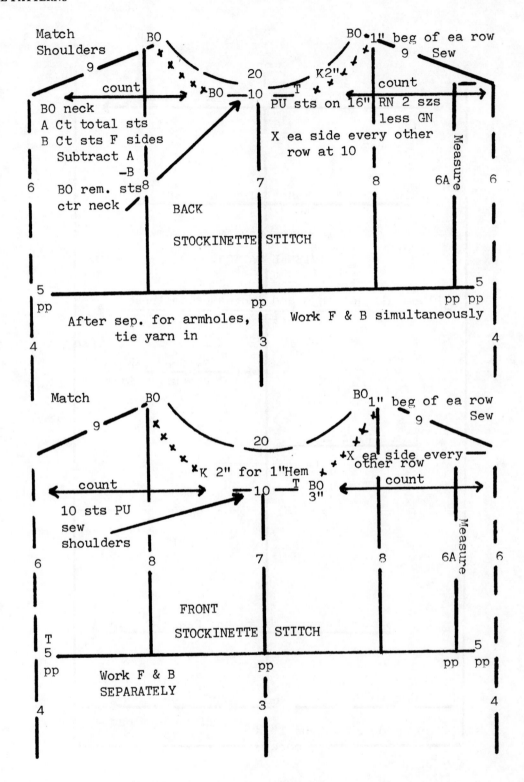

Match
Shoulders
9

BO

count

BO neck
A Ct total sts
B Ct sts F sides
Subtract A
    —B
BO rem. sts
ctr neck

BO
20
BO — 10

BO — 1" beg of ea row
        9   Sew

K 2"
T

count

PU sts on 16" RN 2 szs
                less GN

X ea side every other
  row at 10

6   8   7   8   6A   Measure   6

BACK

STOCKINETTE STITCH

5
pp

pp

pp pp
5

After sep. for armholes,   Work F & B simultaneously
    tie yarn in

4   3   4

Match
9

BO
20

BO — 1" beg of ea row
            Sew
         9

10 sts PU
sew
shoulders

K 2" for 1"Hem
        T BO
           3"

X ea side every
  other row

10

count

6   8   7   8   6A   Measure   6

FRONT

STOCKINETTE STITCH

T
5
pp

Work F & B
SEPARATELY

pp

pp pp
5

4   3   4

Figure 16. Upper sections of Midnight Jewel Visual Pattern.

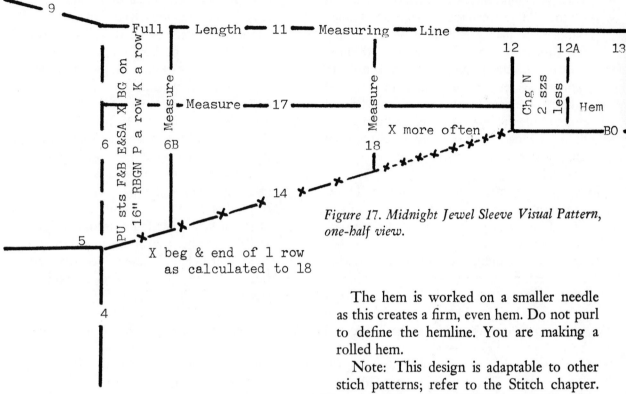

Figure 17. *Midnight Jewel Sleeve Visual Pattern, one-half view.*

REASONS AND TECHNIQUES

Line 1. This is the beginning of your dress. You are the designer, and are considering how you desire your dress to fit: the length and the ease. Ease may range from 1″ to 3″, depending on your size. If you desire a very loose dress, add to the ease allowance. Re-examine your gauge sample. It must be in the yarn, color, stitch pattern, and needles that you intend to use. Write down the stitch count for 1″, 2″, and the complete width. Figure out the exact average, whether for 1″ or 2″. For instance, if you have a 6″ sample and 30 stitches on the needle, you know that you average 5 stitches to the inch. If your larger measurement is 38″ plus 1″ ease, equaling 39″, you will multiply 39 by 5 = 195, thus deriving the number of stitches to cast on. Join your stitches and knit. This design is made straight up to the armholes.

The hem is worked on a smaller needle as this creates a firm, even hem. Do not purl to define the hemline. You are making a rolled hem.

Note: This design is adaptable to other stich patterns; refer to the Stitch chapter.

Line 2. After a good 2″, bend the hem under and measure with a wooden ruler. Change to gauge size needle. Work an additional 2″ and then place pins as detailed on your Visual Pattern.

Line 3. Place pins, horizontally, in the exact center of the front and back. These will aid you in counting and measuring.

Lines 4. Place pins vertically after counting your stitches and dividing them evenly in half, to denote your side folds. (No seams.) Pins will be successively moved up as you work. All increases, decreases, and joinings of yarn should be placed on lines 4. Your pins are a constant reminder. Be certain to work around them carefully. Do not split your yarn or make loose stitches. If necessary, remove the pin, work your stitches, and then replace the pin.

Line 15. This line on your pattern reminds you to measure width and gauge. This measuring determines the success of your design. There may be a slight difference between your work and the desired width. (There is often a difference in the gauge count. Gauge samples are made on straight needles, using the Stockinette Stitch, and you are now knitting in the round.) This is simple to remedy. Refer to your Visual Pattern and your gauge, and determine the additional number of stitches needed. Place them as detailed at Line 19. Allow a few rows between increases or decreases so that the change is gradual.

Line 16. TRY ON! Refer to Chapter Three. Hold the dress in place and study how it fits. If more or fewer stitches are needed, refer to your gauge and line 19.

Line 5. Underarm line. Re-count your stitches and check for correct placement of pins on the side folds (lines 4) and the center front and back (line 3). The pins are your aid in knowing where to separate the front and back for the armholes, measuring for the armhole depth (line 6A), and measuring for the necklines. Try your dress on and make certain that you have your desired length before separating for the upper sections.

T is placed on your pattern to indicate where to tie another strand of yarn in. This enables you to continue working both front and back at the same time. After tying in the second ball, knit across the back half, and then purl back to pin, pick up the first strand and purl the front section; Stockinette Stitch from now on. You now have separated your front and back.

At this point you may be thinking, "What is the matter with her, I have been working on the back and front at the same time all along!" You are correct, but from now on you have two separate halves created by your armholes. The two halves will be absolutely uniform if you work them at the same time.

Look again at line 5. A pin should be placed 2″ in from the right armhole. This will aid you in measuring; remember to refer to your Visual Pattern. Try your dress on,

after measuring, and allow for the shoulder seam before starting to bind off.

Line 5 AGAIN! This row is the measuring point for your necklines. Observe your pattern, and be aware that they start before the shaping of the shoulders.

Line 7. FRONT. You have a line 3″ wide. This represents the center 3″ to be bound off. Each side must have an even number of remaining stitches. Multiply body gauge x 3 to determine the number of stitches to bind off. For instance, if your gauge is 5 stitches to 1″, then 5 by 3 = 15. Add up the number of stitches on your front needle, deduct the 15 (the number you found), and divide the remainder in half. These halves become each side of the neck of your dress. At this point refer to your Visual Pattern.

T on the right side of the horizontal line on line 7 requires you to tie another ball of yarn in, thus enabling you to work both sides simultaneously. If you wish, you may use the other end of the yarn. (Every ball of yarn has a beginning and an end.) This keeps the yarn from tangling.

You also have x's on each side of your neckline. The x's show where to decrease (every other row at the neck-edge) thus shaping your round neck.

Line 7. BACK: Binding off and shaping starts when the back-neck measurement is reached.
A. Count the stitches on the back needle.
B. Count the stitches on both fronts.
C. Deduct the front total from the back.
D. The remaining stitches are bound off for the center back.
E. This makes all neck sides on your dress even.

Refer to your Visual Pattern. T (back neckline), tells you to tie another strand of yarn in. You now have four strands going at once. Do not worry, it is very easy, and diminishes the strain of counting and measuring. You are now shaping the basic Jewel neckline.

Note: Front and Back necklines may be bound off at the same time, as previously discussed. Details for the Visual Pattern have been discussed to enable you to make the pattern and shape the upper back if you so desire. The Upper Section, Visual Pattern and Details are applicable to most designs. This is discussed in Chapter Ten.

Line 9. While you have been shaping your neckline you have reached your armhole length plus ease and seam allowance. Try the garment on and pin the shoulders together before rushing to bind off. Plan on an easy armhole. Bind off 1″ at the beginning of every row, armhole edge only, front and back simultaneously. Your shoulders will match. Do not worry if there is a difference in stitch count towards the end of the binding off. Your shoulders will still match. Sewing your shoulder seams as detailed in Chapter Five will give you a perfect shoulder line. Shoulders must be sewn on the wrong side before picking up the neck stitches.

Line 10. Refer to your Visual Pattern and observe the decreases (x denotes a decrease). By decreasing at the neck edge on every other row you are gradually shaping a Jewel (round) neckline. This neckline is the basis for many designs. This is discussed in Chapter Ten.

A 16″ round needle, two sizes less than gauge, is used to pick up stitches. This is detailed in Chapter Eight. Remember to start, right side out, at the shoulder seam, and to refer to your gauge. (Make a gauge sample with the correct size needles.) This will aid you in knowing the number of stitches to pick up for each inch. Match the number of stitches that are picked up on each side of the center binding off. Knit a good 2″. Allow for doubling under.

Line 20. Measure. Bind off loosely (it may be necessary to use a size needle one size larger). Bend under and sew. Refer to Chapter Five. Always complete the neckline of your garment before making the sleeves, as the finished neckline aids you in properly measuring and fitting the sleeves.

Line 6. Have your dress *right* side out! Look at your armhole. It is a small circle. This necessitates the use of a short (16″) round needle since you do not want to pull on your work. Think of this needle as if it were straight and start to pick up your stitches from the right edge at the underarm. Be certain to use a 16″ round needle in body gauge size. Pick up an even number of stitches on each side of the shoulder seam. Allow for ease and sleeve seam. For instance, if you have a 7″ armhole depth, your calculation is based on 7″ by 2 equals 14″. Multiply 14″ by body gauge and add for seam allowance for the number of stitches to be picked up. After picking up the stitches, purl back. Remember—you have an underarm seam. Work 2″ to line 6B.

Line 6B. Measure for upper-arm width. If you wish, at this point you may change to straight needles of the same size, for ease in knitting. It is at this point that one may work evenly to the wrist if a straight sleeve is desired. Sleeve styles are detailed in Chapten Ten. Plan for this on your Visual Pattern.

Line 14. This line denotes the sleeve seam. Shaping is always done at the seam by decreasing at the beginning and end of a row. Refer to Figure 18.

Formula for Shaping Sleeves

A. Measurement at line 6B. Count your stitches.

B. Width measurement of arm at line 18 (below the elbow).

C. Deduct measurement B from A. The number you have derived is the number of inches to decrease. Refer to your gauge and transpose the inches to stitches. This number is decreased, 2 stitches to a row, spacing decrease rows evenly apart.

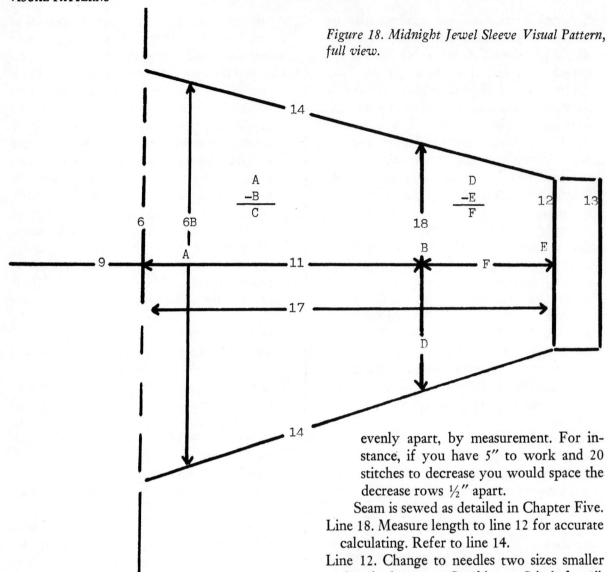

Figure 18. Midnight Jewel Sleeve Visual Pattern, full view.

evenly apart, by measurement. For instance, if you have 5″ to work and 20 stitches to decrease you would space the decrease rows ½″ apart.

Seam is sewed as detailed in Chapter Five.

Line 18. Measure length to line 12 for accurate calculating. Refer to line 14.

Line 12. Change to needles two sizes smaller than body gauge. Stockinette Stitch for 4″. Allow for a good 2″ hem.

Line 13. Bind off loosely. If necessary, use a larger needle. Bend 2″ under, and hem.

Line 17. Depicts where to measure sleeve. Do not skimp. Try your sleeve on as much as possible.

Line 11. This becomes the exact center of the sleeves. Never measure along the edge.

Line 6B. Measure most carefully for adequate width.

Note: Place your sleeve stitches on two 16″ round needles or a strand of yarn to facilitate trying on.

D. Write down the width measurement and number of stitches at line 18.

E. Write down wrist measurement (line 12). Deduct E from D. You now have the number of inches to decrease to reach the desired width.

F. Measure length from line 18 to 12. Refer to your gauge and transpose inches to stitches. Distribute E by decreasing,

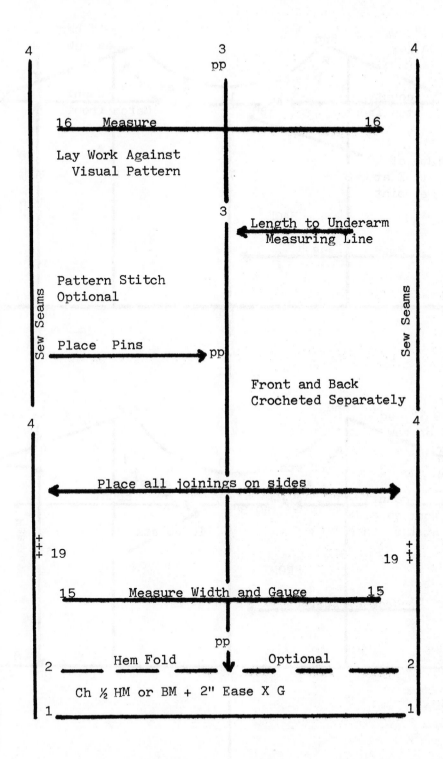

Figure 19. Partial View of Midnight Jewel, Crocheted. This view extends to the underarm.

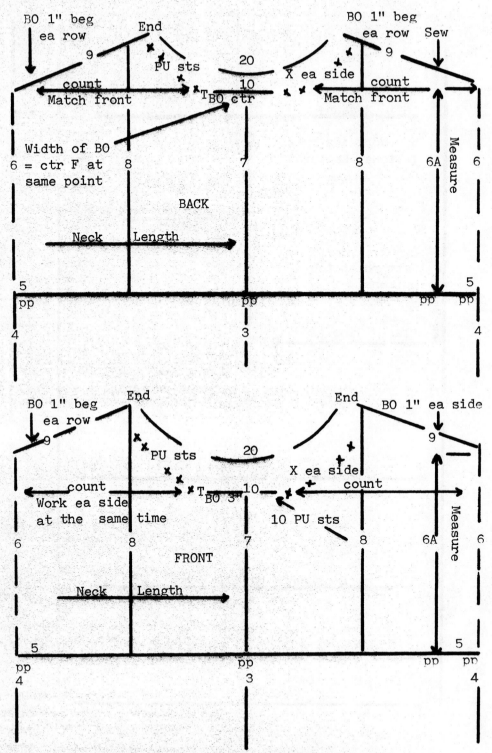

*Figure 20. Upper Sections of Midnight Jewel,
Crocheted. Optional: Front and Back may be
crocheted the same.*

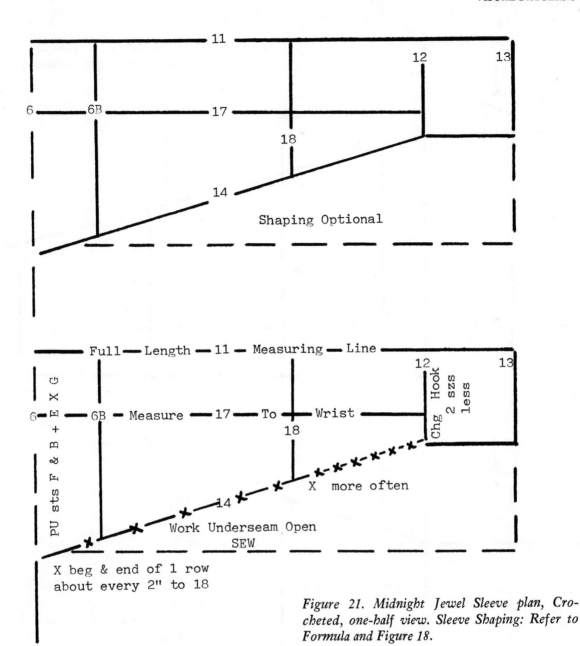

Figure 21. Midnight Jewel Sleeve plan, Crocheted, one-half view. Sleeve Shaping: Refer to Formula and Figure 18.

MIDNIGHT JEWEL—CROCHETED

The secret to success is, again, your *gauge sample*. Note: On Line 1, your chain length is derived from your gauge sample. On Line 7 there is an IMPORTANT CHANGE on your Visual Pattern: Place T at *left* of horizontal line. Refer to Figures 19 and 20.

Visual Pattern

Refer to Midnight Jewel, follow diagrams and directions in Section One. Extra ease and wide seams are recommended. Front and back necklines may be shaped the same. If there is any variation, two full patterns may be needed.

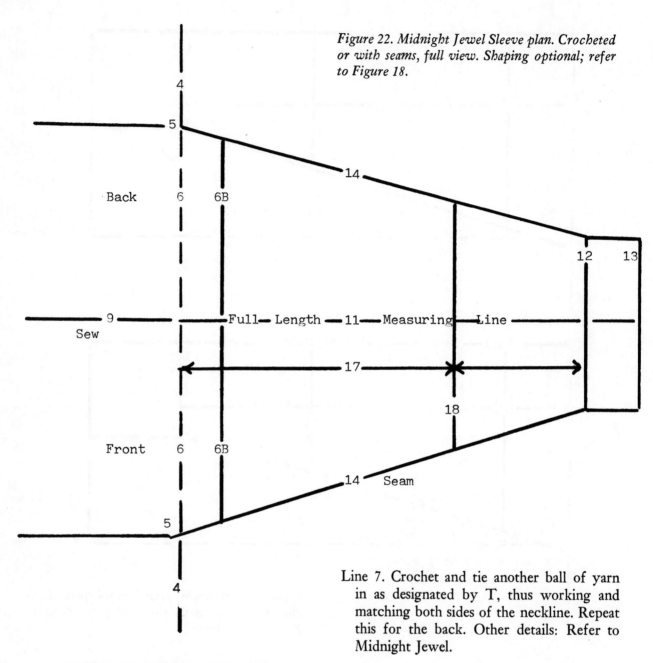

Figure 22. Midnight Jewel Sleeve plan. Crocheted or with seams, full view. Shaping optional; refer to Figure 18.

Line 7. Crochet and tie another ball of yarn in as designated by T, thus working and matching both sides of the neckline. Repeat this for the back. Other details: Refer to Midnight Jewel.

Sleeves

Line 6. Refer to Figures 21 and 22, and to Midnight Jewel. Crochet sleeve edging to match hem and neckband. Sew seams as detailed in Chapter Five.

Visual Pattern Reasons and Techniques

Refer to Chapter Eight, Second Section.

VISUAL PATTERN DETAILS

Line 1. Chain to equal one-half the width of bust or hip measurement plus 2″ ease and seam allowance. Pattern stitch is optional.

Line 2. Hem optional. Refer to Chapter Nine for edgings.

Line 3 through line 6. Refer to Midnight Jewel.

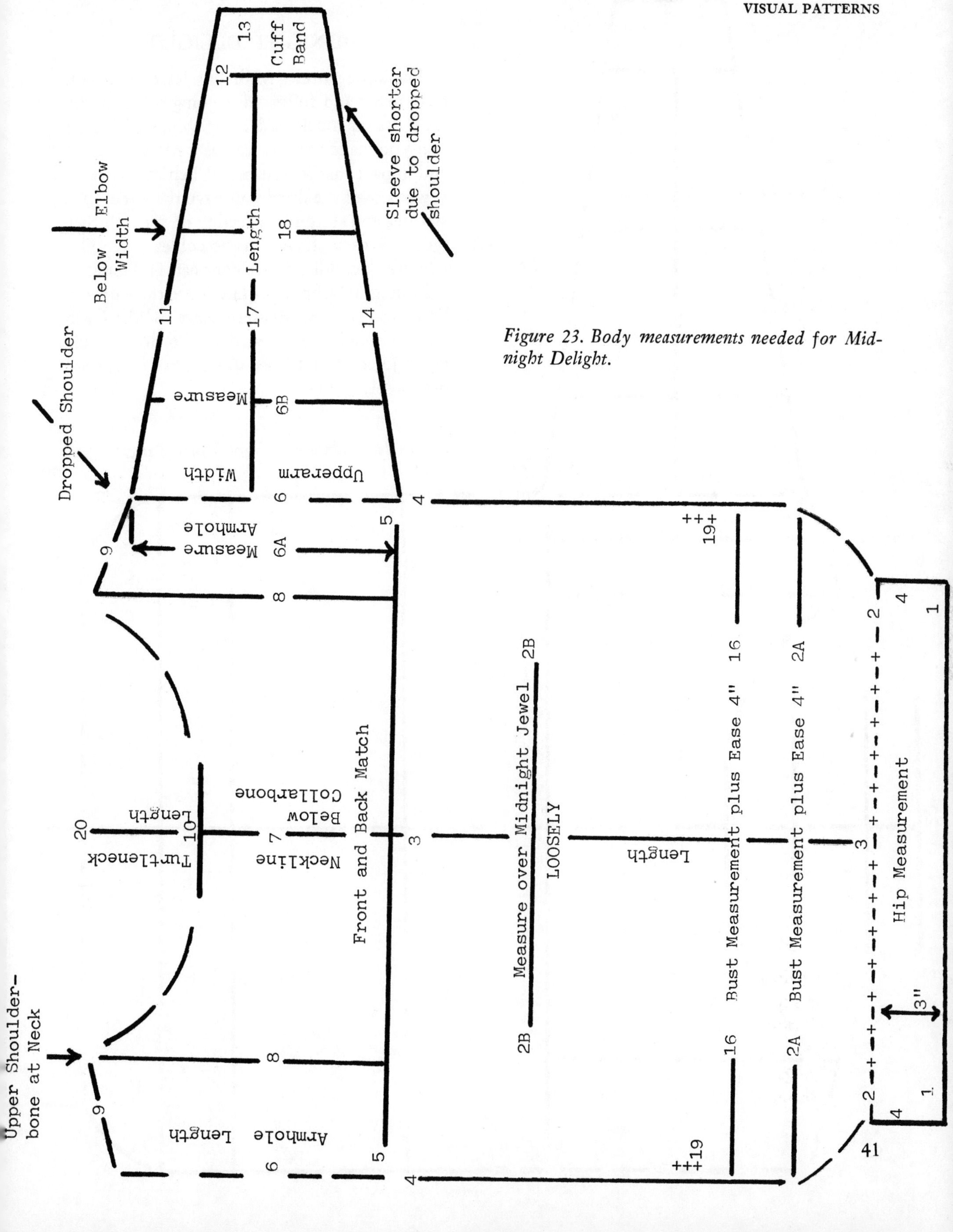

Figure 23. *Body measurements needed for Midnight Delight.*

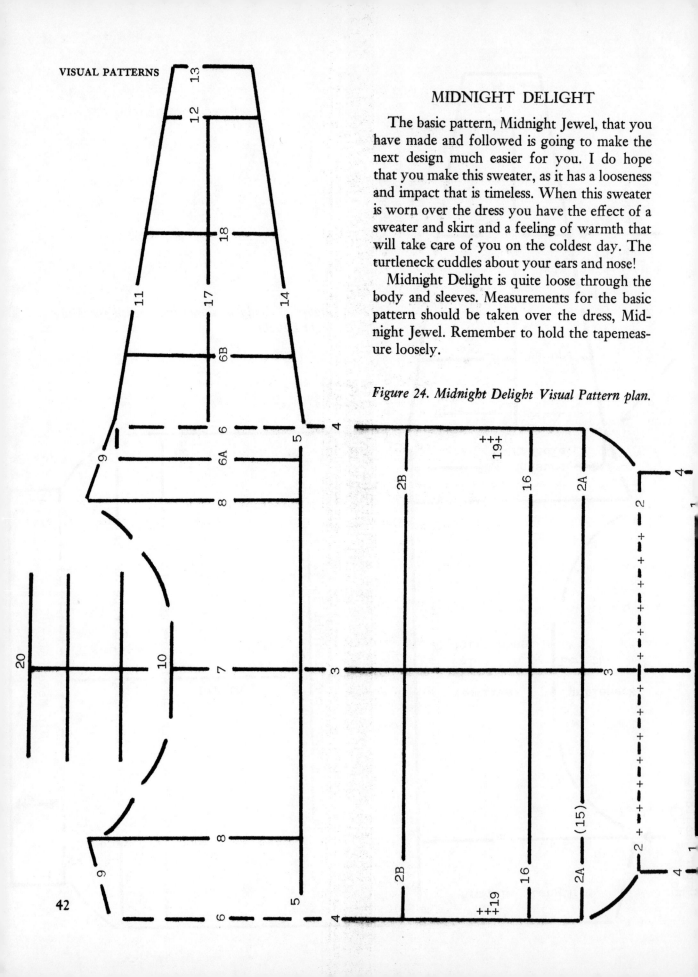

MIDNIGHT DELIGHT

The basic pattern, Midnight Jewel, that you have made and followed is going to make the next design much easier for you. I do hope that you make this sweater, as it has a looseness and impact that is timeless. When this sweater is worn over the dress you have the effect of a sweater and skirt and a feeling of warmth that will take care of you on the coldest day. The turtleneck cuddles about your ears and nose!

Midnight Delight is quite loose through the body and sleeves. Measurements for the basic pattern should be taken over the dress, Midnight Jewel. Remember to hold the tapemeasure loosely.

Figure 24. Midnight Delight Visual Pattern plan.

42

DRAWING YOUR VISUAL PATTERN

Measure your brown paper about one yard long and cut. Prepare your paper as detailed under Midnight Jewel. Look at Figure 24, Midnight Delight, from the *bottom up*. You are going to use your measurements, follow the number sequence, and draw your pattern.

Measurements Needed: Refer to Figure 23. Allow for sufficient ease through the body and sleeves.

Line 1. Start 3" from the bottom. Draw a horizontal line, using the center crease as the middle of your pattern. This line measures one-half of your hip measurement. As you draw, number your lines. Line 1 is the beginning of your sweater.

Line 2. Draw a horizontal line of the same width 3" above line 1.

Line 3. Draw a vertical line, using your center crease, from line 1 up the length to your underarm. This is determined by the length you desire; refer to your measurement chart.

Line 2A. Draw a horizontal line 2" above line 2. This line is the width of your bust measurement plus 4" ease allowance. Line 2A is centered with line 3 as your guide.

Line 2B. Draw a horizontal line 6" above line 2A. Make an arrow at each end of this line pointing to lines 4.

Lines 4. Draw 3" lines at each side from line 1 to line 2. Draw curved lines at each side from line 2 to line 2A. Draw lines at each side from 2A to equal the length of line 3. Refer to Figure 24.

Line 5. Draw a horizontal line from line 4, across the top of line 3, to line 4.

Line 6. Using armhole measurement, plus ease and seam allowance, draw dashed lines at each side over lines 4. Allow for a deep armhole.

Line 6A. Draw a vertical line, the same length as line 6, 2" in from the right of line 6.

Line 7. Refer to your measurement for a lower, round neckline. Draw a vertical line, this length, above line 3. Draw a horizontal line 4" long and centered at the top of line 7. Front and back necklines are the same. Refer to Figure 24.

Line 8. Using measurement from underarm (line 5) to upper shoulder neck edge (collarbone), plus seam allowance, draw a vertical line up *one-third* in from lines 6 at each side.

Line 9. Draw slanted lines across the top from lines 6 to lines 8.

Line 10. Draw curved lines, and x's over the lines, from each end of the horizontal line on line 7 to the top of lines 8. Refer to Figure 24. Note: Add brown paper at each side, using sealing tape on the wrong side to allow for drawing in sleeves.

Line 11. Refer to Figure 23. The length of line 11 is from underarm to wrist. Draw a horizontal line from line 6 where it meets line 9. Figure 23 and the pattern represent a one-half view. (Consider the lower and deeper armhole when measuring.) Continue to number your lines, as this will help when writing instructions.

Line 12. Draw a vertical line, using one-half the wrist measurement, 2" from the lower end of line 11.

Line 13. Draw a vertical line, the same length as line 12, at the end of line 11.

Line 14. Draw a slanted line from line 5 (at meeting point of lines 4 and 6) to line 12. Continue in a straight line to line 13. Refer to Figure 24 and place x's 2" apart on line 14 to line 18. Place x's ½" apart, on line 14, from line 18 to line 12.

Line 16. Draw a horizontal line 3" above line 2A (15).

Line 17. Draw a line down the center of the sleeve.

Line 6B. Draw a vertical line 2" from line 6.

Line 18. Draw a vertical line 8" from line 6.

Line 19. Above line 2A at lines 4. + + + Denotes increasing or placement for decreasing.

Line 20. Draw an 8" vertical line above line 7. This depicts the length of the turtleneck, and is optional. Center a 5" horizontal line

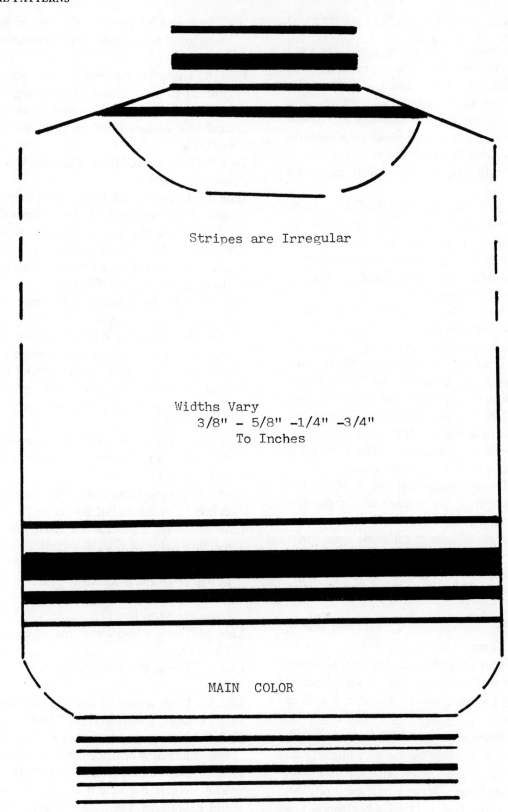

Stripes are Irregular

Widths Vary
3/8" – 5/8" –1/4" –3/4"
To Inches

MAIN COLOR

*Figure 25. Midnight Delight Stripe Plan. Sleeve
band ribbing 2"—½" MC, ¼" Con, alternated.*

3″ above line 10, another line the same width 2″ above, and the last 5″ horizontal line across the top line 20, as detailed in Figure 24.

STRIPE PLAN

Figure 25 details the placement and width of stripes. Draw the stripes onto your Visual Pattern. Decide if you like the placement; make any adjustments on your Visual Pattern.

VISUAL PATTERN DETAILS

Write the following instructions onto your Visual Pattern. Place them *within the pattern*. Prominently place your gauge, needle sizes, pattern stitch, and the type of yarn used for future reference. Abbreviations are used on diagrams; refer to Visual Pattern Key.

Line 1. Cast on hip measurement X ribbing gauge on 24″ round ribbing gauge needle. JOIN. K2—P2 for 3″.

Line 2. Change to body gauge round needle. Knit. Increase in one row to equal bust measurement plus 4″ease allowance. Place pins on lines 4 and line 3.

Line 2A. Measure for Gauge and Width.

Line 2B. Always place joinings of yarn at the side folds.

Line 3. Measure. Place pins horizontally.

Line 4. By Count Divide Stitches in Half. Place pins vertically.

Below Line 5. Refer to Figure 26. By Count Divide Stitches in Half. Place pins at lines 4, 6, 6A, and 3 where they meet line 5. T on line 5, left side (where lines 4 and 5 meet).

Above Line 5. STOCKINETTE STITCH. Work front and back separately, and at the same time. (Method is detailed under Reasons and Techniques.)

Line 6. Pick up stitches front and back plus ease and seam allowance X body gauge on 16″ round body gauge needle. Purl a row, knit a row. (Detailed in Section Three.)

Line 6A. Measure.

Line 6B. Measure.

Line 7 at line 10. Bind off center 4″, T on right of horizontal line. (Make arrows at each side of horizontal line, refer to Figure 26.) Count stitches. Divide evenly.

Note: The front and back are shaped the same.

Line 8 at line 9. Fasten or end.

Line. 9. Bind off 1″ at the beginning of each row, front and back, armhole side. Sew shoulders together on the wrong side.

Line 10. Decrease at each side of the neck edge on every other row. Pick up stitches on 16″ round needle, two sizes smaller· than body gauge. K2—P2 for 3″.

Line 11. Measure.

Line 12. Change to ribbing gauge needles. K2—P2 for 2″.

Line 13. Bind off.

Line 14. Decrease at the beginning and end of one row every 2″ to line 18 or refer to Midnight Jewel, Section Three, Line 14. Measure, leave seam open. Sew.

Line 16. TRY ON. LAY WORK AGAINST VISUAL PATTERN.

Line 17. Measure.

Line 18. Decrease more often to line 12. Measure.

Line 19. Measure for gauge and width. Increase or decrease as needed. Refer to Section Three.

Line 20. At first line: 3″ above line 10. Change to next size 16″ round needle. Continue ribbing 2″.

At second line: 5″ above line 10. Change to body gauge round needle. Continue for 3″. Bind off.

Optional: Changing needles. Refer to Stripe Plan.

Be certain that all written instructions are within the lines of your Visual Pattern. Carefully cut along the outer lines. Use this pattern. Refer to it and lay your work against it.

Remember! Always measure on a flat surface, through the center of your work. Compare to your Visual Pattern.

I have used numbers, step by step, to guide

you to draw the lines for *your pattern* with *your measurements*. The numbers were next used to designate the *instructions* that you were to write on your pattern exactly where needed. Your Visual Pattern Key, using the same number, will now be used to detail the *reasons* and *techniques*.

REASONS AND TECHNIQUES

Line 1. You have decided where, on your hips, you wish your sweater to be. Select this with thought; be critical and do not emphasize the largest part of your body. If you do not wish to attract attention to your hips, eliminate the stripe in the ribbing. Your hip measurement is multiplied by your ribbing gauge without an ease allowance as you want the ribbed border to be snug about your body.

REMEMBER PLACEMENT OF STRIPES. Refer to your Stripe Plan.

Line 2. Ribbed border is measured with a ruler for accurate length. When completed, count and write down the number of stitches on the needle. Write down your bust measurement plus 4″ ease allowance and multiply this by your body gauge. Subtract the number of stitches on your needle. The remaining number is the number of stitches to be increased in one row.

Line 2 designates the change of needle to body gauge size and where you will distribute increases evenly to equal the needed amount. For instance: if you have 180 stitches on your needle and need 20 stitches more, you would increase every 9th stitch. By distributing your increases evenly in one row you create a subtle blousing. Your knitting then continues evenly to the underarm (line 5).

Line 2A, or 15. This line reminds you to measure width and gauge. Your work should equal the width of the pattern. If you have insufficient width, place your increases as shown by line 19. Do *not* place increases through the body.

Line 4. Count your stitches, divide your work evenly in half, for front and back, and keep pins accurately placed at side folds. They are your guide to the underarm. Count your stitches, divide the front and back evenly in half, and place pins designating the exact center (line 3). Move your pins up as you work. Be certain to work around them carefully. Do not split your yarn or create holes. Remove the pin, work, and then replace the pin.

Line 16. TRY ON. Refer to Chapter Three. Try your sweater on over Midnight Jewel. Allow for a deeper armhole and re-measure for accurate length of the body.

Note: Measuring and trying on is done constantly with each stage of your work.

Line 5. Underarm Line. Refer to your Visual Pattern. Re-count for accurate placement of pins. You now have pins on each side, creating the division for upper front and back, pins in the center of the front and back in order to measure accurately for center neck binding off, and a pin two inches in from the right side for accurate armhole measuring. (Line 6A.)

T designates where to tie another strand of yarn in for working the upper back and front simultaneously. Refer to Midnight Jewel, Reasons and Techniques, Line 5.

Line 6, 6A. The importance of this line cannot be over-emphasized! Measuring must *not* be done at the edge; refer to Visual Pattern. Measure carefully, note the deep armhole, and be aware of the dropped shoulder line. This affects the length of the sleeve; re-measure.

Line 7. Front and back necklines are the same for ease in wearing. This neckline is shaped with a lower, wider curve, allowing for a cowl-like turtleneck. Measure carefully for sufficient depth.

Line 10. Shaping the neckline. You have bound off the center four inches (refer to body gauge), leaving an even amount of stitches on each side. You have derived this figure by counting all your stitches, deducting the center stitches, and dividing the remaining stitches in half. On completion of this row purl back and then tie the other ball of yarn in, thus enabling yourself to work both sides of the neckline simultaneously. Refer to your Visual Pattern. Repeat for the upper back. You will now be working with four strands of yarn. Decrease at the neck edge at each side on every other row.

Line 9. Shoulder Binding Off. Try your work on, and do not start to bind off until the armhole is deep enough. Bind off 1″ at a time on each side. All four shoulders will match as they are being worked on at the same time. Refer to Chapter Five for how to sew shoulder seams.

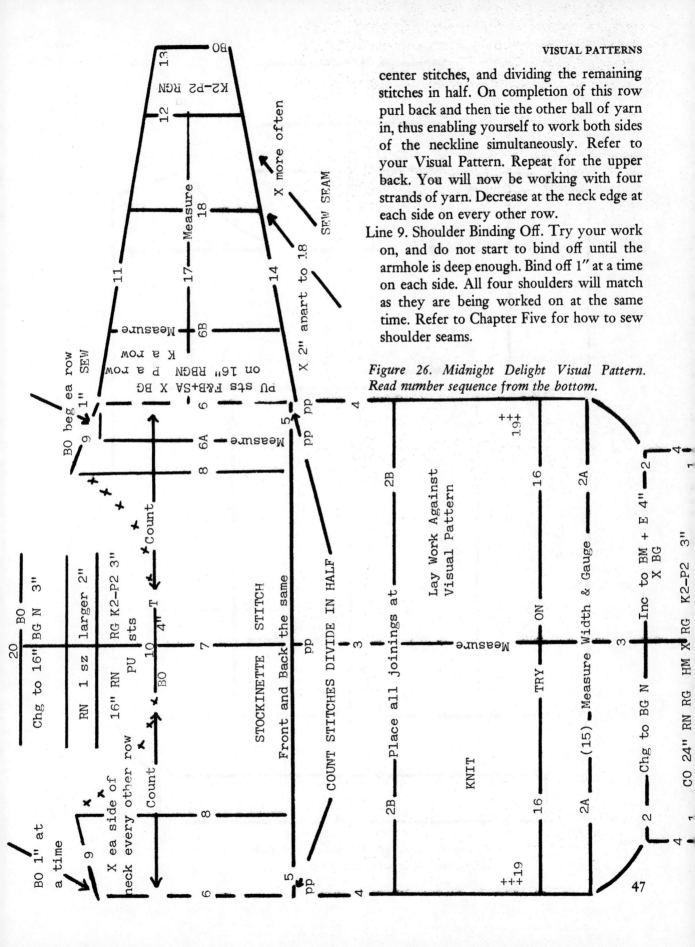

Figure 26. Midnight Delight Visual Pattern. Read number sequence from the bottom.

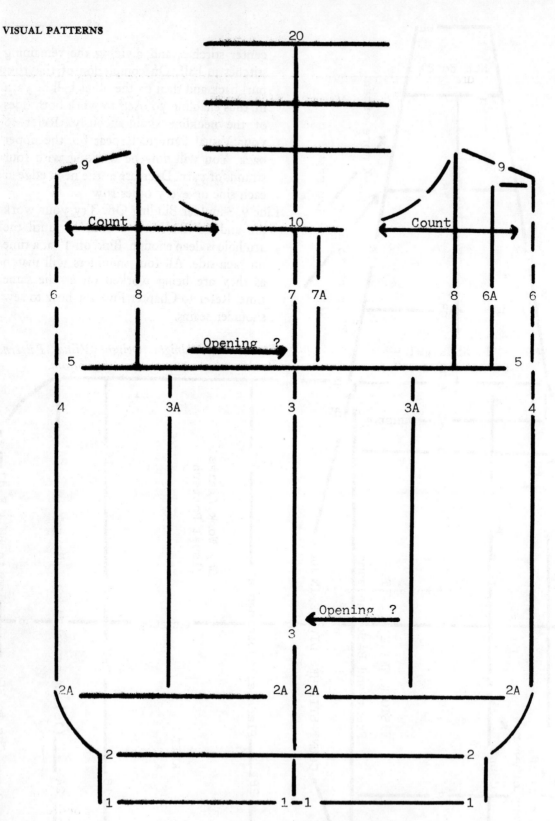

Figure 27. Midnight Delight Visual Pattern, no side seams, optional openings.

Line 8. Look at your Visual Pattern. This line has helped you to draw an accurate pattern. It also shows you where the shoulder ends.

Line 10. AGAIN! Use 16″ round needle, ribbing gauge size. Refer to your gauge and pick up stitches as detailed in this chapter for Midnight Jewel, Line 10 or in Chapter Eight. Ribbing pattern is K2—P2. Refer to Visual Pattern for detailing. Plan on your stripes.

Line 20. Look at your Visual Pattern and observe the three horizontal lines. The first line is 3″ from line 10 and indicates a change to a needle one size larger, and to continue ribbing for another 2″. (Shown on Visual Pattern.) The next line indicates a change to body gauge size needle and 3″ of ribbing to complete the turtleneck. Do not skimp in length, allow for a luxurious look, bind off loosely, and conceal the strand of yarn.

Your sweater is now complete except for your sleeves. Try it on over your dress and re-measure for sleeve width and length. Notice that the sweater sleeves are knit shorter than the dress sleeves, yet when they are worn they will appear the same length. Your dropped shoulder line has caused this. It is a great look!

Line 6. Have your sweater right-side out and pick up stitches for your sleeve as detailed under Midnight Jewel or in Chapter Eight. Remember to use the body gauge size 16″ round needle as if it were straight. Allow stitches for your seam.

Line 6B. After working 1½″, re-measure for accurate width. At this point you may wish to change to the same size straight needles for ease in knitting.

Line 14. If you prefer a straight sleeve or a sleeve bloused at the wrist do not shape the sleeve by decreasing at the seam. Refer to Chapter Ten.

Shaped Sleeves: refer to your Visual Pattern and Midnight Jewel, Reasons and Techniques, Line 14 for Formula for Sleeve Shaping and Figure 18. Suggested decreasing:

Decrease rows approximately 2″ apart for very gradual shaping. Sew seams.

Line 18. Measure length and width. Refer to line 14.

Line 12. Wrist width. Change to ribbing gauge size needles. If necessary, decrease to desired width by distributing decreases evenly apart in one row. Ribbing pattern for 2″ to line 13.

Line 13. Bind off loosely. If necessary, use a larger needle.

Lines 11 and 17. These are drawn on your Visual Pattern to aid you in knowing where to measure.

There is excitement in clever treatment of color. Stripes make the difference between ordinary and imaginative. My version of Midnight Delight matches my Midnight Jewel, and its basic color is black with mink-brown stripes. The stripes are irregular in width and individually placed. The Stripe Plan has positioned them and states the width of each stripe. Adapt this to your own preferences.

Midnight Jewel and Delight were knitted in fine mohair. They are basic designs and are adaptable in cotton, silk, linen, ribbon, or any other yarn or combination of yarn that you may wish. Your pattern remains the same, your gauge approach remains the same, but your look changes with every change of yarn, color, and stitch pattern.

There is no end to the versatility of Midnight Delight. Figures 27 and 28 show you how to convert your pattern to an open sweater, front or back, or a partially open sweater.

MIDNIGHT DELIGHT
OPEN SWEATER—NO SEAMS

Midnight Delight may be made open, either front or back. If you wish a partial opening, this may be planned 8″ up from the bottom, or from the armhole. Decide on the desired opening and determine how you wish to fasten the sweater. Zipper lengths should be planned for

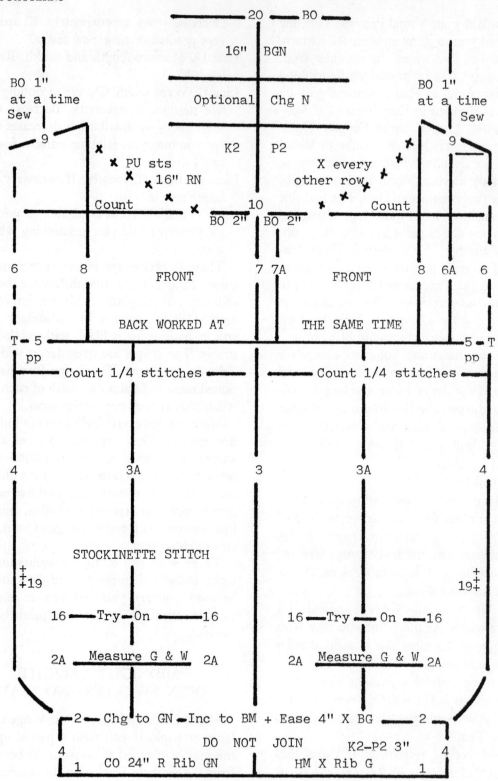

Figure 28. READ FROM THE BOTTOM UP.
Midnight Delight Visual Pattern, no side seams,
optional openings.

Amethyst Delight (page 203)

Amethyst Short Pants (page 203)

Cape Cod Minx Skirt (page 189)

Midnight Delight Long Over-sweater (page 42)

Luscious (page 179)

Amethyst Jewel Sweater (page 202)

Amethyst Skirt (page 200)

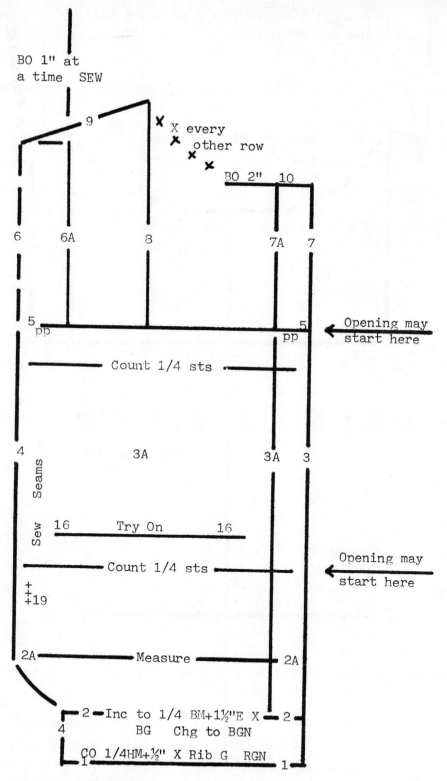

Figure 29. Midnight Delight Visual Pattern, one-quarter view.

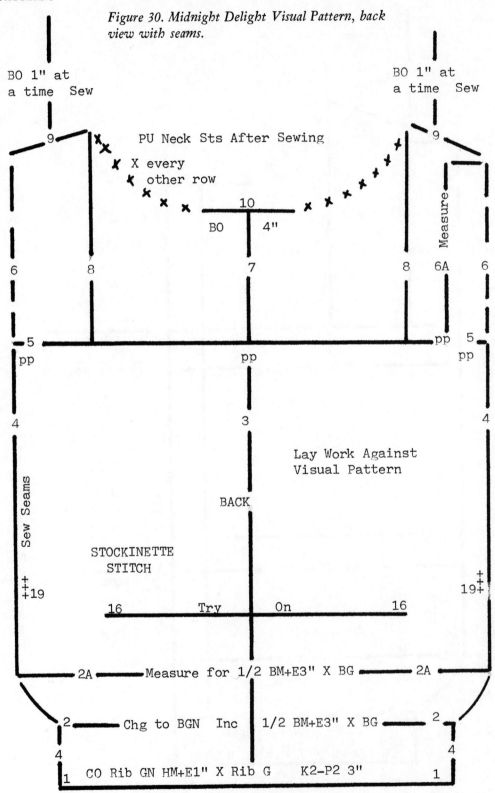

Figure 30. Midnight Delight Visual Pattern, back view with seams.

Optional: Work Back and Two Fronts at the same time. Use three balls of yarn.

on your Visual Pattern and the zipper should be purchased *before* making the sweater.

Refer to Midnight Delight and make your Visual Pattern twice. Cut the desired opening and tape the sides together.

Open From the Bottom

Cast on as previously detailed but DO NOT JOIN. Work on a round needle. Work the ribbing and then change to the Stockinette Stitch.

Line 5. Back equals one-half the total stitches. Each front equals one-quarter of the total stitches.

Open After Eight Inches

Refer to Midnight Delight for 8″.

Line 3. Center opening. Work to line 5.

Line 5. Refer to Open From the Bottom. (Tie yarn in.)

Open From the Underarm

Refer to Midnight Delight and knit to Line 5.

Line 5. Separate at line 7, center, tie yarn in.

Note: Opening Edges. Ribbing pattern may be worked on each side for 1″. Suggested for zipper closings: single crochet or work body stitch pattern.

MIDNIGHT DELIGHT WITH SEAMS OPEN—FRONT OR BACK

Make your Visual Pattern twice. Cut the center of the second pattern on lines 3 and 7. Write your instructions as detailed. Make both fronts simultaneously; use two balls of yarn.

Fronts: Refer to Figure 29.

Line 1. Cast on one-fourth hip measurement plus seam allowance X ribbing gauge on ribbing gauge needle. K2—P2 for 3″.

Line 2. Change to body gauge needle. Increase to one-fourth bust measurement plus 1½″ ease and seam allowance X body gauge. Distribute increases evenly in one row. Stockinette Stitch.

Line 2A. Measure for Gauge and Width. Increase, if necessary, as depicted by line 19.

Line 3A. Front measuring line.

Line 4. Place all increases, decreases, and joinings at the sides.

Line 16. Measure. (Try on after back is completed by pinning together.)

Line 5. Mark with pins on 6, 6A, and 7A.

Line 6A. Measure for armhole depth.

Line 7. Bind off 2″.

Line 7A. Measure carefully.

Line 9. Bind off 1″ at a time at beginning of row on armhole side.

Note: Shoulder seams are sewn together on completion of back.

Line 10. Neckline decreasing starts immediately after binding off at line 7. Decrease at neck edge on every other row.

Line 20. Neckline is resumed after completion of fronts and back.

Back: Refer to Figure 30.

Line 1. Cast on one-half hip measurement plus 1″ seam allowance X ribbing gauge on ribbing gauge needle. K2—P2 for 3″.

Line 2. Change to body gauge needle. Increase to one-half bust measurement, plus 3″ ease and seam allowance X BG. Distribute increases evenly apart in one row.

Line 2A. Measure for Gauge and Width. Increase, if necessary, as depicted by line 19.

Line 3. Back measuring line.

Line 4. Place all increases, decreases, and joinings at the sides.

Line 16. Measure. Try on. Refer to front.

Line 5. Mark with pins on 6, 6A, and 7.

Line 6A. Measure for armhole depth.

Line 7. Measure carefully. Bind off center 4″. Mark with T on right of horizontal line at end of line 7. Tie yarn in. Work both sides of neckline at the same time.

Line 10. Decrease at neck edge, every other row.

Line 9. Bind off, refer to Front.

Detail: Sew shoulder seams.

Line 10. Pick up stitches, fronts and back, X

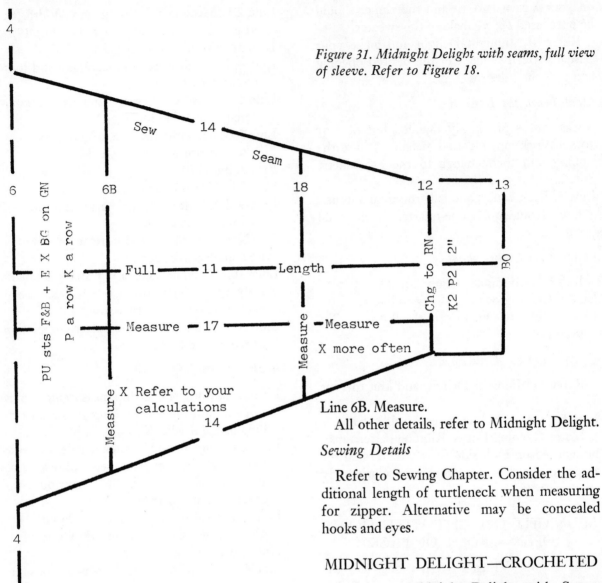

Figure 31. Midnight Delight with seams, full view of sleeve. Refer to Figure 18.

Line 6B. Measure.

All other details, refer to Midnight Delight.

Sewing Details

Refer to Sewing Chapter. Consider the additional length of turtleneck when measuring for zipper. Alternative may be concealed hooks and eyes.

MIDNIGHT DELIGHT—CROCHETED

Refer to: Midnight Delight with Seams, Body Measurements Needed, Visual Pattern Plan, Sleeve Plan, and Stripe Plan.

Remember! When crocheting, your Visual Pattern is your guide, since shape is important! One Visual Pattern will do, as the front and back are the same.

Note: Turtleneck may be crocheted in the round or with one seam; refer to Midnight Jewel—Crocheted.

Visual Pattern—Open Sweater

Refer to Midnight Delight With Seams.

ribbing gauge on ribbing gauge 16″ round needle. Neckband: 1″.

Line 20. Turtleneck: Refer to Midnight Delight.

Sleeves: Refer to Figure 31.

Line 6. Pick up stitches, front and back, plus ease and seam allowance X BG on straight body gauge needles. Purl a row, knit a row (Stockinette Stitch).

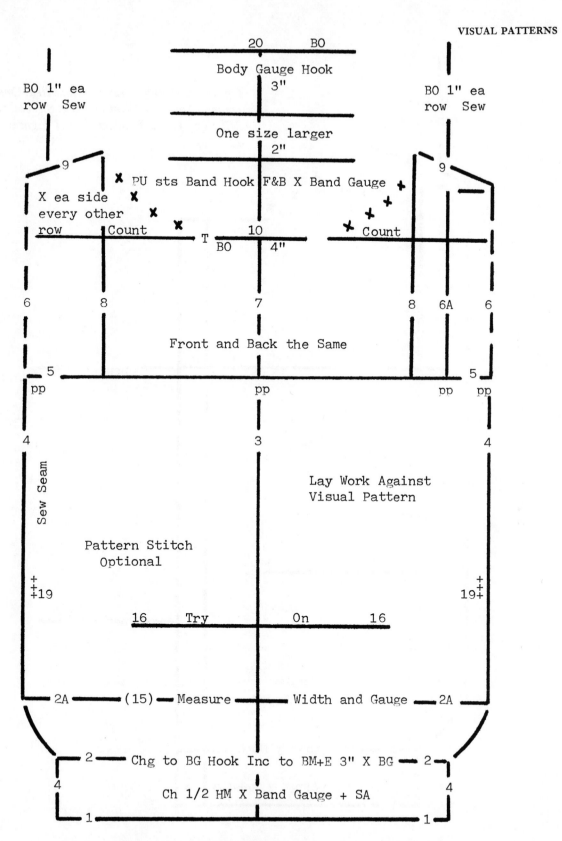

20   BO
Body Gauge Hook
3"

One size larger
2"

✗ PU sts Band Hook F&B ✗ Band Gauge ✚

BO 1" ea
row Sew   9   9   BO 1" ea
                                                                      row Sew

✗ ea side
every other
row   Count   T   10   Count
                                      BO   4"

6   8   7   8   6A   6

Front and Back the Same

5   5
pp   pp   pp   pp

4   3   4

                              Lay Work Against
                              Visual Pattern

Sew Seam

Pattern Stitch
Optional

+   +
‡+19   19+‡
                                                                +
            16   Try   On   16

2A ━━━ (15) ━ Measure ━━━ Width and Gauge ━━ 2A

2 ━━ Chg to BG Hook Inc to BM+E 3" X BG ━ 2
4   4
        Ch 1/2 HM X Band Gauge + SA
1 ━━━━━━━━━━━━━━━━━━━━━━━━━━━━━━ 1

*Figure 32. Midnight Delight, Crocheted with side
seams. Two gauges needed: body and hand. Read
from the bottom up.*

55

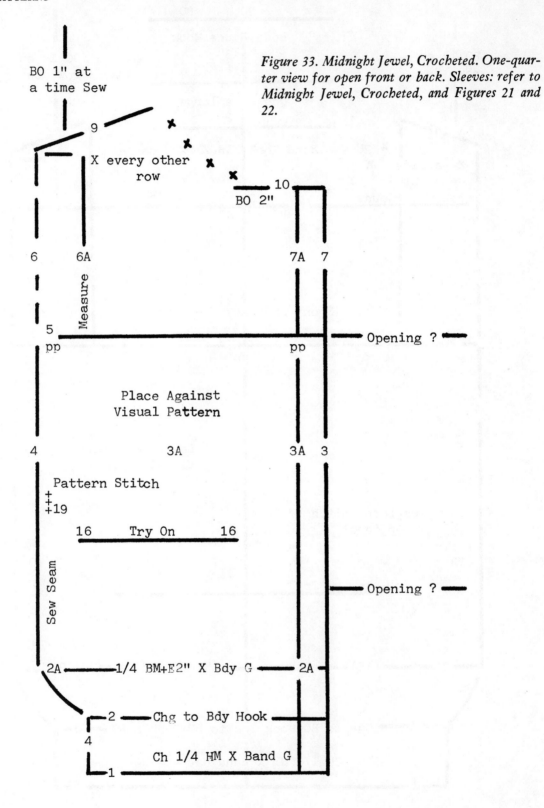

Figure 33. Midnight Jewel, Crocheted. One-quarter view for open front or back. Sleeves: refer to Midnight Jewel, Crocheted, and Figures 21 and 22.

BO 1" at
a time Sew

9

X every other
row

10
BO 2"

6   6A   7A 7

Measure

5   pp
pp

Place Against
Visual Pattern

4   3A   3A 3

Pattern Stitch
+
+
+19

16   Try On   16

Sew Seam

Opening ?

Opening ?

2A ⟵ 1/4 BM+E2" X Bdy G ⟵ 2A

2 ⟵ Chg to Bdy Hook

4

Ch 1/4 HM X Band G

1

Sleeves

Refer to Midnight Jewel—Crocheted and Figures 21 and 22.

Gauge Samples

Two 8″ samples, one for body and one for band.

Hooks

Two sizes. Optional: Three for turtleneck.

Details

Line 1. Chain (refer to gauge) the width of one-half hip measurement X band gauge on band gauge size hook. Crochet 3″. Stitch pattern may be Vertical Single Crochet.

Line 2. Change to body gauge hook. Increase to one-half bust measurement, plus 2″ ease and seam allowance X body gauge. Distribute increases evenly apart in one row. Use the stitch pattern of your choice.

Other Details

Refer to Midnight Delight and Midnight Delight With Seams. Refer to Figures 32 and 33.

Turtleneck

If you desire a fuller turtleneck, decide on the additional inches, plan your increase rows, and space them about 1″ apart.

Note: Stripe Plan may have to be adjusted according to the stitch pattern.

PISTACHIO WHIP

This is a simple variation of Midnight Jewel. The variation in the dress is in the neck-band and sleeves. The neck-band is ribbed K1—P1 for 1″ and the wrist-band is ribbed for 2″. A ribbed hem may also be made by casting on and working the ribbing on a needle one size larger than the body gauge needle. Refer to your Visual Pattern for all other details.

Pistachio Whip is distinctive due to the change in the over-sweater, Midnight Delight.

The change is in the neck-band and the cuffs. The neck is shaped as on your Visual Pattern but is finished with a 1″ ribbing to match Jewel. When this is worn over the dress the neck-band will fit below the dress neck-band and thus create a double ribbed edging.

Sweater Sleeve Detail (Figure 35)

Refer to Midnight Delight but work the sleeve until you are 6″ from the end. Start the ribbing pattern on the body gauge needles and work to the wrist-band. Change to ribbing gauge needles and work an additional 2″. Sew the seam carefully as the ribbing is doubled over, making a bulky cuff, and exposing the wrist-band of Jewel.

JEWEL COAT-DRESS

Truly a jewel! lightweight and supple, a coat that does double-duty and is an absolute joy when traveling. Visualize it in thin mohair or tweedy yarn. Wear it as a coat or blouse it to create a seductive dress.

The secret to making this coat is in measuring fully dressed, as you will then have the needed ease through the body and the armholes. Allow for sufficient ease in the sleeves and consider shaping them straight to the wrists.

I suggest making a muslin pattern and studying the draping of the coat. However, remember that this changes with the texture of the yarn and stitch.

This pattern will be the basic pattern for your cardigans, jackets, and coats. Plan your buttons and buttonhole placement on this pattern. This pattern is adaptable for Chanel-type fronts.

The Jewel is your base. Your Visual Pattern consists of the back and two fronts, even though you may not have seams. If you intend to have seams, add seam allowance to the back and fronts. The front borders, whether worked-in or added later, must be detailed for horizontal or vertical buttonholes with uniform placement; refer to Chapter Five. If you

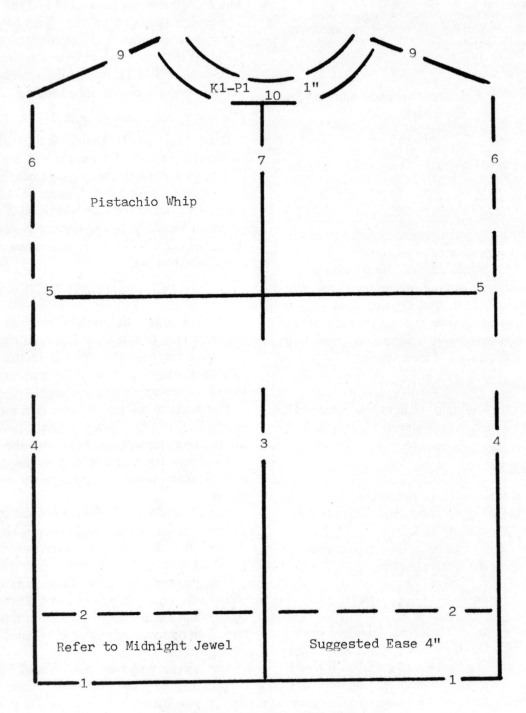

Figure 34. Pistachio Whip Visual Pattern.

Midnight Jewel and Midnight Delight (pages 24 and 42)

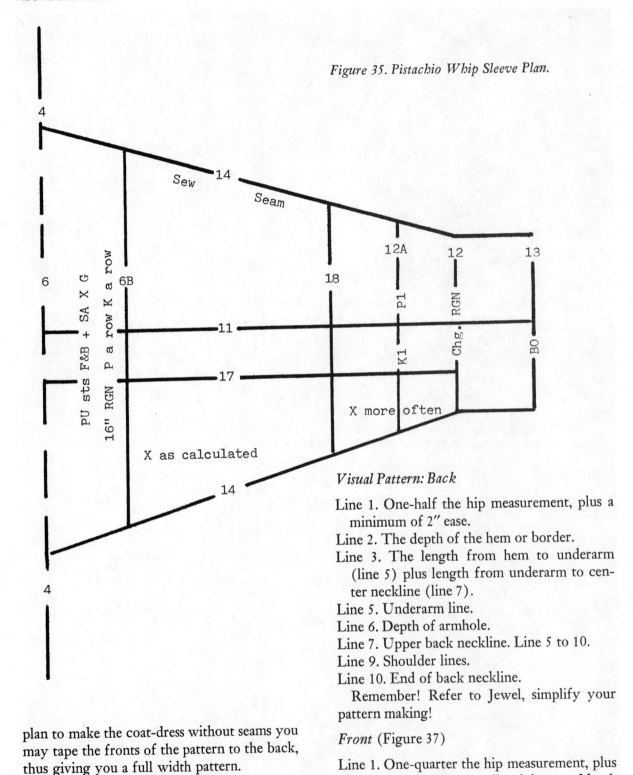

Figure 35. Pistachio Whip Sleeve Plan.

Visual Pattern: Back

Line 1. One-half the hip measurement, plus a minimum of 2″ ease.

Line 2. The depth of the hem or border.

Line 3. The length from hem to underarm (line 5) plus length from underarm to center neckline (line 7).

Line 5. Underarm line.

Line 6. Depth of armhole.

Line 7. Upper back neckline. Line 5 to 10.

Line 9. Shoulder lines.

Line 10. End of back neckline.

Remember! Refer to Jewel, simplify your pattern making!

Front (Figure 37)

Line 1. One-quarter the hip measurement, plus ease and border, 1½″ minimum. Match fronts to back . . .

plan to make the coat-dress without seams you may tape the fronts of the pattern to the back, thus giving you a full width pattern.

Remember! Measurements should be taken over a dress!

60

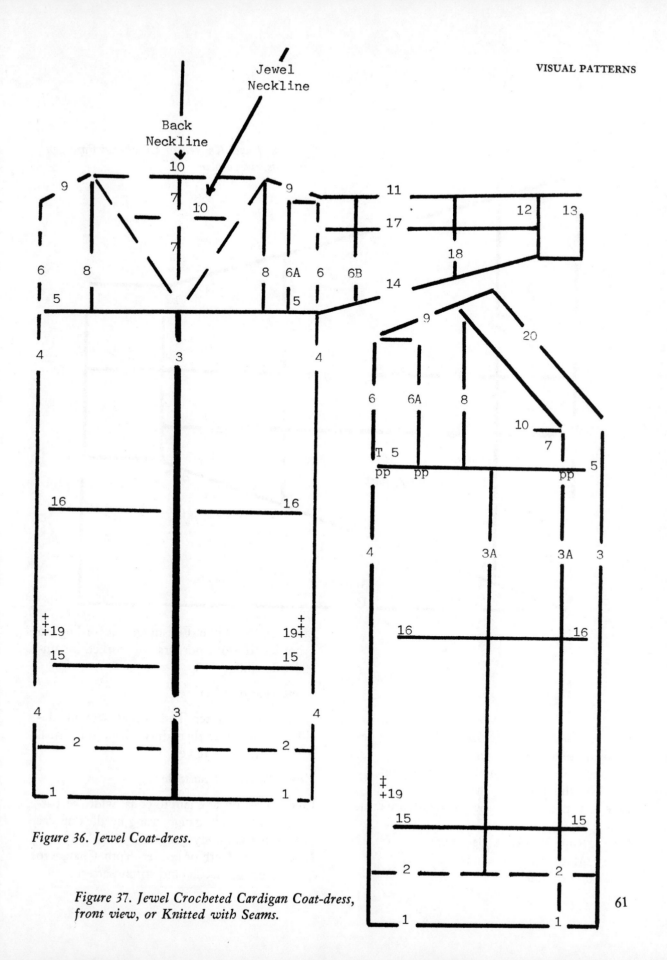

Figure 36. Jewel Coat-dress.

Figure 37. Jewel Crocheted Cardigan Coat-dress,
front view, or Knitted with Seams.

61

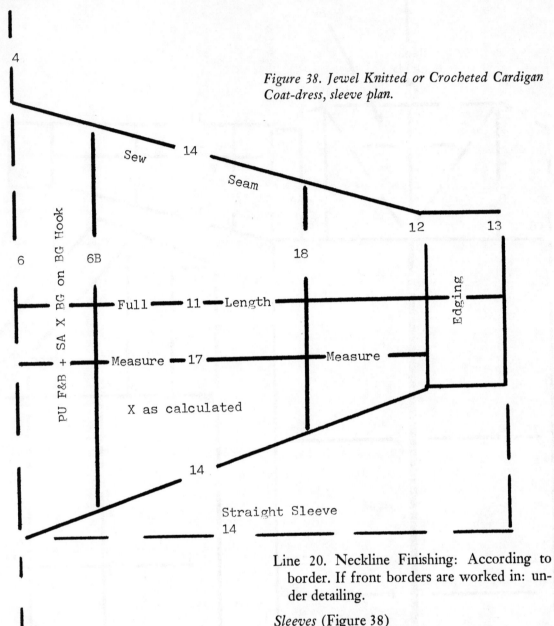

Figure 38. Jewel Knitted or Crocheted Cardigan Coat-dress, sleeve plan.

4

Sew 14

Seam

6   6B   12   13

PU F&B + SA X BG on BG Hook

18

Edging

Full 11 Length

Measure 17 Measure

X as calculated

14

Straight Sleeve
14

Line 20. Neckline Finishing: According to border. If front borders are worked in: under detailing.

Sleeves (Figure 38)

Refer to Chapter Ten, sleeve section, decide on the style, then draw shape on Visual Pattern. Refer to Jewel.

Visual Pattern Details: Back

Line 1. Cast on or chain to equal width of pattern times body gauge, using needle one size smaller than body gauge.
Line 2. Hem depth or border depth. Change to body gauge needle and stitch pattern.

Line 5. Draw desired neckline. (Necklines detailed in Design Chapter.)
Round Neckline: Line 7 to desired spot.
V Neckline: Shaping may start at line 5.
Line 6. V neckline may be started before armhole.
Line 7. Round neckline placement.
Line 9. Match shoulders to back.
Line 10. Neckline.

Line 5. Mark underarm line for proper neck-
line and armhole depth.
Line 6. Armhole.
Line 6A. Measuring line (refer to Jewel)
Line 9. Shoulder binding off.
Line 10. Back neckline bound off.

Front

Line 1. Cast on or chain to equal coat-dress
pattern. (Measurement X body gauge.)
Start front borders or, if making a hem, use
needle one size smaller.
Line 2. Depth of hem, change to body gauge
size needle and body stitch pattern; retain
edging borders. Depth of border, change to
body stitch pattern. Work to . . .
Line 5. V neckline, refer to Necklines in Design Chapter or mark for accurate measuring
for round (Jewel) neckline and armholes;
refer to Jewel.
Line 7. Depth of round neckline.
Line 9. Shoulders shaped (bound off) to conform to back.
Line 10. Completion of shaping neckline.
Line 20. Note: If working borders for V
necklines, place stitches on yarn or pin.
These stitches are to be worked the length
needed to meet (with seam allowance) in
the center back.

Sleeves (Figure 38)

Refer to Jewel and sleeve detailing in Design
chapter. Also refer to your Visual Pattern.
Sewing details in Sewing chapter.

Note: If knitting without seams, use a round
needle, and do not join your work. Separate
for armholes, referring to line 5 and the Jewel.

Buy a large, brown envelope or folder to
keep your patterns intact. Your Visual Patterns
may be used over and over again. Make all of
your notations on them. This approach to knitting and crocheting firmly implants in your
mind the construction of your designs and
gives you the freedom and confidence to plan
designs within a design or different stitch patterns within your designs.

Remember, this book is for you. Follow it
diligently. You will be wearing designer
clothes with *your* label inside. Each design has
very little dressmaking detail, thus eliminating
many problems. I concentrate on proper construction, freedom of movement, and reduce
each design to the basics. Knitting and crocheting do not need detailing! Their beauty
lies in their simplicity. Allow your design,
your yarn, and your hand work to make the
statement.

CHAPTER FIVE

Sewing

Hand-sewing has always been considered the height of luxury. It adds that elegant touch to the hand-knitted or crocheted garment that you created from the very beginning to the very end. Simple sewing stitches—the back-stitch, hemming stitch, and running stitch—are all that you need to know.

Take pride, be painstakingly patient, do not rush, and do not neglect to try your garment on as you assemble it. Work on the reverse, or wrong, side, carefully matching your pieces together, and pin (common pins or safety pins for bulky yarns) allowing a minimum of ½″ for seams.

Seams are functional and a focal point. They are deliberately placed for attractiveness, strength, and to retain the shape of the garment. Seams must be flawless and straight. I do not recommend strengthening seams with tape or ribbon. Many stitch patterns are adaptable to a round needle, although there are definate advantages and functional reasons when designs are detailed with seams.

Basting is done with a *contrasting* color, using doubled mercerized cotton thread, extra long, with a large knot at the end. Do not use the complete length when basting; leave a length dangling. This allows for elasticity and

proper fitting. Your basting stitches will not break or pull out. Examine both sides, matching rows or stitch patterns carefully. Patterns or rows should be counted and pinned at exact intervals to insure matching. Attention to these details guarantees perfection.

Seams are sewn with doubled mercerized cotton thread in the same color or a slightly darker shade. Do not use silk; mercerized cotton is recommended as it does not stretch. When sewing on a combination of yarns, select thread that blends with the predominant hue. The backstitch is used for seams; this is similar to machine-stitching but a little larger. Your stitches should look neat, straight, and unpuckered. Puckering results from pulling on the thread, making tight stitches, winding the work around your fingers, or stretching the edge. Hold the work without tension, firmly yet loosely, within your hands.

The first designs, Midnight Jewel and Midnight Delight, do not have side seams. Shoulder seams should be sewn and the neckline completed before picking up stitches for the sleeves. This is a must for correct measuring. Measuring and fitting are synonymous with success!

When assembling sleeves, pin, baste, and

sew. Sew the ribbing or border first; then backstitch from the underarm to the elbow or mid-point. Resume sewing from the wrist, back to the mid-point. The final touch is to turn your work over and backstitch, from the opposite end, over the complete seam. This seam helps to retain the shape. All seams are approached this way, thus melding the work into a smooth seam. Always press seams, after basting, before your final sewing.

The secret of a successful set-in sleeve is the coordination of the upper arm section, called the sleeve cap, and the armhole. The shape of the outer cap must conform to the armhole. If one is wider than the other, do not rush into sewing. Prepare the wider armhole or cap edge by making little running stitches all around the edge. Pull the thread to bring it to the desired width and fasten securely. You now have tiny puckers all around the outer edge; distribute these evenly. The center top of the cap must align with the shoulder seam. After pinning to make certain that the cap fits smoothly, remove the pins. The sleeve cap or armhole must now be carefully steamed. The puckers will be carefully shrunk in, using your sleeve pad, press cloth, and steam iron. Insert the pad, place your press cloth, and steam lightly. The extra fullness will gradually contract. Allow to dry thoroughly. Remove the running stitches and re-press as previously described.

The sleeve seam is pinned, basted, and sewn as previously detailed. The sleeve is set into the garment by placing the right side of the sleeve inside the armhole, right side to right side, with the wrong side of the garment towards you. Pin carefully, starting at the underarm and working to the shoulder seam, turn, and repeat, working from the underarm to the shoulder seam. Baste and sew in the same manner.

Side seams are approached in the same manner as sleeve seams. If you desire an additional accent you may try sewing, with contrasting yarn, over the seam stitches. Be daring and wear it inside out!

Note: Ripping seams requires extreme caution. Do NOT USE A RAZOR! Use a strong, pointed sewing needle or small, pointed scissors.

The decision to sew a hem or crochet an edging is most important. You must always consider the thickness and the design. Bulky garments should not be hemmed; a simple edging, crocheted or knitted, will enhance the garment. This is discussed in Chapter Eight.

The ingredients for a good hem are a light touch, accurate measuring, and proper preparation. It is vital to pin hems before basting. Pin your hem at the sewing edge and at the fold; common pins are placed horizontally. Measure at different points with a wooden ruler. If you are a beginner or a perfectionist, place common pins vertically between the horizontal pins. This is a must for me. Baste, only after being positive that the hem is smooth and even, at the edge and at the fold.

Sew carefully, with thin needles and short, doubled thread in the correct shade. *Pick* lightly and do not go through to the front, spacing the stitches ½″ apart. Keep the hem stretched out between your fingers, and the thread very loose. When your sewing is completed, your hem will rebound, and you will have retained the resilience of the garment. If you wish, you may hem twice, placing the next set of stitches between those previously sewn. Your stitches will look long and loose on the reverse side; do not be surprised or worried. This is the best method since it avoids a bulky-looking hem or making the stitches obvious. Hand-sewers delight in tiny, invisible stitches, made closely together, as they should. With knits and crochets, that method would be sheer disaster!

Knitted pleated skirts and dresses are exquisite! The secret is in making your pleats permanent. This requires patience, a very fine needle and doubled thread that is not too long. You set your pleats in, permanently, simply by using the running stitch and making small, firm stitches along the *very edge*. Start at the *top*, working until the thread is gone, rethread and start at the *bottom*. Fasten your thread *securely* on the wrong side each time. The strength is in the fastenings. Repeat, working back and forth, as on a sleeve seam. This takes time, but is well worth it. The stitches never show and the dress or skirt never loses its pleats; they lie flat and sharp.

Note: This edge is initially made in the knitting of your pleat; see Chapter Nine. Designs are detailed in Chapter Ten.

Skirts

There are various methods for finishing skirts at the waist. Your design is the determining factor.

1. Ribbed band, either K1—P1 or K2—P2 for desired depth. Elastic, 1″ wide, is then attached on the wrong side. Pin your elastic about your waist before cutting, and wear it for a while. When you are satisfied with the comfort, allow for overlap, and cut. Fit the elastic to the ribbing, stretching and molding them together. Your ribbing must be evenly distributed; after you are satisfied with the pinning, baste and try on. Hand sew firmly—do not machine stitch.

2. Gathering with a casing at the waist. Knit or crochet for twice the depth needed, fold over, and sew. Leave a small section open for inserting elastic. The elastic is measured, cut, and a large safety pin is used to draw the elastic through the casing. Overlap the ends and sew securely. Close the opening. This is a lovely look, especially when a sweater is worn tucked inside the skirt.

3. Crocheted casing on the wrong side. Use matching yarn or mercerized cotton thread; this is detailed in Chapter Eight.

4. Grosgrain belting and zipper on the wrong side. Grosgrain measurement is taken loosely and an allowance of 1″ is added for bending under at each end. Grosgrain is sewn in after installing the zipper.

Zippers

Skirts may be made without zippers but if you wish to use one buy a zipper in skirt weight, one to two inches longer than the opening, with small, metal teeth. Always buy your zippers to match or blend into your yarn. Read the sewing directions on the wrapper and adapt them to hand-sewing. Caution must be taken to avoid pulling on the knitting or crocheting, to match rows or stitch patterns, and to conceal the teeth of the zipper. Sew carefully, do not go through the yarn to the front, and try the garment on before completion. If you notice any puckering or buckling, remove the basting, and install the zipper while the garment is on. Pin it in, baste, check for matching of rows or stitch pattern, and sew. (The extra length of the zipper will give you the needed leeway.) After being completely satisfied, whip-stitch over the teeth of the zipper below the zipper opening, and then cut the excess off. Sewing a zipper in by hand is a couture technique, and is preferred at all times.

Zippers for cardigans and jackets may be purchased in a matching or contrasting color. Your garment should be planned with the zipper in mind: always purchase the zipper first. Do not bind off for your neckline until you have pinned and basted the zipper in and are satisfied. Garments with a ribbed stitch pattern must be on when installing the zipper. Never use a sewing machine; your creation is hand-made.

Ribbon Edging

Ribbon may be used to edge cardigan or jacket fronts, inside or out. Purchase the needed length; this equals the two sides, plus an additional 2″. Cut the ribbon exactly in half, bend it under ½″ at each end, and pin from one end for 4″ and then pin from the other end for 4″. Smooth sweater and ribbon, melding them together, then pin from the center towards each end. Keep the ribbon flat and taunt.

Do not allow any ripples. Place basting and sewing stitches at the edge; use tiny running stitches.

Note: Make certain that the sides match in length between each stage.

Ribbon trim may be used with or without buttons. Buttons may be used with snaps sewn underneath or with buttonholes.

The Chanel-type cardigan or coat is edged without buttons. This is discussed in Chapter Eight and edgings are detailed in Chapter Nine.

Buttons and Buttonholes

Buttons are of the utmost importance! Do not leave this decision until the last moment. A button is more than a way to fasten your garment; it is a decorative accent, and may become the focal point of your design. The proportion of your button determines the spacing; large buttons should be placed further apart. *Do not stitch and cut buttonholes before deciding on the buttons*. This also applies to making buttonholes while knitting or crocheting.

Buttonhole placement should be planned on the Visual Pattern; this completely eliminates any guesswork. The center of your buttonhole should be the exact center of the front neckband.

Horizontal buttonholes are marked in the exact center for button placement. Vertical buttonholes are marked one-eighth of an inch below the top of the buttonhole. These marks must be in a straight line. Sew the buttons securely but not too tightly; allow for a smooth closing.

Knitted or crocheted buttonholes are detailed in Chapter Eight.

Cutting buttonholes into a garment requires patience and accuracy. MACHINE STITCH the desired width, twice, ⅛″ apart, and stitch each end. The distance between the buttonholes should be measured from the exact center of these two lines. Re-check your measuring before stitching and cutting. Carefully cut the center. Finish with matching mercerized cotton thread and the buttonhole stitch.

Buttonholes may be bound with matching or contrasting material.

Lining

Lining knitted and crocheted clothes is a definite art. You are working with two extremes: fabric, which has absolutely no flexibility, and a knitted or crocheted garment with resilience and buoyancy. I learned to do this arduous task to perfection. It always looked beautiful, but never satisfied me, as I did not have the feeling of freedom and comfort that I desired. Nothing equals the fantastic ease and elasticity of unlined knitted and crocheted clothes.

Give no thought to seams showing and allow your design to be free and easy; completely without restraint. Do not worry about "sitting or bagging out," as proper pressing will remedy this.

There are many pitfalls in lining knitted and crocheted clothes. The first is in the selection of the material. If you have taken pains to select a washable yarn, and then combine it with a non-washable fabric, you are completely defeating your purpose. Next, consider the texture of your material, for nothing is worse than a fabric which creates static. This can affect your silhouette and the shape of your design.

Select a durable fabric which will not conflict with your design, since knitted and crocheted clothes last a lifetime. Nothing detracts more from the beauty of a garment than a torn old lining.

Visual Patterns have helped you to create your own original design. They will also help you to line it properly. Use your Visual Pattern as your guide. Enlarge the pattern for ease and seams; patterns for jackets and coats should have a liberal allowance through the back for a center fold (pleat) to give you additional ease.

The next step is to make the lining pattern

in muslin. All adjustments must be made on this. It must fit perfectly! Baste it into the garment and sit in it, walk in it, and comfortably forget about yourself in it. When you have achieved this feeling, then you are ready for the lining.

Your third step is to take the muslin pattern apart. This is your pattern. Keep the grain of the material straight and remember to match any pattern or stripe. Linings are always machine-stitched on the wrong side at the seams and all hems are hand-sewn. Attach wrong side to wrong side, sewing carefully.

I do not line any of my designs as I now feel that linings change the intrinsic quality of hand-knitted and crocheted clothes.

Backstitch

This is done by making two little running stitches, then putting your needle back, through and under, coming up through in front of your last stitch. Make certain that you

Figure 39. Backstitch.

make neat, small stitches, that you come through your work, and do not split the yarn. The front side of your seam will resemble machine sewing, while the back side of your seam will have stitches twice as long. To end the seam, go back, backstitching over several stitches.

Hemming stitch

Take a tiny stitch into the garment and then bring the needle diagonally up through the

hem edge. Take tiny stitches, at least one-half an inch apart. Do not go through to the front. Keep your stitches loose. Keep your thread loose.

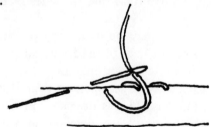

Figure 40. Hemming Stitch.

Running stitch

Take several tiny stitches (if yarn is thick, take one at a time) evenly working the sewing needle in and out. (Tiny basting stitches.) Pull thread through loosely.

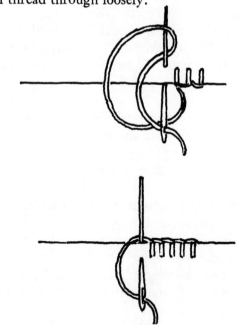

Figure 41. Blanket or Buttonhole Stitch (for edgings).

CHAPTER SIX

Pressing

Pressing is of the utmost importance: it adds the finishing touch to your creation. Pressing does *not* mean ironing. Ironing is when you run your iron heavily in different directions. Pressing means gentle patting, lightness of touch, placing your iron precisely where you want it, and never allowing it to rest heavily on your garment.

Knitted or crocheted clothes should be pressed on the wrong or reverse side as much as possible. Always press over an ironing cloth. (Heavy cotton, linen, or a commercial ironing cloth may be used.) *Never* place your iron, steam or otherwise, directly on your knitting or crocheting.

Set up your ironing board in an area where you will have no interference. Make certain that the board is thoroughly padded. Knubby or tweed yarns require the additional padding of a large, thick towel. This prevents the texture of your garment from being flattened.

The surface of your board, your iron, your ironing cloth, and any additional equipment used must always be spotless.

READ YOUR YARN LABEL CAREFULLY! Press your gauge sample first. Be absolutely positive that your yarn can take heat. Set the temperature dial carefully.

Your ironing cloth may be dry if you are using a steam iron. I recommend a slightly damp (never wet) ironing cloth if you are not using a steam iron. Dampen your cloth carefully by immersing it or sponging it. Roll it with a heavy hand, squeezing the excess moisture out (if necessary press out the extra wetness) until you achieve an even, all-over dampness.

WARNING! Excess moisture will ruin the texture of your garment.

Remember—always start with a cool iron; you may increase the temperature gradually. This will avoid scorching, stretching, or even worse, melting! A hot iron will make your yarn shine. Never rest the iron on one spot. Avoid leaving an imprint. Proper pressing involves a precise combination of pressure, moisture, and heat. The combination of a damp cloth and a steam iron is used when extra steps must be taken. These will be described later in this chapter.

Dressier and metallic yarns must be delicately handled. Caution is the key word, since steam may discolor or tarnish the yarn. Always press lightly, as a heavy hand may cause your threads to become brittle and to break. Proceed cautiously and, if you have any doubts, do not press. Simply lay your garment on your bed and smooth it into shape with your hands. Wear and ease your garment into shape and you will achieve an amazing result.

Ribbon yarns must always be pressed on the wrong side with a *dry* ironing cloth. NEVER on the right side! TEST your gauge sample! Do NOT take any shortcuts!

Mohair, brushed wool, looped mohair, angora, novelty yarns, and yarn combinations require extra care when pressing. Hold your iron *above* (not touching) the cloth, allowing the steam to slowly penetrate, with *no weight* on the garment. This same approach may be used on ribbing. Ribbing should not be heavily pressed as this will affect the elasticity and the look.

I am a firm believer in knitting or crocheting exactly to the required measurements and my Visual Pattern is a constant reminder. Blocking is a term that I feel is misunderstood and mishandled. I do not advocate blocking. Labels on *synthetic* yarns may specify "block" but this may be avoided if they are knit or crocheted properly.

Remember • FIRST TEST YOUR GAUGE SAMPLE.

- Always use an ironing cloth. Never have your iron directly on your work.
- Do NOT OVER-PRESS. This can do irreparable harm by stretching and distorting your yarn.
- Your ironing cloth must not be too wet, or it will ruin the texture and stretch your yarn.
- Do not distort the lines of your knitting or crocheting. Use your hands to keep the grain of your work straight.
- The result depends on you. Do not rush. Allow your creation to dry thoroughly between each step.

Aids to Successful Pressing

1. Set your ironing board at a comfortable height.
2. Pad your board, thickly, and always have a clean surface.
3. Place a heavy towel over the padding before pressing tweed or knubby yarns.
4. Own an iron that you thoroughly understand. Steam irons must have clean water.
5. Ironing (press) cloths must be firm, not torn, but smooth and clean.
6. Sleeve rolls and shoulder pads are invaluable. Make your own by using a clean towel or face cloth and rolling it to the needed size.

Proceed cautiously. You have already tested your gauge sample. Now turn your garment inside out.

Shoulders

Insert shoulder pad and open the seam. Place the press cloth and steam; allow to dry. Repeat for the other shoulder. Dry between each step.

Sleeves

Insert your sleeve roll, open your seam, place the cloth, and steam. Dry. Press the complete sleeve. Repeat for the other sleeve.

Hems

Place the hem flat (do not pull garment onto the board), thus preventing stretching or sagging. Be certain that all common pins or basting threads have been removed as they will leave an impression.

Note: Silk thread may be used, when needed, as it does not mark.

Be certain that each section is placed smoothly, without ripples or wrinkles, and without stretching. Pat your hem into place before putting the press cloth over the section, and then steam. Allow the steam to penetrate while keeping the iron above the cloth. Dry. Gradually shift the hem around, placing it properly before steaming. All hems have rolled (soft) edges.

The garment should be thoroughly dry and right side out before resuming.

Sleeves

Insert the sleeve roll and press. Gently work down to the wrist. Allow to dry and then measure. If more width is needed, insert roll and press horizontally. Press lengthwise when additional length is needed. Dry.

Body

Do not pull onto the ironing board. Place the upper front on the center of the board. Keep the grain of your stitch pattern straight. Do not press to the very sides, or folds—avoid a sharp crease. Gradually press from the top to the hem. Press front and back. Your next step will bring your garment to the desired measurements.

Pull the garment onto the ironing board. Turn, so that the underarm side is workable and smooth, easing this section horizontally before placing the press cloth.

Gradually press from underarm to hem; press both sides. This should remove any creases. Allow to dry.

Compare your garment to the Visual Pattern. It should be identical. If you find that extra ease is needed, go back to the ironing board. Use a dampened cloth and steam horizontally, gently pressing across. Press front, back and sides, paying particular attention to the sides (ease this area horizontally with your hands and steam).

When additional length is needed, run your iron up and down. (Do not forget to use a dampened press cloth.) Concentrate on easing the length evenly.

Study the garment and observe whether the hem is smooth. Correct flared or bumpy hems by placing the section on the middle of the board; do not insert the board. Smooth the hem, working towards the center and creating vertical ripples, and then place your dampened cloth over this and steam. Hold iron above and not on the press cloth. Let the steam do the work. The excess width will contract and shrink in. Constantly use your hands to contract the hem.

This trick is great for a "sat out" dress or skirt. Make your ripples (contractions) longer through the seat and then steam; repeat until your dress looks as good as new.

Narrow hems are widened by using your hands and carefully stretching as you steam. Corrections are an important step, a necessary step, and one must not expect a perfect result with only one pressing.

Lay your garment on a large heavy towel (never try to wear it immediately) and allow it to dry thoroughly. Try it on, dress for it, wear the proper undergarments and shoes. (If trying a coat or jacket wear the dress or skirt.) Look at yourself in a full-length mirror. Do not overlook anything and re-press where needed. Experiment with different undergarments if you observe a roll or bulge, as a tight girdle can create this on the thinnest person.

Sweaters

Follow the previous instructions; and carefully work the point of the iron towards the ribbing. Do not press ribbing.

Skirts

Press on the wrong side. Prepare for the zippered area by placing a pad under the zipper. Close the zipper, place a dry cloth over it, and press lightly. Seams and hem are pressed on the wrong side. Ease the skirt where needed. Re-press on the right side.

Skirts should be pressed before finishing the waistline.

Gathered skirts are pressed before decreasing. Work your skirt onto two round needles and press to the required width. Pressing gathers, after decreasing, is done with the point of the iron. Place the press cloth and work up from full section to the gathering.

Cardigans, Jackets and Coats

Press the reverse side first. Press as previously detailed. Care must be taken not to stretch the front openings: they must hang evenly. Measure as you press.

Extra Steps

Shaping curves should be done gradually, with time allowed between each pressing.

Common pins are used to keep the curve in place on the ironing board, and to help in shaping. Use a damp cloth and a steam iron.

Extra stretching should be done by pinning the garment to the ironing board and pressing horizontally. Dry. Shift the garment, re-pin, and press.

Jewel Coat-Dress (page 57)

CHAPTER SEVEN

Tender Loving Care

Surely you desire to take proper care of your beautiful creations—babying them, handling, and sitting in them gently. Practice caution; never put a soiled garment away. Develop the habit of carefully placing your clothes over the back of a chair, preferably in front of an open window, overnight.

On Cape Cod, we have gray, misty, dewy mornings. I often take advantage of them by simply placing a heavy towel on the courtyard and laying my dress on it, for about an hour, and never in the sun! The air and the dew permeate the yarn, refresh the color, and restore the baby fresh odor of newly washed wool. Airing clothes may be old-fashioned but it is still hard to beat!

Stains often occur in public. Restaurants are usually the site of the mishap but, fortunately, are also the source for the simplest remedies. Be casual but direct! Why live with a spot for the rest of your life? Why spoil a cherished possession? Unobstrusively *blot* your stain; do not rub. Use a napkin and apply warm or hot water for a grease stain, cold water or club soda for a non-grease stain. Then casually continue *blotting*.

The next morning examine your clothes for further treatment or snags. If you have snagged them, simply take a crochet hook and draw the yarn through to the wrong side. If further cleaning is required, read the yarn label that you pinned to your gauge sample. Little did you know, when you first started, how important your gauge samples would be. Gauge samples will be with you for the life of your garments. Always test the recommended treatment on your sample or an inconspicuous spot of your garment. (Try the reverse side of the hem.) Allow the treatment to dry before making a judgment. If any doubt exists, take the garment to a reliable dry-cleaner.

Prior to removing the stain, place a thick towel inside the garment, directly under the stain. Use a sponge or a face cloth to apply your cleaning solution and *pat* the stain. Pat and blot, constantly shifting the face cloth so that you are always working with a clean, absorbent material against the stain. Continue shifting the under towel so that the stain and cleaning solution will be absorbed. Then turn your garment inside out. In trying to remove a stain, always work from both sides. Insert another dry, clean towel when working on the reverse side. Be patient, work slowly, and do not rub. This process will take time because yarn is porous: it is made up of more than one fiber and is not smooth. Remember:

- Test the cleaning treatment on your gauge sample first.
- Do not attempt spot-removal if you are uncertain of the yarn. Synthetics such as ribbons, metallics, and other yarns should be handled differently and as specified on the labels. If dry-cleaning is recommended, do *not* try home remedies.
- Do not use an unknown product without testing it, as it could easily remove the color or cause the yarn to melt.
- Always "spot out" stains before washing any of your hand-knits or crochets. Washing directions are detailed later in this chapter.
- If you have any doubts, use a reliable dry-cleaner. Do not give up!

I remember pressing a beautiful corn-yellow cardigan dress. I had the ironing cloth over it but my iron somehow ran over the edge of the cloth, scorching the wool. I could not believe my eyes! I was heartsick. Tears streamed down my cheeks as I rushed to the nearest dry-cleaner. Holding my breath, I stood over him as he patiently worked on the stain. He slowly applied the solutions, cautiously alert to any change in the yarn. He did not want to fuzz up the yarn or remove any of the color. It was a miracle! The scorch mark gradually left the dress and all that I could see was a ring from the chemicals. The dress had to be dry-cleaned. After wearing it a few times I carefully washed it. This restored the softness and beauty of the sunny yellow yarn. This incident happened years ago and is as vivid in my mind as if it had occurred yesterday.

As you see the beauty of your work and feel the satisfaction that you will derive from a good result, pride will teach you caution and you will baby your wardrobe. You will give it the required care and feel well-deserved pride.

Carefully fold your hand-made garments. Do not ever hang them up. Reserve special drawers and do not cram them in—place them gently with tissue paper between the folds. Use sufficient tissue paper between each garment. This will avoid spotting and needless wrinkling, and will always enable you to wear your favorites at a moment's notice.

I have found that the use of tissue paper and the proper folding of clothes spares me from experiencing mildew and needless wrinkles. My designs look and smell fresh at all times.

Washing

Treat your hand-knits and crochets as gently as you treat the skin on your face!

Washing beautifully handmade clothes must be approached with common sense. Do not combine this with your Monday wash. One careless gesture and your garment could be swept into the washing machine and end up felted or half its size.

I learned a bitter lesson. I had carefully washed my two poodles' sweaters. They were a luscious Italian alpaca in a shade of olive green that looked gorgeous next to their apricot fur. The sweaters were cabled all over and had lush, full turtlenecks that reached their ears. I had designed them to fit perfectly around the neck and chest and had tapered the back to end right at their perky tails. The sweaters had been carefully placed on a towel on top of the dryer to dry. Dry they did! To this day I do not know how it happened, but they were carelessly swept up and thrown into the washer and dryer! They shrunk and felted so that they would not even fit toy poodles!

Profit from my experiences. Be alert and be cautious. Approach your washing as patiently as your sewing or pressing. Do not rush! Always read your yarn label and follow any instructions. Keep the label from your yarn attached to your gauge sample. If you have any doubts, wash your gauge sample. Record washing notes in your notebook; always refer to them.

Prepare a solution of soap and water, and keep this in a bottle for spotting. Always "spot out" your stains before washing the garment.

Use diluted soap solution directly on the spot, especially on soiled areas such as wrists, elbows, inside the neckline, and collars. Work this solution in gently, squeezing it through the soiled areas. Do not rub or fuzz the yarn.

Yarns may be labeled shrink-proof, shrink-resistant, and anti-pilling, but this does not mean that they can be carelessly washed. Many yarns are labeled washable but this does not mean a casual toss into the washing machine with varied and sundry articles.

Handmade garments should be washed by themselves. Attention must be paid to the temperature of the water—the cooler the better. Never, never use a bleaching agent.

If you insist on using your washing machine, please place your garment inside a zippered white pillow case. If you do not own one, fasten the ends of a pillow case with rustproof pins. (Wash your pins first.) Use your gentle cycle, cool water, and Woolite or Ivory Flakes. Do NOT LEAVE THE WASHING MACHINE! Allow the wash cycle to work for a few minutes, stop the motion, and then allow your garment (alone) to soak for about ten minutes. Start the washing machine, rinse and barely spin (shorten the spin cycle). Rinse thoroughly and avoid streaking.

If you must use your dryer, use a low temperature, and open the door often. Feel the garment and do not overdry. BEWARE OF HIGH TEMPERATURES. Avoid shrinking or felting. Do not completely dry your garment. Take it out and lay it smoothly on a large heavy towel. Ease your garment to the desired size; use your Visual Pattern as a guide.

Many of the dressier and metallic yarns are synthetic. Follow the directions on the yarn label and take the added precaution of testing your gauge sample. Ribbons must be dry-cleaned. Always dry-clean if there are any doubts.

My approach is to hand-wash, using mild soaps and cold water, and always holding the garment within my hands and not working it up and down. The heavier wet weight causes stretching. I gently squeeze—never rubbing, never twisting or wringing, just squeezing the sudsy water through. I then rinse many times, until all the soap is removed and the water is clear. I then squeeze out all the excess water, changing the towel if necessary. I dry the garment, changing the towel periodically, away from artificial heat or sunlight. Remember:

- Careless washing creates endless work. Be careful!
- Cool water and mild soap.
- Change the towel and avoid musky odors.
- Refer to your Visual Pattern.
- Follow the directions for pressing.

CHAPTER EIGHT

Techniques

KNITTING

Casting On
Knitting
Purling
Increasing
Decreasing
Picking Up Stitches
Binding Off

CROCHETING

Slip Knot
Chain
Single Crochet
Double Crochet
Increasing
Decreasing
Ending

This is all that you need to know to knit or crochet any design in this book. Use the basic Visual Pattern, Midnight Jewel, as your guide to understanding how to create your own original designs. Use this method, whether knitting or crocheting, since it removes any guesswork.

All arts have their own terminology—there are symbols, terms and abbreviations. These are listed at the end of this chapter. They will be used on design diagrams, stitch patterns, and knitting and crocheting directions only where absolutely necessary.

KNITTING

Casting On

There are many variations. An experienced knitter knows which method to use for the desired result. I am going to detail two methods; if you have your own preference do not hesitate to use it. Bear in mind that this is the beginning of your work and it must have the same resilience as the work to follow. If extra elasticity is needed, cast your stitches onto a larger needle.

1. On one needle, make a slip knot and place it onto needle held firmly in your left palm. *Yarn in right hand, between thumb and index finger and wrapping around index and third finger and under, thus forming a loop. Slip this loop from the back (or left side of loop) onto the left-hand needle, take fingers out of loop, tighten yarn firmly.* Repeat from * for desired number of stitches.

2. On two needles, place a slip knot on left-hand needle. *Yarn in right hand, insert right-hand needle into slip knot from left front, as with knitting, carry yarn under and over right-hand needle. Pull yarn through left loop. Insert left point into loop on right-hand needle, going into loop from right front. Slide right-hand

needle out, leaving loop on left-hand needle.* Repeat from * for desired number of stitches.

For added firmness work your return row by knitting into the back of each stitch. (This becomes the front side.) Do this with the gauge size needle.

When working with round needles, cast on the desired number, *do not join*, knit your return row as previously described. Examine all your stitches from the knit side, have them straight, and then join. For the first inch examine each round to avoid twisting.

Knitting

Knitting and purling may be done in the Continental (German) or English way. If you knit in the Continental manner you may see a difference in the rows. Your purl rows may be looser and your stitches may be reversed. Be critical and strive for perfection.

Continental Knitting and Purling

This is done by holding yarn and needle in the left hand. Right needle pulls yarn *down* and *under* and through the stitch. If yarn is not under the needle, the knit stitch becomes twisted or reversed. When purling, the yarn is still in the left hand and goes over the right-hand needle and is pulled down and through.

English Knitting

The yarn is held in the right hand. Control over the tension is accomplished by weaving the yarn over the index finger of the right hand, under the middle finger, and over the little finger. The yarn moves through the fingers.

Hold the needle with the cast on stitches in your left hand. *Insert the right-hand needle into the stitch from the front. Yarn should be in *back* of your work and under your right-hand needle. Pass yarn over the front point and pull it through, forming a loop on the right-hand needle. Allow the stitch on the left-hand needle to slip off.* You now have one stitch on the right-hand needle. Repeat from * across

the row. When through, put the needle with all the stitches into your left hand. Practice plain knitting, row after row. This is called the Garter Stitch. Learn control of the tension of your yarn.

Purling

Hold your needle with your cast on stitches in your left hand and work with your right hand. *Keep your yarn in *front* of your work and under your right-hand needle. Put your right-hand needle into the stitch from back to front. Pass the yarn, coming from front only, around the top point of the needle and pull loop through the stitch on the left-hand needle. Loop remains on the right-hand needle with previous row stitch just falling off.* Repeat from * across the row. Practice!

Cross Knitting

Insert the right-hand needle into the *back* of the stitch to be worked.

Cross Purling

Insert the point of the right-hand needle into the back of the stitch, going in from the left and with the point coming towards you. Tip: Gently pull work down, holding between thumb and index finger, allowing room for the needle.

Increasing

Knit your stitch as usual but do not take your stitch off the needle. Instead, put the point of your right-hand needle into the back of the stitch and draw yarn through, thus adding another stitch. This creates a small, horizontal bar. This method is most commonly used.

Simple Increase

Use your left-hand needle point and pick up the horizontal strand between the two stitches, and twist the stitch by knitting into the back, thus avoiding a hole. If you desire a hole (similar to a yarn over) do not twist.

Invisible Increase with a Right Slant

Carefully insert only the *tip* of your right-hand needle into the *back* of the stitch, just below the stitch on the left-hand needle, and knit. (The stitch is easily accessible if you angle your left-hand needle towards you.) Knit the very next stitch and proceed as usual.

Invisible Increase with a Left Slant

Carefully insert only the *tip* of your left-hand needle, from *back* to *front*, *under* the stitch just worked on the right-hand needle. Pick up loop and place it onto the left-hand needle. Knit into the back of the loop (avoids a hole), and proceed.

Seams by Symmetrical Increasing

When two increases are made in succession, the first stitch of the second increase will form an attractive chain or seam at the center. This seam may be made wider by working one, two, or three stitches between the increases. The result resembles a full-fashioned seam. This may be used for raglan sleeves, berets, collars, or where desired.

Note: Use the method of increasing that would slant the stitches towards the center seam.

Decreasing with a Right Slant

Simply put your right-hand needle through the *front* of *two* stitches, instead of one (as when knitting), on your left-hand needle and knit the two stitches together.

Decreasing with a Left Slant

Simply put your right-hand needle through the *back* of *two* stitches, instead of one, on your left-hand needle and knit the two stitches together.

Purl Decreases—Right Slant on Knit Side

Simply purl two stitches together.

Purl Decreases—Left Slant on Knit Side

Simply purl two stitches together, the reverse way, working your right-hand needle from left to right.

Variation of Decrease with a Right Slant

Slip two stitches (knitwise) from the left-hand needle to the right-hand needle, pass the yarn over the top of the right-hand needle (as you do when knitting) and bring both slipped stitches over this and off. Very neat. (Same principal as binding off.)

Variation of Decrease with a Right Slant #2

When the two stitches are knit together, by going through the *back* of the two stitches, you have a slightly raised effect.

Variation of Decrease with a Left Slant— Purl Side

Slip the last stitch purled on the right-hand needle onto the left-hand needle. Pass the second stitch on the left-hand needle over the first stitch, as if to purl. Replace the stitch onto the right-hand needle and purl. This decrease is barely discernible and is very good to use, especially when using the Reverse Stockinette Stitch.

Decrease—Preferred Left Slant Variation

Slip the first stitch from left-hand needle (knitwise) to the right-hand needle. Repeat. You now have two slipped stitches on the right-hand needle. Insert the tip of the left-hand needle into the front (right side) of the two slipped stitches and knit together.

Decrease—Left Slant Variation

Slip one stitch, as if to knit (knitwise). Knit the next stitch, then slip the first stitch over and off.

Seams by Symmetrical Decreasing

Slip, knit, and pass over for decreasing at the beginning of the seam (seam may be one, two, or three stitches) and then knit two together. This same approach may be used when shaping armholes.

Slanted decreases are placed to conform to neck edges. For instance, the decreases would follow the angle of the neckline. (Right side, use right slant, left side, use left slant.)

Rounds of decreasing in a seamless skirt should alternate. This prevents the skirt from going off on a bias. This is detailed in the Design Chapter.

Inconspicuous Decreasing—A Must to Know

This method applies to the two stitches to be worked together. Slip the first stitch, as if to knit, from your left-hand needle to the right-hand needle. Repeat; you now have two slipped stitches on the right-hand needle. Insert left-hand needle point into the *fronts* of the slipped stitches and knit them together.

Note: Practice various methods and use the method that gives you the most professional result.

Decreasing Three Stitches Together— Left Slant

Knit three stitches together through the *back* of the stitches.

Decreasing Three Stitches Together— Right Slant

Knit three stitches together through the *front* (as when knitting).

The following methods of decreasing three stitches into one pull the three together, with the *top* stitch slanting to the left or right.

Top Stitch—Left Slant

Slip one stitch, knitwise, knit two together, and pass the slipped stitch over.

Top Stitch—Right Slant

Slip one stitch, knitwise, knit the next and pass slipped stitch over. Place this stitch back onto left-hand needle and pull the second stitch, on the left-hand needle, over the stitch, allowing it to drop off. Put the remaining stitch onto the right-hand needle.

Decreasing Three Stitches Together— Center Stitch

Slip one stitch, purlwise, from left-hand needle to right-hand needle. Drop the center stitch, to the front, off the left-hand needle. Slip (purlwise) the third stitch onto the right-hand needle. Use the left-hand needle point and place the three back onto the left-hand needle; knit the three together.

Note: This method recommended for shaping square necklines.

Stitches may be decreased on the purl side by simply purling together. Practice the previously detailed methods, purling, for triple decreasing. Be aware of the desired direction of the slant.

Slipped Stitches

Stitch patterns usually specify whether the stitch is slipped knitwise or purlwise. When it is not specified, slip the stitch purlwise—regardless of the row. The stitch is then in the correct position for working on the next row.

Knitwise—On a Knit Row

Keep yarn in back, as with knitting, and insert your needle point from front to back and slip onto right-hand needle.

Purlwise—On a Knit Row

Keep yarn in back, as with knitting, and insert your needle point from back to front, as with purling, and slip stitch onto right-hand needle.

Purlwise—On a Purl Row

Have yarn in front, and insert right-hand needle point from back to front, as with purling, and slip onto right-hand needle.

Note: When slipped stitch is used on the knit row as part of the decrease, the stitch must be slipped knitwise or it will twist.

Yarn Over

This stitch is basically an increase. When made, it creates a hole. The yarn over is usually followed, in the stitch pattern, by a decrease. It is easy, since all that you have to do is put your yarn over the needle.

Knitside Yarn Over (YO)

Bring your yarn between the two needles and over the right-hand needle. Knit the next stitch. On the return row, the stitch will be knit or purled into the front. This forms a hole. A hole may also be formed by picking up the strand between two stitches.

Yarn Over Twice

The yarn is wound around the needle twice, making the hole twice as large. This is determined by the stitch pattern. A yarn over twice may also become two stitches on the return row. Yarn over twice is done by bringing your yarn between the two needles, towards you, over the needle away, and then back towards you.

Reverse Yarn Over—Smaller Hole

This is done by bringing the yarn *over* the needle from back to front and to the back again, between the two needles.

The term yarn over (yo) is used in purling, the same as in knitting.

Yarn Over When Changing from Purl to Knit

Keep the yarn in front and knit.

Reverse Yarn Over When Changing from Purl to Purl

Place your yarn in back and then bring yarn towards you and over the needle.

Reverse Yarn Over When Changing from Purl to Knit

Bring yarn in back, between the two needles, and then over the needle and back between the two needles.

Picking Up Stitches

Have your work facing you, right side out. Tie yarn in at the right edge, and hold the work in your left hand. The correct size knitting needle is in your right hand. Keep the yarn in back and *knit* your stitches on; knitting through two loops. Work from right to left, spacing stitches evenly apart and considering your gauge. Do not pick up stitches at the very edge and do not pick them up by taking a strand from previous knitting.

If you are accustomed to picking up stitches with a crochet hook and placing them onto your knitting needle, and you are getting a good result, continue to do so. Remember! Use your yarn and the same size crochet hook as your knitting needle. Do not make holes or split the yarn; if this occurs, re-do the stitch. Take the needle or hook out and insert it in a different spot.

Picking Up Neckline Stitches

This is done after the shoulder seams are sewn; hold the right side of the garment facing you. Tie your yarn in at the right shoulder seam. You will be working from right to left, around and back to the first picked up stitch. A 16″ round needle is usually used. Ribbing is usually done with a needle two sizes smaller than body gauge size. The number of stitches to pick up is based on the measurement desired and the gauge. For instance, if you desire a 20″ neckband you would multiply that number by the ribbing gauge. Space your stitches evenly apart to avoid puckering or rippling. Remember! Do not pick up stitches close to the edge; put the tip of the needle in a little way. Concentrate on the desired shape and accentuate it. If it is straight, keep it straight. If it is shaped, think of the contour, and create it as you pick up the stitches. Necklines are detailed in Chapter Ten.

Picking Up Sleeve Stitches

Sleeve stitches are picked up after the shoulder seams have been sewn and the neckline completed. Always allow for seam allowance and ease. Observe the straight line that is created by going through two loops. If your work looks ragged, or irregular, practice picking up stitches on your gauge sample. Remember that the number of stitches on each side of the shoulder seam must match. This is detailed in Chapter Four. Sleeves are also detailed in Chapter Ten.

Binding Off

Binding off may be done when knitting, purling, or working with a stitch pattern. The process is the same. Be very careful to retain the same tension as your work. Binding off should not be too loose or too tight.

Work two stitches onto your right-hand needle *then with the left-hand needle point lift the first stitch over the second stitch; this leaves you with one stitch on the right-hand needle. Then work another one.* Repeat from * (you are always working with a couplet). When binding off a required number of stitches, it is necessary to work one more stitch. The count is determined by the number of stitches dropped over and off. Fasten by pulling yarn through the last stitch, leaving at least three inches to be worked in on the wrong side.

Be aware! Keep the tension the same as your work. If you find that the binding off is too tight, use a larger needle. If too loose, use a smaller needle. It is the end of your work but not the end of your being careful.

Neck Binding Off

Always bind off in the same stitch pattern.

Shoulder Binding Off

Shoulders are usually bound off gradually; approximately one inch at a time. Perfectly balanced shoulders are achieved by tying another ball of yarn in at the neck edge and working both sides at the same time. This is detailed in Chapter Four.

Dropped Stitch

Constantly look your work over, especially when you first resume knitting. Do not neglect to pick up a single dropped stitch. Use a crochet hook the same size as the knitting needles otherwise there will be a difference in appearance. Insert the hook from front to back through the loop, with the hook facing upwards (knitside), from the back (purlside). Pull horizontal strand of the above row through the loop. Repeat cautiously; do not miss a single horizontal strand. Examine your work, closely, on both sides. Place all the stitches in the proper direction on your needle.

Note: When picking up dropped stitches on the knitside, the procedure is as knitting; when on the purlside, the procedure is as purling.

Ripping Back—One Row

Use the point of your left-hand needle and insert it into the stitch on the right-hand needle. (Point is in front of the back strand of stitch or loop.) Have your yarn in back in the right hand (as with knitting) keeping the tension of the yarn tight as you slip the stitches from the right-hand needle to the left-hand needle. Rip stitch by stitch to the mistake and *beyond*. Always rip a few stitches more. This will keep your work from showing any irregularity. When you resume knitting watch every stitch, as some may be twisted. Use your right-hand needle point to slip the twisted stitches off and replace each one correctly.

Note: Correct placement of stitch for knit or purl. The front strand of stitch (loop) is always to your right and the back strand is to your left and in back of the needle.

Ripping Back—Two Rows

Use the point of your right-hand needle and insert it into the stitch *below* on the left-hand needle. Rip beyond the mistake, to the end of the row. Then take your left-hand needle, yarn in right hand, and correctly re-place the stitches. As you do this the ripped yarn will unwind from the right-hand needle.

Ripping Back a Few Rows

When your error is too far back to work stitch by stitch, do not be afraid to pull the needles out! This is something that all of us do. Anything worth doing is worth doing right. Always rip a few rows more, wind your yarn loosely, and do not be afraid to re-use it immediately. Pick up your stitches with a smaller needle, then work another row off (stitch by stitch) using the proper size needle and placing the stitches correctly. Resume knitting.

Note: If your work has been put away for a long time, do not start to knit blissfully away, for you will not have a blissful result! Always rip back a few rows, otherwise the row where you resumed working will show. Washing or pressing will not rectify this.

Ripping Out

If you are a beginner and find that knitting has its pitfalls, do not be afraid to acknowledge the error, whether in the stitch pattern, workmanship or size. Ripping is not the bug-a-boo that many people think it is. Artists correct and constantly work over canvases, gardeners plant and transplant, and authors write three books for every one they publish. We all learn from our mistakes. Take the needles out. Check and re-check your measurements, gauge, and calculations.

Start over again using the same yarn. Spread the yarn out loosely on the floor. Wind it very loosely around your fingers and make a soft, crunchy ball. Re-use this yarn through the ribbed sections or the hem. Do not use it through the body, unless absolutely necessary. (This rule does not apply if your work has not set and if you are going to use the yarn immediately.)

Ripping a Completed Garment

Another beautiful advantage of handmade knitted or crocheted clothes is that you may wear a garment for a few years, decide on a change of style, rip it out, and re-use the yarn.

When I first started to knit; buying yarn was a problem because money was not too available. My solution was to knit, wear, rip, and re-knit! If ever you desire to completely rip a sweater or dress, do it carefully. Proceed cautiously, and allow yourself enough time. Use a sewing-needle point to open seams; do *not* use a razor. Rip all seams and bound off sections first.

I usually work in a large room, walking around and spreading the yarn out so that it will not tangle. I then rip back to a joining. When one ball or skein has been ripped, I wind it around a chair back. I tie the ends together and then tie the skein (do not make a ball) in three or four different places. This is repeated until all the yarn is skeined.

Refer to your notebook. This is another time when notes, labels and gauge samples will pay off. Read your label or notes and determine if your yarn is washable or if it has to be dry-cleaned. If you do not have your label, or any notes, *test your gauge sample*. Do not wash your yarn unless you are positive that it is washable.

The yarn, if washable, should be placed inside a pillow case, and washed briefly in cool water and with mild soap, on a gentle cycle. Rinse. *Barely spin dry*. Allow your yarn to dry naturally. Hang your skeins, individually with string on a clothesline and in the shade. If you use the dryer, set your dial on cool and keep the yarn inside the pillow case.

Joining Yarn

Do not ignore knots or imperfections. Always cut them out. Do not knot your yarn when joining. Plan your work so that all joinings are at the seams (or sides). If there are no seams, mark the sides with pins (as detailed in your Visual Patterns) so that all joinings may be correctly placed. *Do not place joinings in the middle of your work!* Rip back to the side, if necessary. When you reach the end of your ball or skein leave about four inches and entwine this strand with the yarn from the new ball. The ends of the old and new yarn will be in the back of your work. Work a few stitches, carefully and tightly, with the wound yarn. Do not separate these stitches on the next row.

EXCEPTION: Certain mohairs may be joined in the body, as it will never show. Read about combined yarns.

SECRET: Special thought and time should be given to the stitch pattern when working with lush, soft yarns. Woven stitch patterns will give added firmness and retention to skirts, suits, or items that may easily stretch. In addition to the proper stitch pattern, a great trick is combining the yarn with mercerized cotton thread. This will control the resilience of the fabric that you are making. Take the yarn to the store and match the shade as closely as possible. Wind your yarn and the thread together and examine this shading in the daylight, not under fluorescent lights. You may enhance the yarn by using a slightly different shade of thread. This depends on the yarn, you, and the result that you wish.

When a definite addition to a soft yarn is being considered for shape retention other alternatives are cotton or silk yarns. There is no limit to the combinations that you can achieve.

Combined Yarns

Yarns are combined to create individual, unusual shades and textures. It helps to prepare your yarn by balling it. This means that you loosely wind the different strands around your fingers, forming a ball. When the first color ends, as yardages vary, overlap the matching color for about four inches (do not knot). The combined ball ends with the yarn that goes the farthest; evenly cut the strands.

Once you start to work with combinations you will observe that the overlap facilitates the joining of the yarn. Always make certain that each end remains in back, that the yarn is carefully wound together, and worked in without being separated. Joinings in the middle of a row should not show if carefully worked. As I end each ball I prepare for my joinings at

least three or four yards in advance. I stagger the endings and work them in one at a time. This keeps the joinings invisible. (Exception to the previous rule.)

Another approach to working in a new ball is at the sides. They must be tied in very carefully. (Exception to the previous rule).

Imperfections

Imperfections in yarn are not always visible. Yarn may run thin, have flaws, knots, or be streaky. Cut these damages out, do *not* work them in. You will know imperfect yarn by the way it looks and the way it feels. This knowledge comes with time and experience. Do not continue working, and do not ignore a single imperfection. Rip and omit the bad yarn; it is not useable. If there are too many flaws, return all the yarn. Do not accept the same dye lot.

Ombred Yarns

The beauty of ombred yarns is unique and undeniable. Understanding the *color pattern* of *each* dye lot is most important for a professional result. When working the first ball, make notes and chart the color sequence. All joinings should continue this sequence in order to avoid color blobs. For instance, if your color sequence is white, beige, tan, light blue, dark blue, tan, beige, and white, you must break the new yarn *back* to the shade that will continue the sequence. Do not regret wasting this initial scrap; it pays off in the beauty of your garment. *Do not fail to observe this rule.*

Designs that are worked on round needles must be reassessed if ombred yarns are to be used. There will be a definite change in color and line when you separate for the armholes. If you wish to avoid this change in color pattern, plan your Visual Pattern with seams and use straight needles.

Note: Large garments may be made on round needles but the needle should be used as if it were straight. Skirts may be made without seams on round needles since the yarn works up gradually, and there is no separation and no abrupt change.

The shaping of the neckline requires thought, patience, and planning. Your color pattern should match on each side. Work with two balls of yarn and plan carefully. For instance, if you knit across and end with dark blue at the neck edge, tie dark blue in at the exact sequence on the other side. Think of this as if you were matching stripes in fabric.

Sleeves are also planned for color sequence. Pick up the stitches for your sleeve as detailed on your Visual Pattern. Write down the color and sequence that *ends* the pick up row. This is the color, in sequence, which you will use to *start* the second sleeve.

These details are what make your original design a creation; plan for them. Always purchase extra yarn.

Space-dyed Yarns

Almost the same attention should be paid to space-dyed yarns as ombred yarns. The colors have a tendency to be unpredictable. When you see that a color blob is forming, break your yarn, thus changing the color placement. Carefully join the work in the next shade. Space-dyed yarns form beautiful shadings, cloudlike and dreamy!

Ribbon

The luxury and elegant feeling of ribbon and the change of texture makes working with ribbon a unique experience. Your design should be understated, since the beauty of ribbon and stitch pattern will be sufficient.

If you are using an unfamiliar stitch pattern, practice with medium-weight yarn. Then invest in an extra roll of ribbon for your samples. Study the samples to decide if the stitch pattern enhances or detracts from the ribbon. Decide if you like the texture, resilience, and the size needles used. Make a few samples, changing the stitch patterns and the needles, and learn the uniqueness of ribbon.

As you work with ribbon you will see that it has a mind of its own. Allow the ribbon to be loose, do not control the tension, and let the ribbon rest naturally against the needle. Keep your stitches loose. You will periodically have to fasten the ribbon to the roll, and allow it to dangle. This smooths out the tangles.

Remember to press your gauge sample as detailed in the Pressing chapter. This is a must for an accurate stitch count.

Note: My favorite ironing cloth for ribbon is a white pillow case.

WHYS AND WHEREFORES

If Knitted Garment is Too Large

You did not make a gauge sample. You did not make your Visual Pattern and you did not measure your work as detailed. Perhaps, you have something tucked away, perfectly executed, but completely useless. Do not give up! If you do not wish to rip I will explain how to cut to size.

Knitting must be properly prepared before you pick up the scissors! Garments that are too wide should be double stitched on the sewing machine. Stitch the seam, where desired, and stitch one-half inch away from the seam. The outer stitching is to prevent ravelling. *Do not cut on this line*—cut one-quarter of an inch away. This applies to all seams. You must stitch all seams *twice* and you must have generous seams.

Needles—Straight

When working on a design with seams, the matching piece can be made at the same time, simply by working with two balls of yarn. This avoids constant comparison for uniformity.

Needles—Round, used as straight needles

Two round needles of the same size may be used for larger garments. This keeps the stitches from falling off. Full capes, ponchos, or coats may require three or more.

Needles—Double Pointed

When using double-pointed needles be certain to keep your stitches tight as you go from one needle to another. If you see loose stitches forming, shift the beginning and end on each needle. This is done by continuing into the next needle for two or three stitches. Keep the stitches evenly distributed between the three needles, and work with the fourth needle.

Cable Needle

This is a double pointed needle, the same size. If you find that there are loose stitches on either side of your cabling, use a smaller size.

Needle Change

When a change of needle size is specified, the change should be made stitch by stitch. This does not mean sliding the stitches, it means working the stitches.

Note: Do not interrupt your work in the middle of a row—work to the end or the sides.

Pins

Seams will always match if you mark rows or stitch patterns at exact intervals with pins.

Hems

Never make a purl line to designate the hem. Always knit the hem on a needle one size smaller than the body gauge needle.

Do not hem bulky yarns or ribbing. Many textures or patterns do not look right with hems. Crochet a neat edge. Use a crochet hook one size smaller than your knitting needles. Look closely at your work and if it curls or puckers, change the hook size. There are different crochet stitches that lend themselves to hems. These are detailed in the second section of this chapter and Chapter Nine.

Ease—Larger Women

Larger women should allow for additional stitches through the bust. When calculating your stitches for front and back, divide evenly, deduct the number of stitches that equal two inches from the back, and add this number of stitches to the front. Bind off the added stitches at the armhole. If you bind off one-half an inch at the beginning of each armhole you will have the extra two inches. If you have added more than two inches, decrease in the shaping of the armholes. Plan for this on your Visual Pattern; refer to Chapter Ten.

Lingerie Straps—A Must

Comfort and a well-groomed look can be simply achieved with needle and thread. Plait a chain of the desired length, sew one-half of a snap at the end, and the other half on the shoulder seam of your garment. The strap is attached horizontally on the garment and vertically on the slip.

Plaiting

Attach doubled, mercerized cotton thread or buttonhole twist, and form a loop by making a small stitch. Use your thumb and two fingers of your left hand to hold the loop and, with the needle and thread in your right hand, pull successive loops through, using the second finger of your left hand (similar to crocheting a chain.) Keep the loops tight and work the desired length. Fasten off.

Concealed Eyes for Hooks

Plait with matching thread or crochet a chain with matching yarn.

Threading Large Eyed Needle with Yarn

Loop your yarn, using the needle to pull it tight. Hold the yarn in your left hand between index and thumb; then squeeze yarn through the eye of the needle.

Weaving Stitches Together

No list is complete without this simple method. It may be used at shoulder seams (gradual binding off is eliminated), the toes of socks, and the tips of mittens.

Stitches should be evenly divided between two knitting needles. Naturally, you will start at the pointed end (to your right) and there should be a long strand of yarn remaining that will weave all your stitches together. Thread a large-eyed needle with this strand. There are always *two* steps on each needle but *one* stitch comes off each time.

1. Insert the sewing needle as if to *knit* in the *first front* stitch. Allow this stitch to slip onto the sewing needle and insert the sewing needle into the *next front* stitch as though to *purl*. Pull the yarn through both these stitches. Remember—one stitch is on your knitting needle and one is on your sewing needle.

2. Draw you yarn up close, but not too tight. Insert your sewing needle, as if to *purl*, into the *first stitch* on your *back* needle. Allow this stitch to slip off onto your sewing needle. Insert your sewing needle into the *next back* stitch as if to *knit*. Tighten the yarn through both stitches. Remember—one stitch is on your knitting needle and one on your sewing needle.

Repeat these two steps until all your stitches are taken off your needles. This method may be called the weaving stitch or the kitchener stitch.

Invisible Short Rows

1. Before turning for each short row, slip the next stitch from left-hand needle to right-hand needle, and wrap yarn from back to front around the base of the slipped stitch. Return the slipped stitch to the left-hand needle.

2. Turn. Work the short row (the desired number of stitches).

3. Repeat step #1 at each turning.

4. Whenever working *past* the slipped stitch with the horizontal strand that was created by wrapping yarn on the previous row, place the horizontal strand on the left-hand needle and work with the stitch. Stitch is either knitted or purled, so follow your pattern. When knitting, work into the back loops,

working strand and stitch together. This makes a neat turning.

Buttonholes—Knit In

(Cut-in buttonholes are detailed in Sewing chapter.)

Placement of buttonholes should be planned on your Visual Pattern. Proper placement is determined by the size of the buttons and whether the buttonholes will be horizontal or vertical. Draw your top and bottom buttonhole to exact size on your Visual Pattern. Divide the remaining inches according to the number of buttonholes you wish to make. Measure from the center of one buttonhole to the next center, placing them evenly apart.

Buttonholes—Horizontal

Buttonholes may be knitted in, in one row. If your current method is to use two rows, one for the binding off and the other for the casting on, please try the following method. It is neat and practically flawless. When additional firmness is needed (as when working with soft, fluffy yarns), combine your yarn with matching mercerized cotton thread, single or doubled. The cotton thread is worked in, with the end in back for future knotting, exactly where the buttonhole is to be placed, *one row below* and the working row. Then the end of the thread is knotted, with the beginning, and left in back.

1. Allow sufficient stitches at the edge. Have the yarn in front and slip one stitch from the left-hand needle to the right-hand needle. Drop your yarn in back. Disregard the yarn.

2. Bind off the required number of stitches by slipping stitches from the left-hand needle to the right-hand needle. Use the left point and pick the first stitch and slip it off over the second stitch, thus binding off one stitch. Repeat this for the number you need to take off.

3. Slide the last bound off stitch from the right-hand needle to the left-hand needle and *turn.*

4. Place yarn in back. Cast on the number that you bound off, plus one. The right-hand needle point is inserted between the first and second stitch on the left-hand needle. Pull through a loop and slip this onto the left-hand needle; then place the needle through that loop and the one previously made. Loop through and again place the loop on the left-hand needle, place the needle and pull the loop through the last two loops on the left-hand needle. (Always the last two; towards the point.) Create loops to equal the number bound off, then bring yarn to the front and make a final loop. Turn.

5. Extra stitch is either decreased (worked together), or you can put the first stitch from the left-hand needle to the right-hand needle, and slip the last stitch over it. Continue the stitch pattern and complete the row.

Horizontal buttonholes may also be made by binding off the needed number in one row, and on the return row casting on the same number. Care must be taken when making the end stitches.

Buttonholes—Vertical

Work across to the start of the buttonhole (count the stitches and note them), tie in another strand of yarn by pulling it through the stitch, winding the two strands together, and working three or four stitches (joining). Each side of the buttonhole is worked separately but at the same time. When you have the desired length, carefully tie the additional strand to the first strand of yarn. Cut your extra yarn to about six inches and wind the two strands together. Work a few stitches, leaving a short piece in back. This will be worked in later.

Note: Stitches that are worked with doubled yarn, for securing, will look neat if worked tightly. If you are not satisfied, carefully knot the yarn, and work the end in later. This also takes practice.

Edges for Chanel-type Garments

Edgings may be applied, on completion of the garment, or they may be made as you work. The latter is my preference as I find this method flawless! The border may be made at the very edge or an inch or so from the edge. This border may continue around the neckline and may also be used on the sleeves. Think out your different ideas, place them on the Visual Pattern, and decide if you want the edging to match or contrast.

When working contrast edgings or edgings that require a different ball of yarn, it is wise to fasten your yarn so that the balls do not entangle. Wrap your yarn a few times around the ball and fasten the strand with a safety pin. This may be done to each ball. Unfasten the pin as you use the particular yarn—this is worth the effort.

When changing yarns always hold the yarn that you have just finished working to the *left*, and pick up the next yarn from *underneath*. This crosses your yarn, tightens the stitch, and keeps holes from forming. Be certain to cross firmly and avoid a visible break (loose stitch) between colors.

Corners are worked by marking the center stitch and decreasing at each side of the marked stitch. An alternative is to use a triple decrease (refer to decreases).

Applied borders must be made carefully, pinned accurately, and basted and sewn on carefully. This takes time, thought, patience, and practice.

There is no limit to the imaginative ways you can use fringe, tassels, braid, beads, ribbon, fur, lace stitch, patterns, or cables.

Fringe

Luxuriously full fringe adds tremendously to heavier garments. The length and fullness is determined by the design, so you must always consider proportion and balance. Fringe should be made with its use in mind. Cardigans, dresses, or tabards may be trimmed around the neckline and at the wrists with delicate, contrasting fringe.

Note: When making thick fringe, the outer strands will be longer; trim all strands evenly.

1. Cut cardboard (desired length, plus knot allowance) and use as a form so that the fringe will be uniform.

2. Wind as many strands around the cardboard as needed for the desired fullness. Cut at the bottom.

3. Use a large crochet hook; draw the loop of the combined strands through the edge of knitting. (A loop is formed by the doubling of the strands.) Draw the ends of the yarn through the loop; pull firmly.

4. Place the first fringe at the beginning of the row and the second one at the end. Place them evenly, at least one-half inch from each end—this *must* match.

5. Measure the space between the fringes at each end with a ruler or yardstick and divide by the number of fringe that you wish to place. Mark with pins or contrasting thread so the fringe will be evenly spaced. (Draw this on your Visual Pattern; it will help you.)

6. Be certain to pull all the fringe through from the same side.

Tassels

Cut a cardboard square the size you wish for your tassel. Wind yarn around this square many, many times until you have the desired thickness. (If you are going to make more than one tassel, keep count, and make a note for exact duplication.)

Cut the bottom of the tassel while it is still on the card. Trim ends if necessary. Shake!

Tassels may be made of more than one color or of one color with a different shade wound around the top.

Tie strands of yarn through the top to secure the doubling over and then wind them around and around the top of the tassel. Pull and knot tightly. Conceal the end.

For variety, you can make your tassel striped down the middle, on the outside, or have one color in the center and another one on the outside. Experiment!

Dainty tassels, placed as a yoke around the neckline and around the wrists instead of a ribbing or border will make your sweater or dress uniquely yours!

Fringe and tassels may be made longer and knotted twice, and festoons or knots may be used to create a lacy appearance.

Perfect PomPon

1. Cut two circles, using firm cardboard, to the desired size.
2. Cut a hole exactly in the center of each circle.
3. Place the circles together and wrap them in yarn, drawing yarn through center and over the edge. The fuller the pompon, the more yarn you will wind around. Fill the center openings.
4. Slip a scissor between the two circles and carefully cut all strands along the outside edges.
5. Bring the yarn outward and tie the strands together tightly, at the center between the two circles. Leave a free end for attaching.
6. Remove the disks and fluff!

Easy PomPon

1. Cut the cardboard to the desired depth and place two strands of yarn, horizontally, across the top.
2. Wind the yarn around this; making your pompon as full as possible.
3. Securely tie your horizontal strands together to secure the pompon.
4. Cut the yarn at the other end. Shake! Trim!

Pompons are similar to tassels but they should be lush, full, and not as long.

Beads

The choice of a bead depends on the yarn. Fine beads are for fine yarn and delicate designs. (Heavy beads on fine yarn would definitely pull the yarn out of shape.) Heavy beads are for thick yarn. Beads may be used while crocheting or knitting or they may be carefully sewn on after the completion of the garment. When purchasing beads, determine if they may be washed or if they must be dry-cleaned, then consider the yarn and the use.

CROCHETING

The youth of today have discovered this ancient art and have given it an entirely new dimension. The simplest stitches, single and double crochet, are used with large wooden hooks and rainbow combinations of yarns. The results are original, individual, and priceless! You can develop this talent, as it is latent in all of us. The approach is basic—it is like learning to walk. The most important step is the first step. If you have never crocheted, you are now going to change your life.

Walk into a yarn shop, look at all the colors (not just your favorites), and wind some of them together, combining tweeds, mohairs, ribbons, and novelty yarns. Buy and *try* the different sizes of hooks—especially the wooden hooks. Combine as many as three or four strands and crochet away!

Ideas and designs are inspired by seeing; knowledge is attained through trying. Fascinating yarns are constantly being introduced; be aware of them, try them. Understanding the use of your gauge sample, making your Visual Pattern, and learning the simple techniques in this section will inspire you and spark your enthusiasm.

Most knitting yarns may be used for crocheting. Although crocheting uses more yarn than knitting, it is well worth it. Your rows are deeper, the work goes faster, the result is fascinating, and the additional expense is negligible. Always work with quality yarns, trust your fingers, and listen to what they say as you feel the strands of yarn.

Beginners: proceed with confidence and assurance. If you know how to make a knot, then you know how to start a chain. A chain is a series of loops. Loops become stitches, and stitches become your design.

Start with a medium-sized crochet hook and a medium weight yarn. Do not use a compli-cated yarn, use a smooth and firm one. Concentrate on making the chain and then make sample squares using the single and double crochet. Practice holding your crochet hook as if it were a pencil. Be patient, for it is so easy that after you make your first chain, you will laugh! After you make your first row of single crochet, nothing will stop you!

I have written instructions for the different basic crochet stitches. Refer to them and practice them. Use the stitch that you prefer. Make your designs individually yours. Remember that the beauty of the stitch lies in the even loop formation. Rip out an uneven stitch. Start again if you find that the rhythm of your work has changed the symmetry of your rows. This may happen to anyone. The first three inches may be looser and then the work may tighten up. Do not try to loosen the tension of your stitches to make them match, as you are simply finding your pace. Rip back or discard the sample piece. Never, never settle for anything less than perfection!

Any Visual Pattern or design in this book is adaptable for crocheting. The shape, the design is there. Your figures, both body measurements and gauge calculations, insure your total success.

When you start the garment do not forget to measure after crocheting three or four inches. Always measure on a flat surface, using your Visual Pattern and measuring equipment. Be certain that your work matches the pattern and measures the desired dimensions. It is possible that the tension of your stitches will change when crocheting a larger piece. Do not take anything for granted; measure and compare constantly. If necessary, make adjustments as detailed.

Slip Knot

Sit comfortably, holding your yarn and hook in your hand. Make a loop four or five inches from the end. Hold this loop between the thumb and forefinger of your left hand with the yarn behind the loop. Place the crochet hook in right hand and pull yarn through loop.

Chain

Your chain is the basic row, and is the foundation for anything that you are going to make. Put yarn over hook (YO), and draw yarn through loop on hook, forming a loop of the desired size. You now have one loop on the crochet hook and the working yarn over the left-hand index finger. Repeat. The left hand holds your work and the yarn. Your right hand holds the hook. Learn to control the yarn as it moves through your fingers. Keep the tension of the yarn even, and not too tight or too loose. Chain the desired length, keeping your loops even.

Turning Post

A row with any stitch requires a turning post. A turning post may be made at the end of a row before turning or at the beginning of a row after turning. The turning post is always counted as the first stitch and the stitch immediately following is usually skipped. At the end of each row the last stitch is worked into the turning post of the previous row. A turning post consists of one, two, or more loops. The number of loops depends on the height of the row you are going to crochet. (The height of a row is determined by the thickness of the yarn, the stitch, and the hook.) When crocheting with bulky yarns, chain one loop less than required on average weight yarns; this makes a firm edge and keeps the sides of the garment from sagging. A turning post may also be made by working the similar stitch. This does not apply to single or double crochet. Single crochet requires two loops and double crotchet requires three loops. As you practice you will see the need for the extra loop.

Note: Always count the stitches in each row. Be positive that you have not omitted one. This is easy to do and must be avoided.

Single Crochet

Hold chain or work horizontally. Insert the hook into the second loop on the chain (turning post), put yarn over the hook (YOH), draw yarn through the loop (this gives you two loops on the crochet hook) then yarn over (YO) and draw through both loops, resulting in having one loop remaining on the crochet hook. This completes one stitch. *Insert hook into next chain stitch, put yarn over the hook, draw yarn through the loop (this gives you two loops on the crochet hook) then yarn over and draw through both loops, resulting in one loop on hook.* Repeat from *. At the end of row, chain two for turning post and turn.

Note: Always insert hook from front to back. Always insert hook under the *two* top loops (unless directions specify otherwise). Do not work tightly. One loop will always remain on your hook on the completion of a stitch.

Second Row

The turning post has been made, work is turned, and the reverse side is facing you. Single crochet as previously described between *—*. Remember to count the stitches. You will gradually see the straight edge and your eye will guide you.

Single Crochet—Variation

Patterns that specify going through only *one* loop create a different appearance. As your work progresses you will see a line or ridge form. This ridge is created by only going through the *back* loop. This is very effective when working with bulky yarns and a large hook.

Single Crochet for Edging

This may be used for edging necklines, sleevees, hems and edges. The best result is achieved by using a crochet hook that is one size smaller than the knitting needles.

1. Always have the garment with the right (front) side facing you.

2. Tie yarn in at the right side since you are going to crochet from right to left. (Reverse if left-handed.)

3. Always go through two loops of the edge, spacing stitches evenly apart. Refer to your gauge, as you do not want any puckering or pulling. (Puckering is the result of too many stitches, and pulling of not enough stitches.) The first row is the most important row of the edging.

4. Crochet the desired rows.

5. Fasten your work by pulling yarn through the last stitch. Leave at least four inches of yarn and work this end in on the reverse side.

Note: Corners are made by making one extra stitch, exactly on the point. Be precise.

Tip: Be painstakingly precise when starting the edging. Do not place the stitches too closely or the edging will curl. Crochet for about six inches, examine the edging closely, and make a judgment. Your eyes will tell you when it is not right. The crocheted edge should blend smoothly into your garment.

Double Single Crochet

Crochet your chain. Insert the hook into the second loop from the hook, draw yarn through, yarn over hook, draw yarn through one loop, yarn over hook, draw yarn through two loops. *Insert hook into next loop, draw yarn through, YOH, draw yarn through one loop, YOH, draw yarn through two loops.* Repeat from * to end. Make your turning post, turn.

Second Row: Work as between *—*.

Half-Double Crochet

Chain. Allow extra loops for turning post. *Yarn over hook, insert hook into the next stitch, YOH, draw yarn through, making a loop, YOH, draw yarn through the three loops at once. One loop remaining.* Repeat from * to the end. Make your turning post, turn.

Second Row: Work as between *—*.

Double Crochet

Crochet the chain longer than the desired length. Allow for turning post (two or three loops, depending on the height of the row). *Yarn over hook, insert hook into the loop, YOH, draw yarn through loop (there are now three loops), YOH, draw yarn through two loops (two loops remaining on hook) YOH, draw yarn through two loops. One loop remaining.* Repeat from * to end. Make your turning post, turn.

Second Row: Crochet the same, work as between *—*, except for crocheting into the stitch below (instead of a loop of the chain) going through two loops.

Double Crochet—Variation

Patterns that specify going through one loop only (the back loop) create ridges. This is most effective when working with combined yarns.

Note: Different yarns and combinations of yarns require different stitches. In time you may wish to know them. All stitches start with a slip knot and the chain, and all stitches require a turning post.

Triple Crochet

You are going to pull yarn through two loops, *three times*. Have chain longer than desired length; allow for turning post (four or five loops. *YOH twice, insert hook and draw yarn through, four loops on hook. YOH, draw yarn through two loops, YOH, draw yarn through two loops, three times in all, one loop remaining.* Repeat from * to end of row. Make your Turning Post, turn.

Second Row and Following Rows: Insert hook into the second stitch (first stitch is the turning post) crochet as between *—*. At end of row, always work into the turning post of the previous row.

Double Triple Crochet

This stitch is one loop taller than the Triple Crochet. Consider this when making the turning post. *YOH *three times*, insert hook into stitch, draw loop through, five loops on hook. YOH, draw yarn through two loops, *four times*. One loop remaining.* Repeat from * to end of row. Make your turning post, turn.

Treble Triple Crochet

Chain, allowing extra loops (six or seven) for turning post. This stitch is the loosest. *YOH *four times*, insert hook and continue as in the Triple Crochet with two extra steps. (You now have six loops on your hook. YOH, draw through two loops, *five times*.* Repeat from * to end of row. Make your turning post, turn.

Slip Stitch

This is a joining stitch. It is also used to strengthen edges. It does not add to the height of your previous work. Chain. *Insert hook, YO, and with a single motion draw yarn through the stitch and the loop on the hook.* (This is one-half of the single crochet.) This is used to join a chain, thus forming a circle.

Round or Ring

The basis of most circles. Make a short chain and join with a slip stitch. Work stitches for the first round by going into the center of the ring. This forms a neat circle.

Increasing

Crochet two stitches into the same stitch. Use the stitch that you are working with. For instance, if you are double crocheting, do two double crochets in the same stitch. Plan to place increases at the beginning and end of rows. You may also increase by not skipping the stitch immediately after the turning post. If possible, avoid increasing through the body of the garment.

Increasing Several Stitches or Casting On—Beginning

Crochet a chain equivalent to the number of desired stitches plus stitches for the turning post. For instance, if you need five stitches, chain five plus the number needed for the turning post.

Casting On at the End—Method #1

Chain the number of stitches needed at the beginning of the previous row; slip stitch over stitches.

Casting On at the End—Method #2

I find this method is the best when working with bulky or combined yarns. At the end of the row, I tie another strand (or strands) of yarn in at the base of the last stitch, and I chain the needed number. I fasten the last loop, break the yarn, retie, and proceed to finish the row. Each side is perfectly balanced.

Note: Always count the stitches in the row before increasing or decreasing, then count the stitches in the row where you increased or decreased. This is where mistakes easily occur; place pins to help you count and to aid you in measuring. Be accurate.

Decreasing

Plan to do your decreasing at the beginning and end of the row. Irregular edges are lost in proper sewing of the seams. Decreasing is done by crocheting two stitches together or skipping two stitches after the turning post.

Decreasing Several Stitches or Binding Off—Beginning

To decrease several stitches at the beginning of the row, slip stitch over the number to be decreased. Crochet the turning post.

Binding Off at the End

Crochet to the end, *minus* the number of stitches to be bound off, make the turning post, turn, and work the row.

Fasten Off

Simply pull the yarn through the last stitch. Always leave about four inches and work the end carefully (on the reverse side) through a few stitches. Never cut an end too short.

Shoulder Shaping

Refer to your gauge and decide on the number of stitches to be bound off. This must be done on each side at the beginning and end of the same row to be balanced. At the beginning of the row, slip stitch the number to be bound off and at the end of the row do not work that number. Make the turning post and turn.

Note: Remember to consider yarn, stitch, crochet hook, and gauge.

Joining Yarn

Do not knot. Plan to make all joinings at the seams. Joinings are detailed in the knitting section. If it is absolutely necessary to join the yarn in the middle of the row, wind your yarn together carefully, work this in at the yarn over, and lay the old and new ends on top of the row. Work these ends in as you crochet; crochet over them.

Note: Always attach new balls or skeins at the beginning or end of a row. Plan for this.

Knots

Cut all knots out; do not ignore a single one. Refer to joinings and imperfections in the knitting section.

Joining Combinations of Yarns

Refer to the knitting section. Place the joined yarn in the middle of the stitch that you are crocheting, through the yarn over and the loops. Your joinings will melt into your work. This method leaves the old and new ends in back; refer to Joining in this section (above).

Note: Preparing combinations of yarn is detailed in the knitting section.

Crocheted Edgings

Crocheted borders and edgings are detailed and illustrated in Chapter Nine. They are also discussed in Chapter Five. I am now going to list a few musts!

1. Carefully measure your garment. Know the exact length needed for your edging.

2. Draw the placement of the trim on your Visual Pattern. Decide whether you want the trim at the exact edge or set in about an inch.

3. Make your gauge sample. This will aid you in knowing how long the basic chain should be.

4. Study your edging design, determine how you will shape it, and plan to start and end in an inconspicuous place.

5. Corners may have to be mitred. This mitre may be made while crocreting the border or two strips may be crocheted and butted at the corner.

Two Strips—Butted (See Figure 42.)

The corner is carefully bent under, basted, and tacked down with concealed stitching. All stitching must be done loosely to avoid puckering. Carefully butt the second strip to the first.

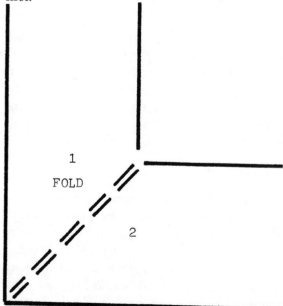

Figure 42. Two strips—butted.

Crocheted Mitred Corner

1. Measure your gauge sample and determine the length needed for the basic chain.

2. Refer to your Visual Pattern and your garment and determine exactly where you want the corner.

3. Mark this spot on your chain. Use contrasting thread.

4. Your chain becomes the *innermost* corner.

5. The corner is made by chaining two every other row at this point. Count your stitches. (Mark with a pin, ten stitches before and after the two loops. These two loops become one stitch on each side of the strip. This will help you to see the shaping.)

6. Stitches may be crocheted into the loops or around the loops. If worked around the loops, a small hole is formed.

Mitred Corner—Chain the desired length

1. *Single Crochet to loop before the marked loop (corner), chain two, single crochet (stitch optional) to the end*.

2. *Crochet to chain 2, work the two, and continue to the end*. Repeat these two rows.

Circle Formula

When shaping any circle there is one basic formula that will keep it flat. This basic formula is to use six increases to a round. If increasing every other round, there would be twelve increases. If every third round, increase *nineteen* stitches. This will keep your work flat and eliminate ripples or puckers.

Crocheted Buttons

There will be times when you will want your buttons to blend with your garment. Beads, old buttons, or button forms may be used. Work with matching or contrasting yarn. Make a slip stitch and a short chain, join, and single crochet a little circle. Set your form within the circle and crochet, shaping to the width and then decreasing to enclose the form.

Fasten your last stitch, leaving a length for sewing. Conceal this end if you wish to sew the button with mercerized cotton thread.

Buttonholes

Draw the buttonholes on your Visual Pattern. Read about this in Chapter Five and in this chapter under Knitted Buttonholes.

Buttonholes—Horizontal

Crochet in, counting the stitches so that the edge will be uniform, at least one-half to three-quarters of an inch. (Make a note of the number of stitches.) Crochet a chain, the loops to equal the desired width of the buttonhole, and then continue crocheting to the end of the row.

Return Row at the Chain: Crochet to the chain. Stitches may be worked around the chain, to equal the number, or into the loops. (Encasing the chain is determined by your stitch pattern. Try both and use the method that looks the best.) Crochet to the end. These two rows are repeated wherever the buttonholes are desired.

Buttonholes—Vertical

Crochet to the exact spot, keeping the edge uniform, and tie another strand of yarn in. You are now working two separate pieces at the same time. (Turning posts will be required.) Make the turning post and continue crocheting to the end of the row.

Return Row: Crochet to buttonhole (separation), pick up the other strand, make turning post and work with edging stitches. Continue crocheting the two sides for the length of the buttonhole. Then re-join the two sides by carefully tying and crocheting the wound strands for a few stitches. Conceal the end on the reverse side. Repeat the vertical buttonholes where needed. Be accurate.

Note: Crochet turning posts firmly for they are the exact edge of your buttonhole. Buttonholes should be practiced, as any flaw will show. Your buttonholes are very obvious and must look professional.

Skirts—Waistbands

Knitted and crocheted skirts may have an additional crocheted waistband. This is usually done in the single crochet for about one inch. Elastic may be attached on the wrong side. This is detailed in Chapter Five.

A chain may be made and attached to the inside of the waistband. Chain the number of stitches needed to span from the top to the bottom of the band, tack this down with your hook and a stitch (slipstitch), and repeat, going back and forth at an angle. Proceed around the waistband. This creates a diagonal chain to thread your elastic through either by drawing it through or by encasing it. This diagonal chain may be made with mercerized cotton, using the plaiting method, or crocheted (chain) with matching yarn (See Figure 43.)

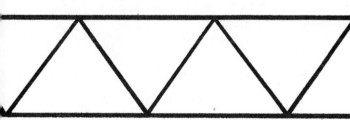

Figure 43. Diagonal chain to hold elastic inside waistband.

An alternative to the diagonal chain is vertical posts, made of chains crocheted closely together or the triple crochet.

These types of casing do not conceal the elastic.

Cords

Cords for belts, cords for bags, cords to attach mittens and gloves, cords for trimming—there is no limit to their uses. Chain a small circle, join, and work the number of stitches you desire around the circle; encase the circle for a neat beginning. Do not slip stitch at the end of the round, but continue crocheting, using single or double crochet, to create a spiral effect. Work the desired length. Fasten.

This cord looks stunning as a belt when knotted at each end.

Assembling Crocheted Garments

Remember • Consult the Sewing chapter.
- Always match rows at the seams.
- Although both sides may look alike, your ridges must match. For instance, there is a strand from the foundation chain to your right, and this becomes the outside front. The end of the foundation chain for the outside back should also be to the right. If they are not placed properly, your ridges will not line up.
- Consult the Pressing chapter.

There is no limit to the articles and garments that may be crocheted. Chapter Nine is your treasure chest. A complete wardrobe may be created in an extraordinarily short time: gloves, hats, and scarves in one sitting, sweaters and skirts in a week.

ABBREVIATIONS AND SYMBOLS
KNITTING

B	Back of Stitch
Beg	Beginning
BG	Body Gauge
BGN	Body Gauge Needle
BO	Bind Off
Chg	Change Needles
CN	Cable Needle
CO	Cast On
Con	Contrasting Color
Dec	Decrease (x = symbol)
DPN	Double Pointed Needle (same as Cable Needle)
G	Gauge
GN	Gauge Needle
GS	Garter Stitch
Inc	Increase (+ = symbol)
K	Knit
MC	Main Color
N	Needle
P	Purl
PSSO	Pass Slip Stitch Over

ABBREVIATIONS AND SYMBOLS
CROCHETING

PU	Pick Up Stitches
Pat	Pattern
RN	Round Needle
Rem	Remainder or Remaining
RG	Ribbing Gauge
RGN	Ribbing Gauge Needle
Rib	Ribbing
Rep	Repeat (* = symbol)
SKP	Slip, Knit, and Pass
Sl	Slip Stitch
SN	Straight Needles
SS	Stockinette Stitch
T	Tie Another Strand In
TBL	Through Back Loop
TFL	Through Front Loop
Tog	Together
WE	Work Even
YB	Yarn in Back
YF	Yarn in Front
YO	Yarn Over
YO—3	Yarn Over—Number Represents YO's

Beg	Beginning
Ch	Chain
Cl	Cluster
DC	Double Crochet
Dec	Decrease
DSC	Double Single Crochet
HDC	Half Double Crochet
HTR	Half Triple Crochet
Inc	Increase
Lp	Loop
Pat	Pattern
PR	Previous Row or Round
Rep	Repeat (* used)
Sk	Skip
Sl St	Slip Stitch
Sp	Space
St	Stitch
Tog	Together
Tr	Triple Crochet
YOH	Yarn Over Hook
YRH	Yarn Round Hook

Symbols

x	Decrease
+	Increase
*	Repeat
* *	Repeat within

Symbols

x	Decrease
+	Increase
*	Repeat
* *	Repeat Within

CHAPTER NINE

Stitches

Knitters and crocheters have individual reactions to yarn and stitch patterns, just as art collectors have individual reactions to paintings. Think about your reactions, as they are the key to deciding on stitch patterns. The exhilaration that you will feel when you are creating your design is truly wonderful. There is no limit to the uniqueness of your design; the look depends on you. You select the yarn, stitch pattern, and the size of knitting needles or crochet hook. Stitch and yarn must be in harmony.

Yarns immediately change the character of a stitch pattern. If you have decided on a stitch pattern, you must select a yarn that is compatible. If you have decided on the yarn, you must select a stitch pattern that will enhance the texture and color. The combination of yarn and stitch must also suit your purpose.

Try the same stitch pattern with various yarns and various sizes of knitting needles and crochet hooks. Always strive for an innovative result from your combination of yarn, stitch pattern, needles, and hooks.

KNITTING

Think of the challenge of knitting and purling. Straight knitting or straight purling cre-
ates the Garter Stitch, the stitch for beginners. Do you know that this stitch can create a beautiful sweater? Knitting a row, purling a row creates the Stockinette Stitch, and is the look that we most commonly think of as knitting. This stitch is incomparable for novelty yarns, mohairs, chenilles, and cashmeres. Variations of this stitch are indispensable when working with ribbon. Its hidden beauty is in its subtle simplicity and evenness. There is also another side to the Stockinette Stitch; the wrong side, the reverse side. However, what makes it reverse or wrong? Call it the Reverse Stockinette Stitch and you have another way to exhibit your yarn.

Make a six-inch sample. Knit a row and purl a row, and on the knit side simply knit into the back of each stitch. You now have the Crossed Stitch variation. Make another six inch sample. Knit a row and purl a row, and work into the back loop of each stitch. You now have the Twisted Stitch variation.

Knitting and purling also creates ribbing. Ribbing is most commonly used to edge garments. Plan your ribbed border to coordinate with your body stitch pattern. Whenever possible, continue the knit or purl of the ribbing into the knit or purl of the body pattern. This is a little detail, but is worth attention. Countless variations in ribbing patterns are attained by changing the number of stitches in the knit and purl ribs, by twisting the stitches, by crossing the knit stitches every other row, or by slipping stitches. Ribbings may also be made by cabling or yarning over.

We have discussed knitting, purling, ribbing, and variations. Knitting and purling also become vertical ribbing and may be used to make horizontal ribbing, ridging, or welting. Plan your individual stitch pattern by varying widths.

Consider your experience when selecting a stitch pattern. Do not select a complicated pattern if you are a beginner. Study the stitch patterns and select a simpler version. All patterns have a logical sequence. Your fingers and your mind will work together and you will gradually learn to understand the most intricate stitch patterns. Learning new patterns requires the proper approach. Prepare yourself: work with lightly colored yarns and medium-sized needles. Have patience and persevere.

Learning a Stitch Pattern

1. Cast on sufficient stitches. Allow for a minimum of six patterns.

2. The number of stitches to cast on is determined by the number of stitches in the pattern. (The number within * — *.) This is called the multiple. Patterns may also have plus or extra stitches. Your total stitches should be divisible by the multiple, plus the extra stitches.

3. Stitch patterns may consist of more than one row. All patterns clearly state the number of rows.

4. Stitch patterns consist of the multiple plus the number of rows. This becomes the repeat when completed.

5. The proper size needle must be used. Experience will teach you that needles too large create holes, limpness of texture, and affect the stitch pattern. Experience will also teach you that needles too small create hard textures, absorb lace patterns, and diminish the

intrinsic value of the yarn and stitch pattern.

6. Always have a pencil and notebook.

7. Avoid interruptions. If you are interrupted, mark the spot on your directions and note down the row number.

8. Break down the pattern directions by writing them down. Emphasize the rows that are different.

9. Work, work, work; do not quit! Put your work aside, review the pattern and resume.

10. Practice the pattern stitch. Always bind off continuing the stitch pattern.

11. Make a fresh gauge sample in the yarn, color, and needles that you plan to use. (Yarn labels may suggest a size needle but *you* must experiment with sizes; strive for the best result from your combination of yarn, stitch pattern, and needles.

12. Study the fresh sample and re-assess it. Do you still like the look, the texture, and the feeling?

Note: Several stitch patterns may be combined in one garment. Each stitch pattern requires a gauge sample.

Suggestion for Dreamers

1. List the numbers of the rows in your stitch pattern.

2. Cross off the corresponding number as you work each row; continue doing this until you are familiar with each row.

Converting Stitch Pattern for Round Needle

1. Cast on the number of stitches needed to equal the required measurement which is divisible by the multiple. Do not include extra or plus stitches. Consider the repeat.

2. Mark the beginning of the round; consider this a side of the garment.

3. Place all increases or decreases on the sides.

4. Consider the increase or decrease when working the stitch pattern. If it cannot be included make a side seam-line as detailed on your Visual Pattern.

5. Stitch patterns usually alternate with a purl row, when working on a round needle, do the opposite and knit. Meaning: do the opposite of what is specified for alternate rows.

6. When stitch pattern consists of more than two rows, write the stitch pattern on a piece of paper, converting the alternate rows.

7. Slipped stitches are worked as specified. Do the opposite on all alternate rows. Slipped stitches, when not part of a decrease, are slipped purlwise on a knit row.

Logic of Lace Patterns

The knowledge of how to knit lace patterns is at your fingertips! Do not allow the written page or chart to inhibit you! Read it through *twice*, keep paper and pencil by your side, and relax as you pick up your yarn and needles. Your fingers will work with your mind and you will soon see the simplicity of the pattern. The pattern will gradually come to life, the form will be visible, and you will see definite lines, shapes, or figures. These are created numerically, and if you mis-count the error will show blatantly. Look at the error, think about it, and start over again. Do not rip; knit two rows and resume practicing the stitch pattern. Work at the pattern until it is familiar to you. Your stitches and patterns will definitely benefit from practice.

Fine yarns, thin mohair, ribbon, and silk yarns lend themselves beautifully to lace patterns. Do not make your gauge sample too small. You will have a better result if you measure the individual pattern and the full width of your gauge sample.

Tip: When shaping sleeves or the body of your garment, retain the lines or patterns by increasing or decreasing the size of the needles. If you wish to diminish the size, use smaller needles; if you wish to enlarge, use larger needles.

Pressing Lace Patterns

There is no rule for this. Experienced knitters press according to the desired look. I do not care for anything that has been stretched or pressed to the fullest. I prefer making my work wider. The simplest answer to pressing is to experiment on your samples. The first step is as detailed in Chapter Six.

The second step may be pressing in the direction that you think your lace may stretch thus affecting the length or width of the garment. Therefore, you would press in this direction, removing any give in the knitting. Think about what you want. This must be done on your gauge sample so that you will be able to calculate accurately for your Visual Pattern.

CROCHETING

The basic crocheting stitches are detailed in the preceding chapter. I have selected crocheted stitch patterns that I consider the essence of beautiful and elegant crocheting. As you work them, ideas for their use will inspire you. Enjoy the fun of crocheting and store them carefully in your treasure chest!

Learning a Stitch Pattern

1. Chain sufficient loops. Make your chain at least ten inches long. Do not skimp.

2. The total number of loops must be divisible by the multiple, plus extra stitches. Always considering your gauge.

3. Crocheting starts with the chain. Stitch patterns may have one or two basic rows before the repeat. (Repeat consists of the multiple and the total rows in the stitch pattern.)

4. Read the directions carefully. Always count the turning post as one stitch and do not work the stitch immediately after it, unless specified otherwise. Always work the last stitch in the row into the turning post of the previous row. *Count your stitches!*

5. Try the same stitch pattern with different crochet hooks to determine the best size. Look at your work carefully and think about this decision. It must satisfy *you*.

6. Remember! The directions within * — * are repeated as detailed.

7. Always measure the full width of each stitch pattern and the full width of the gauge sample in order to average out an accurate gauge. Do not measure at the start; measure across the middle. Tension and work changes after the first few rows.

8. Try different stitch patterns. They will glow and come to life in your hands!

9. Press carefully and then measure for gauge; refer to Pressing.

Note: ALWAYS ALLOW FOR WIDER SEAMS.

Each stitch pattern has many facets. Make the same pattern many times, allowing the colors and assorted textures to show you the intrinsic value of each sample, stitch by stitch. Become a collector, and enrich your approach to designing.

Allow this collection to grow, reflecting the yarns that interest you and the stitch patterns that have inspired you. As the samples move through your hands you will know how they feel, how to make them, and how to use them.

The stitch patterns that I have detailed have been selected with you in mind.

KNITTING STITCHES

1. Garter Stitch
2. Stockinette Stitch
3. Reverse Stockinette
4. Crossed Knitting
5. Twisted Knitting
6. Ribbing: K1—P1
7. Continental Ribbing
8. Moss Stitch
9. Ribbing: K2—P2
10. Slipped Stitch Ribbing
11. Broken Ribbing
12. Spiral Ribbing: K2—P2
13. Spiral Ribbing: K3—P3
14. Teardrops
15. Teardrops Variation
16. Ladybug
17. Brioche
18. Mother's Favorite
19. Horizontal Ridges
20. Vertical Wide Ribbing

21. Finesse
22. Gathers
23. Knitted Pleats
24. Francoise's Twist
25. Baby Cable—Left
26. Baby Cable—Right
27. Baby Cable—Both Directions
28. Baby Twist Fabric
29. Double Twist Rib
30. Cable—Right
31. Cable—Left
32. Cable—Both Directions
33. Cable—Entwining
34. Petite
35. Reverse Petite
36. Slipped Ribbed Fabric
37. Flat Ribbed
38. Alternate Weave
39. Slipped Stone
40. Pearl Drops
41. Ripples
42. Mildred's Couplet
43. Woven Couplet
44. Luscious Loops
45. Diamond Smocking
46. Lace Faggot
47. Fragile
48. Alternating Faggot
49. Muffy's Tiny Bell Lace
50. Tiny Favorite
51. My Favorite Lace
52. Laburnum Stitch—Eyelet Rib
53. Quaint Lace
54. Diamond Lace
55. Melissa Jane's Favorite—Van Dyke Lace

1. Garter Stitch. (Figure 44.)
   Knit each row.

2. Stockinette Stitch: Debby's Favorite. (Figures 45 through 50.)
   Row 1. Knit.
   Row 2. Purl.
   Repeat these two rows.

3. Reverse Stockinette Stitch. (Figures 51 and 52.)

Figure 44. Garter Stitch.

Figure 48. Stockinette Stitch—two yarns.

Figure 45. Stockinette Stitch.

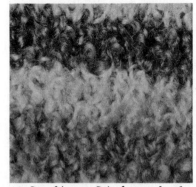

Figure 49. Stockinette Stitch—ombred yarn.

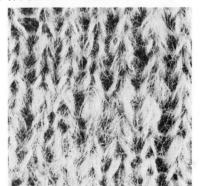

Figure 46. Stockinette Stitch—space dyed yarn.

Figure 50. Stockinette Stitch—ribbon.

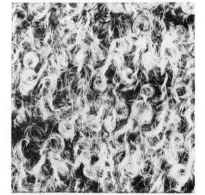

Figure 47. Stockinette Stitch—looped mohair.

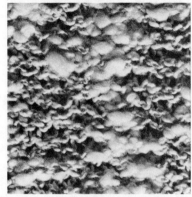

Figure 51. Reverse Stockinette Stitch.

101

The opposite side of Stockinette Stitch.

4. Crossed Knitting. (Figure 53.)
Row 1. Knit into the back loop of each stitch.
Row 2. Purl.
Repeat these two rows.

5. Twisted Knitting. (Figure 54.)
Row 1. Knit into the back loop of each stitch.
Row 2. Purl into the back of each stitch.
Repeat these two rows.

6. Ribbing: K1—P1. (Figure 55.)
Even number of stitches: *K1—P1*. Repeat from *.

7. Continental Ribbing. Multiple of 2, plus 1 (Figure 56.)
Row 1, *P1, Kb 1*. Repeat from *, end P1.
Row 2. *K1, P1*. Repeat from *, end K1.
Repeat these two rows.
European hand knitters prefer this ribbing as they like the appearance and the retaining quality of the stitch. Consider your yarn.

8. Moss Stitch: for odd number of stitches. (Figures 57 and 58.)
K1—P1. Repeat from *.

9. Ribbing: K2—P2. Multiple of 4. (Figure 59.)
K2—P2. Repeat from *.

10. Slipped Stitch Ribbing. Multiple of 4, plus 2. (Figure 60.)
Row 1. *K2—P2*. Repeat from * end K2.
Row 2. P2 *Slip the next 2 (purlwise) P2*. Repeat from *.
Repeat these two rows.

11. Broken Ribbing. Multiple of 4, plus 3. (Figures 61 and 62.)
K2—P2 Repeat from * end K2—P1.
Repeat this row.
Ribbon (optional)—knit into the back loops and Reverse Purl.

Figure 52. Reverse Stockinette Stitch—ribbon.

Figure 53. Crossed Knitting.

Figure 54. Twisted Knitting.

Figure 55. Ribbing: K1—P1.

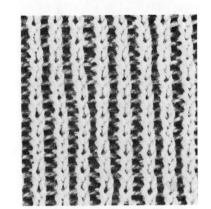

Figure 56. Continental Ribbing.

Figure 57. Moss Stitch.

Figure 58. Moss Stitch—ribbon.

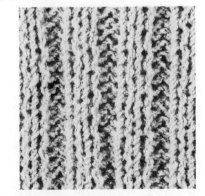

Figure 59. Ribbing: K2—P2.

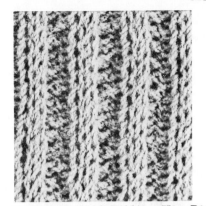

Figure 60. Slipped Stitch Ribbing: K2—P2.

Figure 61. Broken Ribbing.

Figure 62. Broken Ribbing—ribbon.

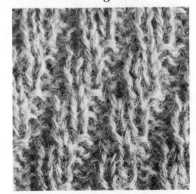

Figure 63. Spiral Ribbing: K2—P2.

103

12. Spiral Ribbing: K2—P2. Multiple of 4. (Figure 63.)
    Use round or double pointed needles, shift 1 stitch to the left every 3rd or 4th row.

13. Spiral Ribbing: K3—P3. Multiple of 6. (Figure 64.)
    Use round or double pointed needles.
    Rows 1, 2, and 3: *K3—P3*. Repeat from *.
    Rows 4, 5, and 6: P1 *K3—P3* Repeat from * end P2.
    Rows 7, 8, and 9: P2 *K3—P3* Repeat from * end P1.
    Rows 10, 11, and 12: P3 *K3—P3* Repeat from *
    Continue ribbing, shifting 1 stitch to the left, every 4th row.

Figure 64. Spiral Ribbing: K3—P3.

14. Teardrops. Multiple of 3, plus 2. (Figures 65 and 66.)
    Row 1. *K2, K1 winding yarn twice*. Repeat from * end K2.
    Row 2. *P2, slip 1 dropping long loop*. Repeat from *end P2.
    Row 3. *K2, slip 1 (purlwise) *. Repeat from * end K2.
    Row 4. *K2, yarn in front, slip 1 (purlwise), yarn in back*. Repeat from * end K2.
    Repeat these 4 rows.

Figure 65. Teardrops.

15. Teardrop—Variation. Multiple of 5, plus 4. (Figure 67.)
    Row 1. *K4, K1 winding yarn twice*. Repeat from * end K4.
    Row 2. *P4, slip 1*. Repeat from * end P4.
    Row 3. *K4, slip 1*. Repeat from * end K4.
    Row 4. *K4, yf, slip 1, yb*. Repeat from * end K4.
    Repeat these 4 rows.
    Delightful with two shades of yarn.
    Teardrop Ribbon Variation: knit into the back loops and Reverse Purl. Slip all stitches purlwise.

Figure 66. Teardrops—ribbon.

Figure 67. Teardrops Variation.

16. Ladybug: Brownie's Favorite. Multiple of 3, plus 2. (Figure 68.)
    Great for fluffy cardigans, caftans, and scarves.
    Row 1. K2 *P1—K2*. Repeat from *.
    Row 2. P2 *K1—P2*. Repeat from *.
    Row 3. Repeat Row 1.
    Row 4. Repeat Row 2.
    Row 5. Repeat Row 1.
    Row 6. P2 *Allow your next stitch to drop down and unravel with 4 horizontal strands, these are then picked up by putting your needle through the front of the dropped stitch and under these horizontal strands. Knit the stitch, P2*. Repeat from *

    Repeat these 6 rows.
    This stitch is adaptable to various yarns and ribbon.
    Ladybug Ribbon Variation (Figure 69.): #9 needles recommended. K and P as usual. Steam lightly.

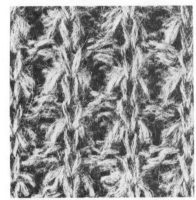

Figure 68. Ladybug.

Figure 69. Ladybug—ribbon.

17. Brioche Stitch: for even number of stitches. (Figures 70 through 72.)
    This is great for scarves, as it is reversible. This pattern consists of slipped stitch and yarn over. It stretches in both directions. When using this pattern for ribbing, start by casting on your stitches onto a needle one size larger. Cast on an even number.
    Optional: For the basic row, knit into the back loops.
    First Row Only: *Have right-hand needle under your yarn. This makes the first YO, slip 1 (purlwise), K1*. Repeat from *.
    Pattern Row: Have right-hand needle under your yarn. *YO, slip 1 and K2 tog*. Repeat from *.
    Note: The K2 tog. are always the stitch and the yarn over. Mark the side that you knit into the back loops; this becomes the right side (front). (Basic Row.)
    Bind off loosely.

18. Mother's Favorite: for even number of stitches. (Figures 73 and 74.)

Figure 70. Brioche Stitch.

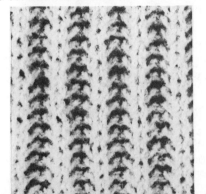

105

Figure 71. Brioche Stitch—small needles for ribbing.

Brioche with a Twist.

This pattern is reversible. Fine yarn and large needles are recommended. Delightful when worked with fine mohair and #10½ needles.

Row 1. K1 *YO, slip 1, yb K2 tog*. Repeat from * end K1.

Row 2. Repeat Row 1.

Row 3. K1 *K1, skip 1, knit the YO stitch and leave it on your left-hand needle, then work the skipped stitch. (The stitch that is closest to the point of the left-hand needle.) Slip the couplet off together.* Repeat from * End K1.

Repeat these three rows.

19. Horizontal Ridges: Stockinette and Reverse Stockinette. (Figure 75.)

Pattern: Six rows of each stitch pattern.

Rows 1 through 5. Stockinette Stitch.

Rows 6 and 7. Purl. This reverses the stitch pattern.

Rows 8 through 11. Stockinette Stitch Stripe.

Rows 12 and 13. Knit. This resumes the alternating of the stripes. Count your rows; keep your stripes even.

Note: Plan your own widths; you may desire a wider knit ridge alternating with narrow Reverse Stockinette Stripes.

20. Vertical Ribbing. Multiple of 14. (Figure 76.)

K7 P7. Repeat from *.

Steam lightly! Do not stretch when measuring for gauge; allow the ridges to be slightly raised.

Note: Vertical ribbing may be varied by changing the number of stitches in either rib. If you desire your knitted rib to stand out, make your purled rib narrower. This ribbing is most attractive for skirts or dresses.

Round Needles: Multiple of 14.

21. Finesse. (Figure 77.)

Stockinette Stitch on normal size needles

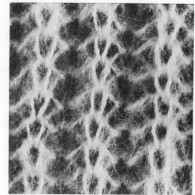

Figure 72. Brioche Stitch—mohair.

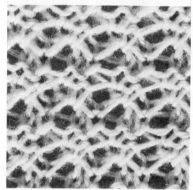

Figure 73. Mother's Favorite: Brioche with a twist.

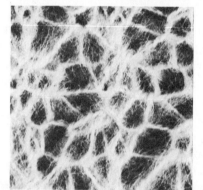

Figure 74. Mother's Favorite—mohair and large needles.

Figure 75. Horizontal Ridges.

for selected yarn. Work Stockinette Stripe the desired width. Change to needles #13, K for 2 rows. Resume Stockinette Stitch with previously used needles.

With very little effort you have a superb stitch pattern; stunning on both sides! Steam lightly.

Illustrated: *Stockinette Stitch, #4 needles, 6 rows. Garter Stitch, #13 needles, 2 rows*. Repeat from *.

22. Gathers: for even number of stitches. (Figure 78.)

Adapt this method to any width of stripes. Stockinette Stitch—any width. Right Side.

Gathers: K1 *Pick up next stitch, right loop exactly below the stitch to be knit, put this loop onto left-hand needle and knit into the back. Then knit into the immediate next stitch.* Repeat from * end K1. (This avoids holes or bars from being formed by your increasing. Also detailed in Chapter Eight). The next stitch is the stitch that you would have normally worked. Purl back and resume Stockinette Stitch. Work your Gathered Stripe the desired width. Then on the next Knit row, K every 2 stitches tog. Resume Stockinette Stitch Stripe.

Figure 76. Vertical ribbing.

Figure 77. Finesse.

Figure 78. Gathers.

Figure 79. Knitted Pleats.

107

Note: When increasing, insert right-hand needle point into loop from back to front and place this onto left needle, then carefully knit into the back loop. Increase is invisible.

This pattern is versatile. Use it for sweaters or as a stunning border at the hem of a skirt.

23. Knitted Pleats. (Figure 79.)
    Terms: Pleat or Overlay—the top of the pleat.
    Underlay—section under the pleat.
    Inner Fold—bending or folding over, created by Purl Rib.
    Edge—sharp edge of pleat, created by Slipped Stitch, every other row.

    Pleated skirts or dresses are usually made on round needles. The following pattern is based on a gauge of 8 stitches to 1″.
    Pattern: Multiple of 29.
    Row 1. *P4, K8, sl 1 (purlwise), K16*. Repeat from *.
    Row 2. *P4, K25*. Repeat from *.
    Repeat these two rows.

    Note: Required width for one complete pleat equals three times the pleat width. (Underlay must always be double the width of the pleat.)
    Plan for the width of your pleat and make your gauge sample. This is a must!
    Gauge Sample—Straight Needles
    Row 1. *P4, K8, sl 1 (purlwise), K16*. Repeat from * end row with P4.
    Row 2. *K4, P25* Repeat from * end K4.
    Repeat these two rows.
    Exact details for figuring the number of stitches to cast on is detailed in Chapter Ten.

24. Francoise's Twist: for even number of stitches and two sizes of needles. (Figure 80.)
    Couplet Combination of crossing. The second stitch is crossed over the first and then knit. Knit the second stitch. Each stitch is dropped off the needle individually. Cast on with the smaller needle.
    Row 1. Use the larger needle; Purl.
    Row 2. Use the smaller needle. *Cross right, lifting the stitch over, before knitting, knit, and then knit the next stitch.* Repeat from * to the end.
    Repeat these two rows.
    Superb! Try using four strands at once; #9 and #11 needles. Have fun!

Twisted Patterns Without Cable Needle

Left Twist—Method #1

Using the right-hand needle point; knit into the back loop of the second stitch from the point. Do not drop this off the left-hand needle. Bring the point of the right-hand needle to the front and knit the first stitch. Slip both stitches off. Tip work towards you so that it will be easier to see the back loop.

Method #2

Knit into the back loop of the second stitch from the left-hand needle point; do not drop off the needle. Bring the point of the right-hand needle to the front and knit the first stitch. Slip both stitches off.

Right Twist

Knit two stitches together; do not drop off. Insert the right-hand point between the two stitches (just worked together on the left-hand needle) and knit the first stitch, (closest to the point) again. Slip both stitches off the needle.

Twisting stitches is simply working the second one from the tip of the needle first. The methods detailed determine the direction in which the twist will slant.

25. Baby Left Twist. Multiple of 4, plus 2. (Figure 81.)
    Row 1. K2 *P2—K2*. Repeat from *.
    Row 2. P2 *K2—P2*. Repeat from *.
    Row 3. Repeat Row 1.
    Row 4. P2 *Left Twist (Method #2), P2*. Repeat from *.

Twist is in every K2.
Repeat these four rows.

26. Baby Right Twist. Multiple of 4, plus 2. (Figure 82.)
Rows 1, 2, and 3. Same as Baby Left Twist.
Row 4. Right Twist in every K2.
Repeat these four rows.

27. Baby Twists in Both Directions. Multiple of 4, plus 2. (Figure 83.)
Row 1. K2 *P2—K2*. Repeat from *.
Row 2. P2 *K2—P2*. Repeat from *.
Row 3. Repeat Row 1.
Row 4. P2 *Right Twist, P2*. Repeat from *.
Row 5. Repeat Row 1.
Row 6. Repeat Row 2.
Row 7. Repeat Row 1.
Row 8. P2 *Left Twist, P2*. Repeat from *.
Repeat these eight rows.

28. Baby Twist Fabric. Multiple of 4, plus 2. (Figure 84.)
Row 1. Purl.
Row 2. K1 *Twist Left, K2*. Repeat from * end K3.
Row 3. Purl.
Row 4. K3 *Twist Right, K2*. Repeat from * end K1.
   Note: Twist may also be called cross. Use Method #1 for Left Twist.
This pattern creates a fabric-like texture and requires more yarn. Experiment with different size needles. Increases and decreases should be made at the beginning and end of rows; if using round needle, place them on the sides.

29. Double Twist Rib. Multiple of 6. (Figure 85.)
Row 1. *P2, yb, slip 1 (purlwise), K1 and do not take off the left-hand needle, psso, and finish by knitting into the back loop of the partially knit stitch. The next couplet: twist by knitting into the back

Figure 80. Francoise's Twist.

Figure 81. Baby Left Twist.

Figure 82. Baby Right Twist.

Figure 83. Baby Twists in Both Directions.

of the second stitch on the left-hand needle and then knit the first stitch in the usual manner and drop the couplet off.* Repeat from * to end.

Row 2. *P4, K2*. Repeat from * to end.

Repeat these two rows.

Try knitting with your yarn doubled; the bulkier the better!

Cables

Follow your stitch pattern carefully. It will tell you the number of stitches to place on your cable (double pointed) needle and where to hold it, front or back. The placement of the cable needle determines the slant direction.

Variations are limitless. They may be made by changing the number of stitches in the cable, in the purl or separating rib, the number of rows between the cabling, the direction of the twists, or the alternating of the cables.

Cabling is very popular and there are many interesting combinations. Gauge sample must be made wider because cabling will definitely contract your work. Measure the complete width to average out the gauge.

Have fun; work out your own cable patterns. This detailing is the method for cabling.

30. Cable—Right. Multiple of 6, plus 2. (Figure 86.)

    Row 1. P2 *K4—P2*. Repeat from *.

    Row 2. K2 *P4—K2*. Repeat from *.

    Row 3. Repeat Row 1.

    Row 4. Repeat Row 2.

    Row 5. P2 *Place first 2 stitches onto dpn, hold in back, K the next 2, then K the 2 from dpn, P2*. Repeat from *.

    Repeat Rows 2 through 5 for your pattern.

    Remember that cable width is optional.

31. Cable—Left. Multiple of 6, plus 2. (Figure 87.)

    Pattern: Read Cable—Right, but change Row 5.

    Row 5. P2 *Place first 2 sts. onto dpn, hold in front, K the next 2 sts. K the 2 sts. from the dpn. P2*. Repeat from *.

Figure 84. Baby Twist Fabric.

Figure 85. Double Twist Rib.

Figure 86. Cable—Right.

Figure 87. Cable—Left.

Practice and become familiar with the use of the double pointed needle.

32. Cable—Alternating. Multiple of 6, plus 2. (Figure 88.)

Rows from 1 through 4 as previously detailed.

Row 5. P2 *Place first 2 sts. onto dpn, hold in *back*, K next 2 sts, then K2 from dpn, P2*. Repeat from *.

Rows 6, 7, and 8 are rows 2, 3 and 4 of previously detailed cable.

Row 9. Work as Row 5, but hold the dpn in *front* of your work.

Pattern: Rows 2 through 9 are repeated.

Figure 88. Cable—Alternating.

33. Alternating and Entwining Cables. Multiple of 4, plus 2. (Figure 89.)

Pattern: Ribbing of K2—P2 and cabling every inch.

Row 1. P2 *K2—P2*. Repeat from * to end of row.

Row 2. *K2—P2* Repeat from * end K2. These two rows are repeated throughout. Count rows between cabling. Be exact.

Cable #1: *P2, put the next 4 sts onto dpn, in *back* of your work, K the next 2 from the left-hand needle, then *P2, K2* from dpn.* Always keep pattern going. Repeat from * to end of row.

Cable #2: P2, K2 *P2, put the next 2 sts. onto dpn and hold in *front* of your work, K2, P2 and then K2 from the dpn*. Repeat from * end row P2, K2, P2.

Cable #3: *P2, slip next 4 sts. onto dpn, hold in *back*, K next 2 sts. then P2, K2 from dpn.* Repeat from * end P2.

Pattern: Keep K2—P2 Ribbing going, at all times. Repeat Cables #2 and #3 for pattern. Sleeves are shaped by using smaller needles where needed. Turtleneck is worked from smaller 16″ round to larger sizes. Keep pattern going.

Figure 89. Alternating and Entwining Cables.

Woven Stitches

Woven stitch patterns are usually firm, with very little elasticity, and resemble fabrics in

Figure 90. Petite—linen.

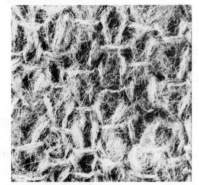

Figure 91. Petite—mohair.

111

texture. Stitch patterns should be cast on and bound off with the size needles that are normally used with the selected yarn.

The slipped stitch is often used and the tension of the yarn must remain the same. Stitches are slipped purlwise unless directions specify differently. The use of the slipped stitch definitely contracts your work, and you must therefore use needles two to three sizes larger than normally used with the selected yarn. Make your samples and decide on the look that *you* prefer.

Woven stitch patterns look best when used with designs that have seams. Increases and decreases should always be at the seams.

Remember to cast on sufficient stitches. Do not try to stretch your work; calculate the number of stitches needed very carefully.

34. Petite. (Figures 90 through 93.)

This stitch pattern is the star of the collection. Its glow never ceases to amaze me. When worked with fine yarn the result is a petite linen-like fabric (petite point); when worked with mohair, tweed, or ribbon the result is incomparable. Either side may be used, allowing various textures. This stitch pattern is worked on needles three to four sizes larger than those normally used with the selected yarn. Stitches should be cast on and bound off with the size needles that would normally be used.

Petite requires a gradual transition of needle size when changing from a ribbed border. This is detailed under Amethyst Tweed.

> *Pattern:* Straight needles require an even number. Round needle requires an odd number and only work Row 1.
>
> Row 1. *K1, yf, slip 1 (purlwise), yb*. Repeat from *.
> Row 2. *P1, yb, slip 1 (purlwise), yf*. Repeat from *.
> Repeat these two rows.

Remember! Steam lightly on the opposite side. It will not be easy to decide which side to use: you will have to make two garments!

112

Figure 92. Petite—tweed.

Figure 93. Petite—ribbon.

Figure 94. Reverse Petite.

Figure 95. Reverse Petite—ribbon.

35. Reverse Petite. The opposite side of Petite. (Figures 94 and 95.)

Straight Needles: Refer to Petite.

Round Needle: I recommend working Row 2 for full control of the appearance of Reverse Petite; especially when working with bulky yarns.

Increases and decreases are made at the seams.

Increasing if necessary: This may be done on the knit side and is barely discernible. Insert right-hand needle point into stitch as to knit, do not take stitch off, bring yarn in front, then knit into the back of the stitch (reversely) and remove the stitch from the needle. Repeat this process in the very next stitch, thus having two increases in succession and allowing for continuation of pattern. Reverse procedure for increasing on the purlside.

Decreasing: Reduce three stitches to one; refer to Chapter Eight.

36. Slipped Ribbing Fabric: for odd number of stitches. (Figures 96 through 98.)
Row 1. *K1 into the back loop, yf, sl 1 (purlwise), yb*. Repeat from * end K1.
Row 2. Purl.
Repeat these two rows.

Note: Slip stitch row is the only row that you knit into the back of the stitch.
Round Needles: Even number of stitches.
Row 1. *K1 into the back loop, yf, slip 1 (purlwise), yb*. Repeat from * for one round.
Row 2. Knit into each stitch.
Repeat these two rows.

37. Flat Ribbed Fabric: for odd number of stitches. (Figure 99.)
Row 1. K1 *Yf, slip 1 (purlwise), yb, K1*. Repeat from *.
Row 2. Purl.
Repeat these two rows.

This pattern has very little elasticity. Experiment with bulky yarns. Think about using it horizontally! Stunning for

Figure 96. Slipped Ribbing Fabric.

Figure 97. Slipped Ribbing Fabric—mohair.

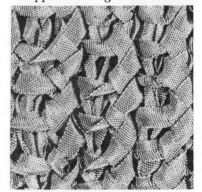

Figure 98. Slipped Ribbing Fabric—ribbon.

Figure 99. Flat Ribbed Fabric.

113

cardigans and cardigan dresses.
Round Needles: even number of stitches.

38. Alternate Weave: for even number of stitches. (Figures 100 through 102.)
Row 1. *K1, yf, slip 1, yb*. Repeat from *.
Row 2. Purl.
Row 3. *Yf, slip 1, yb, K1*. Repeat from *.
Row 4. Purl.
Repeat these four rows.

This is most effective when yarns are combined. Illustrated: Fine mohair combined with a knubby cotton worked on #10 needles. This creates a firm but porous fabric which is delightful to wear, even on a summer night!

39. Slipped Stone. Multiple of 4, plus 2. (Figure 103.)
Row 1. WRONG SIDE. *K1—P1*. Repeat from *.
Row 2. *P1, yb, slip 1 (knitwise), K2, yo, psso the K2, and yo*. Repeat from *. Last 2 sts. P1, K1.
Row 3. *K1—P1* Repeat from *.
Row 4. P1—K1 *P1, yb, slip 1 (knitwise), K2, yo, psso the K2 and yo*. Repeat from *.
Repeat these four rows.
Stunning in tweed, doubling the yarn.

40. Pearl Drops. Multiple of 4, plus 3. (Figure 104.)
Row 1. *K3, sl 1 (purlwise)*. Repeat from * end K3.
Row 2. *K3, yf, sl 1 (purlwise), yb*. Repeat from * end K3.
Row 3. K1, sl 1 (purlwise) *K3, sl 1 (purlwise)*. Repeat from * end K1.
Row 4. K1, yf, sl 1 (purlwise), yb, *K3, yf, sl 1 (purlwise), yb*. Repeat from * end K1.
Repeat these four rows.

Remember! Slipped stitches make a firm fabric. Work this stitch pattern with needles one or two sizes larger than usual.

Figure 100. Alternate Weave.

Figure 101. Alternate Weave—mohair and cotton combined (two yarns).

Figure 102. Alternate Weave—ribbon.

Figure 103. Slipped Stone.

Select the look that you care for. This pattern is firm, dense, and has very little elasticity. Think of it as a fabric. Wonderful for suits, skirts and coats.

41. Ripples: for even number of stitches. (Figure 105.)
Row 1. Knit.
Row 2. *K1, sl 1 (purlwise)*. Repeat from * end K2. Yarn in back when slipping stitches.
Row 3. Knit.
Row 4. K2 *sl 1 (purlwise) K1*. Repeat from *.
Repeat these four rows.
Ripples—Ribbon Variation. (Figure 106.) Knit into the back loop of the knit stitches.
Round Needles: Slip stitch row is the right side. Ripples alternate every other row. Odd number.
Row 1. Knit.
Row 2. *P1, yf, sl 1 (purlwise)*. Repeat from *.
Row 3. Knit.
Row 4. *Yf, sl 1 (purlwise), P1*. Repeat from *.
Ripples—Variation on Straight Needles. (Figure 107.)
Knit Row: Use a needle three to four sizes smaller than Pattern Row. Bind off with smaller needle.

42. Mildred's Couplet: for even number of stitches. (Figures 108 and 109.)
Cast on with normal size needles. Work on needles three to four sizes larger. Work two stitches together but allow only one to slide onto the right-hand needle. The other one remains on the left-hand needle. This stitch becomes the first stitch of the next couplet. Work loosely and stitches will be easier to manipulate. Bind off with smaller needle.
Basic Row: Knit into the back loop of each stitch.
Row 1. *P2 tog., slide 1 off*. Repeat from

Figure 104. Pearl Drops.

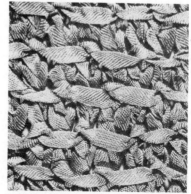

Figure 105. Ripples.

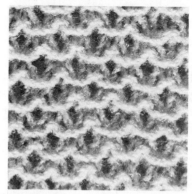

Figure 106. Ripples—ribbon.

Figure 107. Ripples—variation on straight needles.

115

* P last stitch.
Row 2. *K2 tog. tbl, slide 1 off*. Repeat from * end K1.
Repeat these two rows.

Bind off on purl side. Do not neglect to work the last stitch of each row. Decreases should be made in the direction of the stitch; placed at sides.

Figure 108. Mildred's Couplet.

43. Woven Couplet: for even number of stitches. (Figures 110 and 111)
Cast on with normal size needles. Work on needles two to three sizes larger.
Basic Row: Knit into the back loop of each stitch.
Row 1. P1 *P the 2nd st, then the 1st. Drop both off.* Repeat from * end P1.
Row 2. *K the 2nd st. tbl, K the 1st st. in the front (regular knitting). Drop both off.* Repeat from *.
Repeat these two rows.
Bind off with normal size needle.

Note: This stitch pattern uses more yarn. Super for coats, suits and jackets.

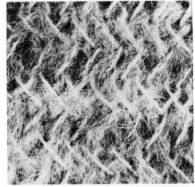

Figure 109. Mildred's Couplet—mohair.

44. Luscious Loops: for even number of stitches. (Figure 112.)
Garter Stitch is the background. Pattern starts after the first three rows. Loops are made on one row. Garter Stitch rows may be worked the depth of your loops. For instance, if you worked *3 rows for the Garter Stitch and 1 row of loops*, this would be the pattern. Optional: Seam allowance is made by not working the first and last 2 stitches on the loop row. Loop is formed on the wrong side. Do not rush! This stitch is worth all your effort!
Loop Formation: do this loosely!
*Insert right-hand needle, as to knit, and wind yarn around the needle and two fingers (first and second), three times. The third wind does not go completely around, draw loops through the stitch and place them onto the left-hand needle. Work these three loops and the original stitch to-

Figure 110. Woven Couplet.

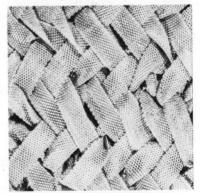

Figure 111. Woven Couplet—ribbon.

116

gether through the back. Slide off*. Repeat from *. Gently ease the loops.

This stitch pattern may be used for trimming. I plan to make a mink-brown mohair topper!

45. Diamond Smocking. Multiple of 6. (Figure 113.)

This stitch pattern is a must for your collection. Use it with flair and imagination. It may be used for borders, collars, cuffs, pocketbooks, etc. Truly great as an all-over pattern for sweaters, cardigans and toppers! Double pointed needle needed.

Row 1. (Wrong side) P2 *K2—P4*. Repeat from *. End last 4 sts. K2—P2.

Row 2. K2 *Sl 2 (purlwise), K4*. Repeat from *. End last 4 sts., sl 2, K2.

Row 3. P2 *Sl 2 (purlwise), P4*. Repeat from *. End last 4 sts., sl 2, P2.

Row 4. *Slip first 2 sts. onto dpn, keep in back, K1, K2 from dpn, slip next stitch onto dpn, keep in front, K the next 2 and then the stitch on dpn*. Repeat from *.

Row 5. K1, P4 *K2, P4*. Repeat from *. Last stitch K1.

Row 6. Sl 1, K4 *Sl 2, K4*. Repeat from *. Last stitch sl 1.

Row 7. Sl 1, P4 *Sl 2, P4*. Repeat from *. Last stitch sl 1.

Row 8. *Slip the first stitch onto dpn, keep in front, K2, K the stitch from dpn, sl the next 2 sts. onto dpn, keep in back, K1, K2 from dpn* Repeat from *.
Repeat these eight rows.

Ribbon Notes: Knit into the back loops. # 9 Needles recommended.

46. Lace Faggot: for even number of stitches. (Figures 114 and 115.)

One row makes this pattern. It is a simple combination of a decrease and a yarn over.

Yo, K2 tog.. Repeat from *. End K1.

Stunning in thin yarns, fine mohair, and thin worsted. Cashmere would be sublime!

Figure 112. Luscious Loops.

Figure 113. Diamond Smocking.

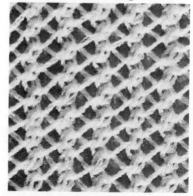
Figure 114. Lace Faggot.

Figure 115. Lace Faggot—casual yarn.

117

With ribbon, #6 needles are recommended.

47. Fragile. Multiple of 4, plus 2. (Figures 116 and 117.)
Row 1. Purl.
Row 2. K1 *Yo K1 yo, SK2 tog. P*. Repeat from *. End K1. (Slip stitch purlwise, then K2 tog. and pass the slip stitch. Thus SK2 tog. P).
Row 3. Purl.
Row 4. K1 *SK2 tog. P, yo K1 yo*. Repeat from *. End with yo K1 yo K1.
Repeat these four rows.

The character of this stitch pattern changes with every change of needle size. Fine yarn and fine needles become Fragile Lace for your best dresses. Mohair and larger needles may be used for scarves, cardigans, and caftans. This stitch pattern is reversible.

48. Alternating Faggot. Multiple of 3. (Figure 118.)
Row 1. *K1, yo twice, K2 tog*. Repeat from *.
Row 2. P each stitch, dropping 1 yo. (YO becomes one long stitch.)
Row 3. *K2 tog, yo twice, K1*. Repeat from *.
Row 4. Repeat Row 2.
Repeat these four rows.

49. Muffy's Tiny Bell Lace. Multiple of 8, plus 2. (Figure 119.)
Optional: Basic rows of Stockinette Stitch.
Row 1. K2, turn, P2, turn, *K2, (yo twice, K1) 6 times in all, yo twice, K2, turn, P2, turn, K2*. Repeat from * to last 2 sts. K2. (YO twice; refer to Chapter Eight.)
Row 2. Attention! The yo twice becomes one long loop. *P2, turn, K2, turn, P2, as you drop one yo slide your long purl stitch, 6 times, over to the right-hand needle (6 long purl stitches), place the 6 longs back on the left-hand needle and purl the

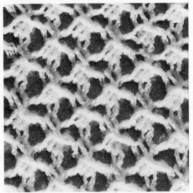

Figure 116. Fragile.

Figure 117. Fragile.

Figure 118. Alternating Faggot.

Figure 119. Muffy's Tiny Bell Lace.

6 longs together as one stitch. Drop last yo*. Repeat from * Last 2 sts. P2.

Row 3. *K2, yo twice, increase in stitch (over bell) yo twice*. Repeat from *. Last 2 sts. K2.

Row 4. Purl all stitches and purl both yo loops. (The second yo is worked as a reverse purl stitch.) Your purl stitches should equal the number cast on.

Repeat these four rows.

Variation: If you desire a finer line between the bells, change the K2 turn P2 formula to K1 turn P1. The multiple would then be 7, plus 1. This stitch pattern looks fantastic upside down! Experiment with different size needles and various yarns. Wonderful for Caper (see Chapter Ten) caftans, and shawls. Use your imagination!

50. Tiny Favorite. Multiple of 6, plus 1. (Figures 120 and 121.)

Wrong Side: Purl Rows 1, 3, 5, and 7.

Row 2. K1 *yo, sl 1 (purlwise), K1, psso, K1, K2 tog., yo K1*. Repeat from *.

Row 4. K1 *yo K1, sl 1 K2 tog, psso, K1, yo, K1*. Repeat from *.

Row 6. K1 *K2 tog, yo, K1, yo, sl 1, K1, psso, K1*. Repeat from *.

Row 8. K2 tog *K1, yo, K1, yo, K1, sl 1, K2 tog, psso*. Repeat from *. Last 5 sts. K1, yo, K1, yo, K1, SKP (Slip, knit, and pass).

Repeat these eight rows. Bind off loosely.

51. My Favorite Lace. Multiple of 10, plus 1. (Figures 122 and 123.)

Wrong Side: Purl Rows 1, 3, and 5.

Row 2. K1, *yo, K3, sl 1, K2 tog, psso, K3, yo, K1*. Repeat from *.

Row 4. K2 *yo, K2, sl 1, K2 tog, psso, K2, yo, K3*. Repeat from *. End yo, K2.

Row 6. K2 tog *yo K1 yo K1, sl 1 K2 tog psso, K1 yo K1 yo, sl 1 K2 tog psso*. Repeat from *. End K1, yo, K1, yo, SKP. Slip stitches purlwise.

Repeat these six rows.

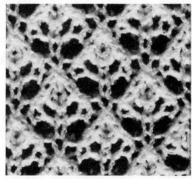

Figure 120. Tiny Favorite.

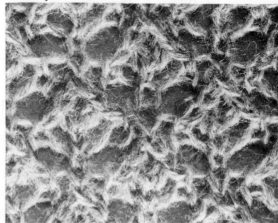

Figure 121. Tiny Favorite.

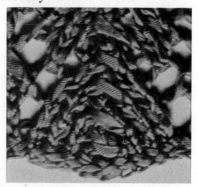

Figure 122. My Favorite Lace.

Figure 123. My Favorite Lace—ribbon.   119

If you desire a pointed hemline, emphasize the beginning of your pattern by knitting into the back loop of each stitch for the first row. Purl back and start the pattern with Row 2. This is lovely in thin yarn, mohair or ribbon.

52. Laburnum Stitch or Eyelet Rib. Multiple of 5, plus 2. (Figure 124.)
Row 1. P2 *yf, sl 1 (purlwise), yb, K2 tog, psso, yo twice, P2*. Repeat from *.
Row 2. *K2, P into the front and then into the back of the yo stitches, P1*. Repeat from * end K2.
Row 3. P2 *K3, P2*. Repeat from *.
Row 4. *K2, P3*. Repeat from *. End K2.
Repeat these four rows.

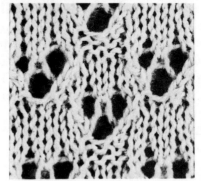

Figure 124. Laburnum Stitch.

53. Quaint Lace. Multiple of 8, plus 4. (Figures 125 and 126.)
Row 1. K2 *K2, K2 tog, yf, K4*. Repeat from *. Last 2 sts. K2.
Row 2. Purl.
Row 3. K2 *K1, K2 tog, yf, K1, yf, (K2 tog tbl), K2*. Repeat from *. Last 2 sts. K2.
Row 4. K2 *K2, P5, K1*. Repeat from *. Last 2 sts. P2.
Row 5. P2 *P1, K5, P2*. Repeat from *. Last 2 sts. P2.
Row 6. K2 *K2, P5, K1*. Repeat from *. Last 2 sts. P2.
Row 7. K2 *K6. K2 tog, yf*. Repeat from *. Last 2 sts. K2.
Row 8. Purl.
Row 9. K2 *yf, (K2 tog tbl) K3, K2 tog, yf, K1*. Repeat from *. Last 2 sts. K2.
Row 10. P2 *P3, K3, P2*. Repeat from *. Last 2 sts. P2.
Repeat these ten rows.

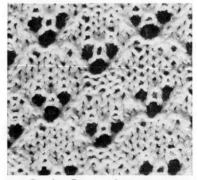

Figure 125. Quaint Lace.

This is delightful whether worked with fine yarn and small needles or mohair and large needles.

Figure 126. Quaint Lace—fine yarn.

54. Diamond Lace. Multiple of 10, plus 1. (Figure 127.)
Even Rows: Purl
Row 1. K4 *yo, SK2 tog P, yo, K3, yo,

Figure 127. Diamond Lace.

SKP, K2*. Repeat from *. End yo, SK2 tog P, yo, K4.

Row 3. K2, K2 tog, *yo, K3, yo, SKP, K3, K2 tog*. Repeat from * End yo, K3, yo, SKP, K2.

Row 5. K1, K2 tog *yo, K5, yo, SKP, K1, K2 tog*. Repeat from * End yo, K5, yo, SKP, K1.

Row 7. K2 tog *yo, K3, yo, SKP, K2, yo, SK2 tog P*. Repeat from *. End yo, K3, yo, SKP, K2, yo, SKP.

Row 9. K2 *yo, SKP, K3, K2 tog, yo, K3*. Repeat from *. End yo, SKP, K3, K2 tog, yo, K2.

Row 11. K3 *yo, SKP, K1, K2 tog, yo, K5*. Repeat from *. End yo, SKP, K1, K2 tog, yo, K3.

Twelfth row is purled.

Repeat these 12 rows.

This stitch pattern has intrinsic value. It is aptly named Diamond Lace.

55. Melissa Jane's Favorite: Van Dyke Lace. Multiple of 12. (Figure 128.)

Even rows: Purl.

Row 1. *K3, yo, sl 1, K1, psso, K2, K2 tog, yo, K1, yo, sl 1, K1, psso*. Repeat from * to end.

Row 3. *K1, K2 tog, yo K1 yo, sl 1 K1 psso, K1, K2 tog, yo K1 yo, sl 1, K1 psso*. Repeat from * to end.

Row 5. *K2 tog, yo K3 yo, sl 1, K1, psso, K2 tog, yo K1 yo, sl 1, K1, psso*. Repeat from * to end.

Repeat these six rows.

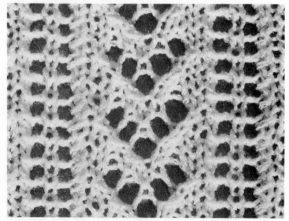

Figure 128. Melissa Jane's Favorite: Van Dyke Lace.

Suggestion: Knit the Stockinette Stitch on both sides for seam allowance when using straight needles.

CROCHET STITCHES

Single Series

1. Single Crochet
2. Single Crochet Back Loops Only
3. Single Crochet Ribbing
4. Double Single Crochet
5. Little Couplet
6. Leaf-like Couplet
7. Single Basket Weave
8. Picquot Fabric
9. V Fabric

Double Series

10. Double Crochet
11. Double Crochet Back Loops Only
12. Half-Double Crochet
13. Simplicity
14. Delicate Lace #1
15. Delicate Lace #2
16. Delicate Lace #3—Back Loops Only
17. Shimmering Autumn Leaf
18. Double Basket Weave
19. Clusters #1
20. Clusters #2
21. Francesca
22. Double Diagonal
23. Double Shell

Triple Series

24. Triple Shell
25. Triple Diagonal
26. Loops—Single
27. Loops—Double

1. Single Crochet. (Figures 129 through 131.)
   This is detailed in Chapter Eight.

2. Single Crochet—Back Loops Only. (Figure 132.)
   This is detailed in Chapter Eight.

3. Single Crochet Ribbing. (Figure 133.)
Single Crochet in back loops only; use vertically.

4. Double Single Crochet. (Figure 134.)
This is detailed in Chapter Eight.

5. Little Couplet. Multiple of 2, plus 1 (Figure 135.)
Motif: SC, ch 1, SC.
Chain: Desired length.
Optional: First row may be SC. TP (ch 2) turn.
Basic Row: *1 SC, 1 ch, 1 SC into 1 lp (or st), sk 1*. Repeat from * to last st. Crochet SC, ch 1, SC into last st. Ch 2, turn.
Pattern: *1 SC, 1 ch and 1 SC, into each ch 1 of the previous row.* Repeat from * to end. Ch 2, turn.

Count your couplets—do not lose a single one! If you wish a firmer edge, slip stitch before making TP (ch 2). Lovely vertical patterns are formed. Small hooks and fine yarn create a fabric-like appearance. Large hooks create lace.

6. Leaf-like Couplet. Multiple of 2, plus 1. (Figures 136 through 138.)
Chain: Desired length.
Basic Row: 2 SC into 3rd loop from hook. Sk 1 ch. *2 SC into the next loop, sk 1 1p*. Repeat from * to end. 2 SC into last st TP, turn. (TP ch 2)
Pattern Row: *SK 1 SC, 2 SC into 2nd st of couplet.* Repeat from *. TP, turn.

Concentrate on working all loops evenly. This is most important when working with fine yarn and a large hook. This stitch is adaptable to any yarn; try crocheting it with ribbon!

7. Single Basket Weave. Multiple of 4, plus 3. (Figure 139.)
Motif: 3 SC into the back loops of each stitch and 1 long-looped SC. (Stitch on hook should be normal size. Long-loop, allow yarn to be double in length.) Long-loop is made by working into stitch ex-

Figure 129. Single Crochet.

Figure 130. Single Crochet—ribbon.

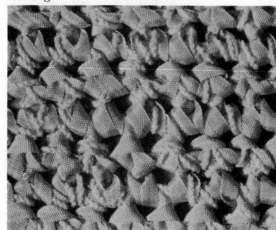

Figure 131. Single Crochet—ribbon and yarn combined.

Figure 132. Single Crochet—Back Loops Only—ribbon.

Figure 133. Single Crochet Ribbing.

Figure 137. Leaf-like Couplet.

Figure 134. Double-Single Crochet.

Figure 138. Leaf-like Couplet.

Figure 135. Little Couplet.

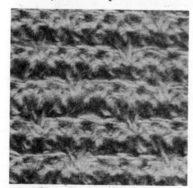

Figure 139. Single Basket Weave.

Figure 136. Leaf-like Couplet.

Figure 140. Picquot Fabric.

123

actly below the working row. Control looseness by holding stitch between thumb and index finger.

Chain: Desired length

Basic Row: SC into 2nd lp from hook. SC to end, TP, turn.

Turning Post: (Ch 2) It is optional whether TP is made before or after turning.

Pattern:

Row 1. SC into each stitch, TP, turn.

Row 2. SC into the back lps of the next 2 sts. *1 long-loop (as previously detailed), SC into the back loops of the next 3 sts.* Repeat from *. TP, turn.

Row 3. Repeat Row 1.

Row 4. *Long-looped st, SC into the back of the next 3 sts*. Repeat from * to last 2 sts. End with 1 long-loop and 1 SC. TP, turn.

Repeat these four rows.

Caution: Before making long-loop, concentrate on the size of the loop on the hook. Do not allow it to sag.

8. Picquot Fabric: for even number of stitches. (Figure 140.)

Chain: Desired length

Basic Row: Insert hook into 2nd lp from hook and SC to end.

Turning Post: Ch 2, turn.

Pattern: *Insert hook into front lp, pull yarn through, then insert hook through both loops of the same stitch (there are 3 lps on your hook) yo, and pull yarn through*. Repeat from * to last st, SC in last st (TP of previous row). TP, turn.

9. V Fabric: for even number of stitches. (Figure 141.)

Chain: Desired Length

Basic Rows: 1. SC to end, ch 2, turn.
2. *SC, ch 1, sk 1*. Repeat from * to end.

Turning Post: Ch 2, turn.

Pattern: *SC into ch 1 of the previous row, ch 1*. Repeat from * to end. TP, turn. Count your stitches!

Figure 141. V. Fabric.

Figure 142. Double Crochet.

Figure 143. Double Crochet—four strands.

Figure 144. Double Crochet—ribbon and yarn combined.

10. Double Crochet. (Figures 142 through 145.)

   Directions in Chapter Eight. Yarn in any weight and hooks in any size may be used. Superb when used vertically! Combine ribbon with yarn, silky-textured yarn with mohair, and yarns doubled, tripled, or quadrupled for magnificent shading and textures.

11. Double Crochet—Back Loop Only. (Figure 146.)

   Refer to Chapter Eight, Crochet Section.

12. Half-double Crochet. (Figure 147.)

   Refer to Chapter Eight, Crochet Section.

   Do not neglect crocheting these stitches —the slight variations make them worth knowing. Learn to use them.

13. Simplicity. (Figure 148.)

   Before you decide on a crocheted stitch pattern trying this one is a must!
   Right Side: Row 1. SC
                     Row 2. HDC
   Repeat these two rows. That is all that there is to it!

14. Delicate Lace #1. Multiple of 2, plus 1. (Figures 149 through 153.)·

   Motif: 1 SC, 1 DC, alternating over each other.
   Chain: Desired Length
   Basic Row: SC into 2nd lp from hook. *1 DC into the next lp, and 1 SC into the following lp*. Repeat from * to end. TP (height of row), turn.
   Pattern: *1 SC directly over the DC of the previous row, and 1 DC over the SC of the previous row*. Repeat from * to end.

   Note: COUNT YOUR STITCHES. Do not skip stitch after TP. This pattern has a subtle elegance especially when worked in the back loops only.

15. Delicate Lace #2. Multiple of 4, plus 2. (Figure 154.)

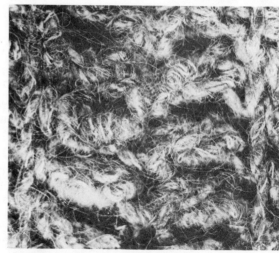

Figure 145. Double Crochet—vertical.

Figure 146. Double Crochet—Back Loops Only.

Figure 147. Half Double Crochet.

Figure 148. Simplicity.

125

Motif: 2 SC, 2 DC, alternating over each other.

Chain: Desired length. Allow for TP (ch 2)

Basic Row: YOH, insert hook into 3rd lp from hook *DC in next 2 lps, SC into the next 2 lps.*. Repeat from * to end. TP (needed height) turn.

Pattern: *2 DC directly over the 2 SC of the previous row and 2 SC directly over the 2 DC of the previous row.* Repeat from * to end.

Note: Do not skip a stitch after turning. Turning post may be stitch to be used instead of a chain or two.

16. Delicate Lace #3. (Figure 155.)
Crochet into back loops only.

17. Shimmering Autumn Leaf: for even number of stitches. (Figures 156 and 157.)
Chain: Desired length. Allow for TP (ch 3)
Basic Row: Work 1 DC into the 4th lp from hook. *Sk 1, 2 DC into next lp*. Repeat from * to end.
Turning Post: Ch 3, turn.
Pattern Row: (TP counts as 1 st) 1 DC between the 1st and 2nd DC of the previous row. *Crochet 2 DC between each couplet of the previous row*. Repeat from * to end. Pattern row is crocheted throughout.
Suggestion: Use smaller hook and create a stunning fabric!

18. Double Basket Weave. Multiple of 3, plus 1. (Figures 158 and 159.)
Motif: 3 Successive long DC and 3 successive DC.
Long-looped DC: This is made by inserting hook into space below the previous row of SC. Looped rows have a row of SC between and the long DC alternate; thus creating the basket weave.
Chain: Desired length
Basic Row: SC into the 2nd lp from hook and SC to the end. Ch 2, turn.

Figure 149. Delicate Lace #1.

Figure 150. Delicate Lace #1.

Figure 151. Delicate Lace #1.

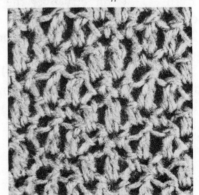

Figure 152. Delicate Lace #1.

Figure 153. Delicate Lace #1.

Figure 154. Delicate Lace #2.

Figure 155. Delicate Lace #3.

Figure 156. Shimmering Autumn Leaf.

Figure 157. Shimmering Autumn Leaf—ribbon.

Figure 158. Double Basket Weave.

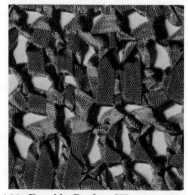

Figure 159. Double Basket Weave—ribbon.

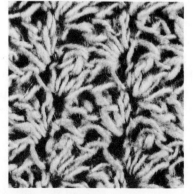

Figure 160. Clusters #1.

127

Pattern:

Row 1. SC into each st, ch 3, turn.

Row 2. 1 DC into the next 2 sts. (TP is counted as one st.) *Work long DC into next 3 sts, 3 DC into next 3 sts.*. Repeat from * to end. TP (ch 2) turn.

Row 3. Repeat Row 1, TP, turn.

Row 4. After TP, 2 long DC *1 DC into the next 3 sts, then work 3 long DC*. Repeat from * to TP, turn.

Repeat Rows 1 through 4 for pattern.

Figure 161. Clusters #1.

19. Clusters #1. Multiple of 3. (Figures 160 and 161.)

There are many patterns for grouping stitches; this is one of my favorites. It may be worked as closely as you desire. The most ordinary yarn becomes unique!

Chain: Desired length

Basic Row: YOH and insert hook into the 3rd lp and crochet 2 DC, sk 2 lps and *1 SC 2 DC into the next lp, sk 2 lps*. Repeat from *, end row with 1 SC.

Turning Post: Ch 2, turn.

Figure 162. Clusters #2.

Pattern Row: 2 DC into first SC *1 SC 2 DC into each SC of the row below*. Repeat from *, end with 1 SC.

Repeat pattern row throughout.

Tip: This pattern is another exception to the rule. Do not skip a stitch immediately following the turning post.

At end of row: The last SC in the row is made in the TP of the previous row.

At the beginning of the row: The first 2 DC are made in the SC that you previously worked in the TP.

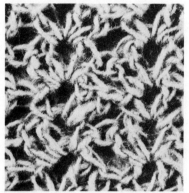

Figure 163. Clusters #2—ribbon.

20. Clusters #2: for even number of stitches. (Figures 162 and 163.)

Chain: Desired length

Basic Row: YOH and insert hook into 3rd lp and make 1 DC, ch 2, 1 SC into the next lp *Sk 2 lps, 2 DC into next lp, ch 2, 1 SC into next lp*. Repeat from * to end.

Turning Post: Ch 2, turn.

Pattern: *Crochet combination of 2 DC, ch 2, and 1 SC, into the next ch 2 of the

Figure 164. Francesca.

previous row*. Repeat from * to end. This pattern row is worked throughout.

Tip:

1. Observe closely and crochet slowly, as turning your work puts the ch 2 on the opposite side. Your combination of (2 DC, ch 2 and 1 SC) are only made in the ch 2 of the previous row.

2. Be certain to put the last SC into TP.

This pattern creates swirls that go in opposite directions. Great for tweeds, ribbons, or mohairs.

21. Francesca. (Figure 164 and 165.)

Try this stitch with more than one color or type of yarn, at the same time, on a wooden hook. You are always working on the front. Do NOT TURN!

Chain: Desired length

Pattern:

Row 1. DC into each lp to the end. Do not turn. TP, ch 2 or 3. (This depends on the yarn or combination.)

Row 2. *Reverse DC into first and every stitch to the end.* TP at the end of rows. These two rows are repeated throughout.

Note: Double Crochet Rows: Place your stitches between the vertical stitches and the horizontal strands of the previous row.

Reverse Rows: Work your Reverse DC into both lps of the previous row.

22. Double Diagonal. Multiple of 3, plus 1. (Figure 166.)

Chain: Desired length

Basic Row: SC into 2nd lp from hook and into each lp. Ch 2, turn.

Pattern:

Row 1. *Sk 1 SC, DC into the next 2 sts, (go back and make a DC in the sk. st.) insert hook from *back* to *front*.* Repeat from * to end. Ch 1, turn.

Row 2. SC into each st. Ch 2, turn.

Repeat these two rows. COUNT YOUR STITCHES.

Figure 165. Francesca—two strands.

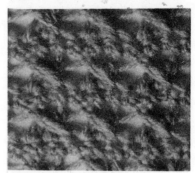

Figure 166. Double Diagonal.

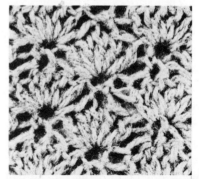

Figure 167. Double Shell.

Figure 168. Double Shell—ribbon.

129

23. Double Shell. Multiple of 6, plus 1. (Figures 167 and 168.)

Chain: Desired length

Basic Row: 2 DC in 4th lp from hook. (Half shell) *Sk 2 lps, 1 SC in next lp, sk 2, 5 DC in next lp*. (Shell 5 DC). Repeat from * to end. End chain with sk 2 lps, SC in last loop.

Turning Post: Ch 3, turn.

Pattern: 2 DC in 1st SC of previous row *SC in 3rd DC of previous row, 5 DC into SC of previous row*. Repeat from *. End row with SC in TP. Make TP and turn.

Repeat pattern row throughout.

24. Triple Shell. Multiple of 6, plus 1. (Figures 169 and 170.)

Chain: Desired length

Basic Rows:

1. DC into 2nd lp from hook, continue to end, ch 1, turn.

2. *Sk 2 DC, work 5 Tr into next DC, sk 2 sts, DC into next st*. Repeat from * to end, ch 3, turn.

Pattern:

Row 1. 2 Tr into TP. *DC into the center st of the shell. (5 Tr of previous row) and work shell into the DC of previous row*. Repeat from *. End row with 3 Tr in the last stitch of the shell, ch 1, turn.

Row 2. *5 Tr into the DC and DC into the center of each shell*. Repeat from *. End with TP, ch 3, turn. These two rows are your pattern. Shell consists of 5 Tr. Turning Post is either ch 1 or 3; depending on height of row to be worked.

25. Triple Diagonal. Multiple of 3, plus 2. (Figure 171.)

Chain: Desired length

Basic Row: DC into 3rd lp from hook. DC into each lp to end. Ch 3, turn.

Pattern:

Row 1. *Sk 1 DC, Tr into the next 2 sts, go back to the sk st and make a Tr, inserting your hook from *back* to *front**.

Figure 169. Triple Shell.

Figure 170. Triple Shell—ribbon.

Figure 171. Triple Diagonal—threaded.

Figure 172. Loops—One Loop to a Stitch.

Repeat from * to end. Ch 2, turn.
Row 2. DC into each st, ch 3, turn.
Repeat these two rows for your pattern.
Variation: Weave ribbon or strands of yarn under the crossed stitch. Use matching or contrasting ribbon or yarn.

26. Loops—One Loop to a Stitch. (Figure 172.)
Basic Background: Single or Double Crochet. Loops are formed on the wrong side.
Loop Formation: The depth of your loop determines the width of your cardboard strip. For instance, if you desire a 1″ loop you would cut a 6″ x 1″ strip. Cut the desired depth and width; using firm cardboard.
Loop Row: Crochet 4 or 5 sts (seam allowance) before starting loops. (Wrong Side) Hold the cardboard strip in back of your work. Yarn in front of cardboard, behind work. *Insert hook into the next stitch, wind yarn over (front to back) the strip and draw through loop (now there are 2 lps on hook), yoh, and pull through.* (As if you were making a SC.) Repeat from *. Crochet the last 4 or 5 sts (seam allowance). Make the TP the needed height. Turn.
Background Stitch: Crochet the number of rows desired between the loop rows.
   Note: Loops are formed while working on the wrong side.

27. Loops—Two Loops to a Stitch. (Figure 173.)
Refer to and understand Loops, One Loop to a stitch (pattern 26).
Make your first lp into the back lp of the stitch and then work the 2nd lp in the front of the same stitch. Repeat from *.
Return Row: Be certain to work through both loops of each loop stitch in the previous row or crochet every other stitch. Your stitch count will then be decreased back to the original count (as in the basic rows).

Figure 173. Loops—Two Loops to a Stitch.

This may be used as an edging for collars and cuffs, or as an all-over pattern for garments. Have fun and plan a design with rows of loops creating stripes.

ACCENTS

Knitted

1. Picquot Hem
2. Bias Strip
3. Cable Strip
4. Braid
   (Suggestion: Refer to Stitch Patterns.)

Crocheted

1. Chain—Four Strands
   Eight Strands
2. Double Crochet Braid
3. Reverse Single Crochet
4. Reverse Double Crochet
5. Double Shell
6. Triple Shell
7. Picquot Edging #1
8. Picquot Edging #2
9. Loop Trim
10. Scallops
11. Baby Scallops
12. Cluster Border
13. Cluster Triple
14. Bias Edging
15. Cord

Trimmings, borders, and edgings are the final touch, but they never should be the result of the final thought! Think, and plan your finishing details before you start your garment. Your accents should be an integral part of your design. Do not allow an afterthought to completely throw your design out of balance.

Plan in advance, draw your ideas on your Visual Pattern, and study the effect. Planning in advance insures a flawless result. Knit or crochet various borders and edgings and decide on which one you prefer for the design in mind. It may be that you will achieve the best result by working the accent into your garment, completely eliminating pinning, basting, and hand-sewing. Study your stitch patterns and think of the many ingenious ways to use them. Perhaps the Diamond Lace pattern as a yoke and borders or a thick cable running down the sleeves and around the neckline.

Whether knitting or crocheting, the simplest edging may be just the right touch; think of single crochet, combining your yarn with shimmering ribbon, and it may be perfect for your design.

Trimmings, edgings, and borders should relate to the yarn, design, and the use of the garment. Fringes, tassels, pompons, braid, velvet ribbon, beads, etc.—there is no limit to the choice. Always purchase your trimming first so that your design will be coordinated. Lace sweaters look lovely with delicate beads and tweed sweaters look lovely with fur collars and cuffs. Fur collars and cuffs may be purchased with fabric backing so that they may be easily sewn.

Beautiful edgings may be made by making double crocheted or triple crocheted strips and threading ribbon through them. Dust the edges, here and there, with seed pearls or rhinestones. Use your metallic yarns to create thin chains or braids that you can carefully arrange and tack on.

Applied edgings must be accurately made and carefully sewn on.

I will now detail my favorite finishing touches!

Knitted Accents

1. Picquot Hem. (Figures 174 and 175.)
   Knit the depth of your hem.
   Right Side: One row only, K1 *yo, K2 tog.*. Repeat from *.
   Straight needles: Resume pattern stitch
   Round needles: Multiple of 2
   Row 1. *YO, K2 tog.*. Repeat from *.
   Row 2. Resume stitch pattern.
   Hem is bent under at the yarn over row. This displays your serrated edge. This edging may be used on sleeves, necks, and hems. Sewing is detailed in Chapter Five.

Figure 174. Picquot Hem.

Figure 175. Picquot Hem.

2. Bias Strip Edging—Stockinette Stitch. (Figure 176.)
   Cast on stitches to equal 1″
   Row 1. P2 tog, P to the end. (Wrong side.)

Figure 176. Bias Strip Edging: Stockinette Stitch.

Figure 177. Cable Strip.

Pattern: Garter Stitch the first and last three rows and the sides (a minimum of 2 sts).

Row 1. K2, P6 (optional), K2

Row 2. K10 sts. (The center 6 sts. will be cabled.)

Repeat these two rows; start cabling as soon as possible to prevent flaring. Also end the strip with a cable close to the Garter Stitching.

Cable as often as you desire; twists may alternate. Experiment with different cables and widths. Cable strip may be placed at the very edge or in 1".

4. Braid. (Figure 178.)

Decide on the desired thickness; the number of strands of yarn you use can be varied. Fasten yarn, braid, and fasten securely after you have braided the needed length. For added dash, allow your ends to become fluffy tassels.

Row 2. K inc. in 1st st, (insert your right-hand needle into the stitch below *back* to *front* and twist it onto the left-hand needle. This method of increasing makes a fine edge.) K to end.

Repeat these two rows.

Moss or Seed Stitch may be used.

3. Cable Strip. Width Optional. (Figure 177.)

Double your yarn; emphasize your cable!

Figure 178. Braid.

133

Crocheted Accents

1. Chain—Four Strands (Figure 179.)
   Combine 4 strands of yarn and ch the desired length. Fasten.

2. Double Crochet Chain—Four Strands. (Figure 180.)
   Chain the desired length and DC. Fasten.

3. Reverse Single Crochet Edging. (Figure 181.)
   Pick stitches up evenly as any little deviation will show, or chain the desired length.
   Row 1. SC.
   Row 2. Finishing row: DO NOT TURN YOUR WORK! TP, work from *left* to *right*; SC into each st. Fasten.
   Optional: Row 2 may be crocheted over more than one row of SC. Pattern row must be crocheted with front side of work facing you.

4. Reverse Double Crochet Edging. (Figure 182.)
   Knitted edges should be picked up and complemented with a row of SC. I am detailing the final row.
   Pattern: Work from *left* to *right*. Always start with a TP, the correct height, and DC into each stitch. Fasten.

5. Double Shell Edging. Multiple of 6, plus 1. (Figure 183.)
   Pick up stitches or chain the desired length.
   Front Side:
   Pattern: Make your TP (ch 3) or needed height. 2 DC into the next st (half shell). *Sk 2 sts, SC into the next st, sk 2 sts, 5 DC into the next st (shell)*. Repeat from * to end. Fasten.
   Note: Rows of SC may be used before crocheting shell edging. This edging may also be crocheted separately and appliqued. It is beautiful when trimmed with beads or pearls.

Figure 179. Chain—four strands and eight strands.

Figure 180. Double Crochet Chain—four strands.

Figure 181. Reverse Single Crochet Edging.

Figure 182. Reverse Double Crochet Edging.

Figure 183. Double Shell Edging.

Figure 184. Triple Shell Edging.

6. Triple Shell Edging. Multiple of 6, plus 1. (Figure 184.)
Pick up stitches or ch the desired length.
Basic Row: SC or DC
Front Side—Pattern: Ch 4 (TP) and then make 2 Tr into the next st (half Tr Shell) *Sk 2 sts, 1 DC into the next st, sk 2 sts, 5 Tr into the next st*. Repeat from * to end. Fasten.

Figure 185. Picquot Edging #1.

7. Picquot Edging # 1. (Figure 185.)
Pick up stitches or ch the desired length.
Basic Row: SC
Front Side—Pattern: (Optional: SC instead of DC). *Sl 2 sts, 1 DC, ch 3 and 1 sl st in the previously made DC*. Repeat from * to end. Fasten. Yarn may be doubled; think of the effect you wish.

8. Picquot Edging # 2. (Figure 186.)
Pick up stitches or ch the desired length.
Basic Row: SC
Front Side—Pattern: (Optional: SC instead of DC). 1 DC *Ch 3, 1 sl st in base of DC, sk 1 st, 1 DC*. Repeat from * to end. Fasten.

Figure 186. Picquot Edging #2.

9. Loop Trim. (Figure 187.)
Pick up stitches or ch the desired length.
Background Stitch: SC or DC.
Pattern: Refer to Crocheted Loop; edging may be more than one row.

Figure 187. Loop Trim—double loops.

10. Scallops. Multiple of 6, plus 1. (Figure 188.)

Pick up stitches or ch the desired length.

Basic Row: SC

Front Side—Pattern: TP. *Sk 2, Scallop (1 SC, 1 DC, 1 Tr, 1 DC. 1 Sc)*. Repeat from * to end. Fasten. If you wish you may start row with one-half of the Scallop. (1 DC, 1 SC) sk 2 and start with full Scallop.

Figure 188. Scallops.

11. Baby Scallops. (Figure 189.)

Pick up stitches or ch the desired length.

A basic row is optional.

Front Side—Pattern: *Ch 5 and make a DC into the first lp of the ch 5, sk 1, sl st into the next lp or st*. Repeat from * to the end. Fasten.

Optional: SC instead of DC for finer Baby Scallop.

Figure 189. Baby Scallops.

12. Cluster Border. (Figures 190 and 191.)

SC along your garment edge. This border is made with the right side of your work facing you. Matching or contrasting yarn or ribbon may be used.

Pattern: TP. *1 DC, yoh and insert your hook behind the first DC, draw lp through, this is done 3 times in all, yoh and draw through the 7 lps on your hook, ch 1, sk 1*. Repeat from * to end with DC.

Variations: Thickness of cluster is dependent on yarn. Different effects may be achieved by using the HDC or SC instead of the DC.

Bulky clusters may necessitate the use of Tr and skipping 2 stitches between the clusters. Make short strips and decide on your preference.

Figure 190. Cluster Border.

13. Cluster Triple. (Figure 192.)

Cluster or popcorn is formed on the wrong side by *YOH, insert your hook into designated stitch, draw lp through, this is done three times in all, YOH and

Figure 191. Cluster Border—ribbon.

Figure 192. Cluster Triple.

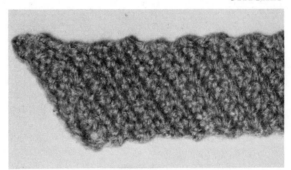

Figure 193. Bias Edging—Single Crochet.

draw through 7 loops on your hook.* Repeat from *.

Pattern:

Row 1. SC into each st.

Row 2. SC *form cluster in next st, SC in next st*. Repeat from * to end. Fasten.

Repeat these two rows until you have three rows of clusters.

Optional: DC may be substituted. Colors may also be changed by breaking the yarn at the end of a cluster row and tying in a contrasting color.

14. Bias Edging—Single Crochet. (Figure 193.)

1″ Strip. Chain: Example—ch 9.

Basic Row: Insert hook into 2nd lp from hook and SC to end. (8 stitches.) Ch 1, turn.

Pattern:

Row 1. SC into 2nd st and SC the next 6 sts. In the last st, SC twice. (Increase.) ch 1, turn.

Row 2. SC into the very first st and SC to the end. (8 in all), ch 1, turn.

Repeat these two rows.

Simply said: Increase Row. Skip first stitch and increase in the last stitch.

Alternate Row: SC the total number to equal the desired width.

Count your stitches! Avoid mistakes! Double crochet may also be used. (Figure 194.)

15. Cord. (Figure 195.)

Refer to Chapter Eight.

Figure 194. Bias Edging—Double Crochet.

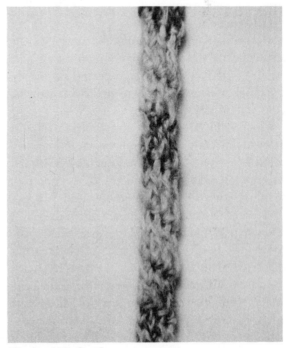

Figure 195. Cord.

CHAPTER TEN

Design

With ideas for a dress or coat formulating in your mind, a definite picture will emerge. Whether you doodle it, sketch it, stitch a sample, or make a paper pattern, you must have an idea of what *you* want to make. This, combined with the excitement of making your own original design, will inspire you and lead you to success.

I would like you to take advantage of the sequence of the following thoughts and patterns, for they will create an awareness within you that will enable you to make a wardrobe that is uniquely yours.

Once you have made and worn Midnight Jewel and Midnight Delight you will understand why these designs are so named. You will also understand the simplicity of calculating, shaping, and subtly changing your pattern, thus creating a new design. Draw your Jewel and Delight patterns, making any of the adjustments needed, since only after wearing them will you know if you are satisfied with the ease allowance, armhole depth, and neckline placement. Learn to allow for more ease when making a garment in soft, luxurious texture, for you want your design to drape

fluidly. Learn to coordinate ease and texture for each individual design. As we proceed, step by step, your adjusted Jewel and Delight patterns will be used as the base.

Draw your own ideas for placing borders or stripes on your Visual Pattern. Make more than one pattern, express and detail more than one design; then allow a day or two to pass and you will be amazed at the new ideas that will come to mind. The basic Jewel pattern will encourage your imagination and clarify your design. Figure 196 depicts simple borders, which immediately change the appearance of the design. The borders may be achieved through use of a contrasting yarn, stitch pattern, or crocheting. Review the different stitch patterns and think of how they relate to your yarn and the use of your garment.

Look at the striped diagram (Figure 197); it deliberately draws the eyes to the neck, bust, and hem, and away from the hips. Mathematics is an integral part of design: an inch or two can create an illusion, camouflage your waist, hips, or bust, and enhance your figure. Draw your pattern with symmetrical horizontal stripes and study it—do you like it? Draw

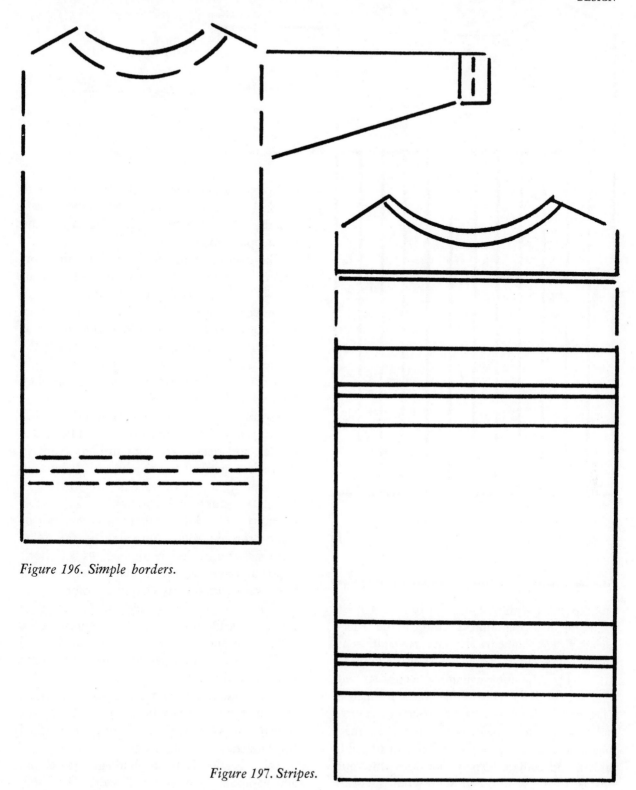

Figure 196. Simple borders.

Figure 197. Stripes.

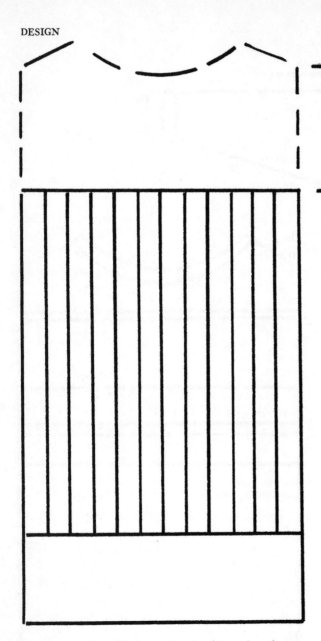

Figure 198. Yoke, border, and short sleeves.

close together or shades of the same color with unusual accents. Colors definitely create moods; moods that may be exciting to you and the people you are with.

The diagram with yoke, border, and short sleeves (Figure 198) must be copied on your Visual Pattern. Yoke depth is measured from shoulder seam to the most attractive point on your bust. Draw a horizontal line on your Visual Pattern. Draw a horizontal line for the border at the hem, matching the yoke depth. The vertical stripes are not drawn, since they are created by your stitch pattern.

I want you to study the lines and then think about the following description. The yoke, border, and sleeves are done in Garter Stitch. The stitch pattern for the body is a knit rib separated by a narrow purl rib, for instance, a 1″ rib (8 stitches) and a purl rib (2 or 3 stitches). The knit stitches are twisted or cabled for one row before starting the yoke. I emphasize this design for it gives you horizontal and vertical lines which create an exciting design without any change in color.

Make another Jewel pattern, referring to Figure 199. Draw a horizontal line low on the hips, and shape in short sleeves and the desired neckline. Plan for stripes or ridges through the top; draw them. Length is optional, but I see this dress swirling about your ankles. Imagine your design in creamy beige or pearl gray, or perhaps in ivory with bands of gold worked through the horizontal ridges.

Skirt Details: Refer to Midnight Jewel and add a minimum of 6″ to 8″ ease. The stitch pattern is *K5—P2*, creating a dramatic rib.

your pattern with irregular horizontal stripes; thinking of a predominant color as the background. You immediately have two different designs; you may even decide to make both of them. Think about owning an evenly striped chemise in red, white and blue—a timeless classic. Think of interesting groups of colors, such as navy blue, beige, and caramel outlined in black. Another group could consist of gold, green, and brown. Experiment with different shades of gray accented with your favorite color. Try different shades of colors that are

Figure 199. Stripes and a swirling skirt.

Top Details: Your top is a continuation of the skirt (refer to Jewel). It fits straight and loosely, and simply drops over your head. Place the first horizontal ridge or stripe strategically on your hips. Do not place ridges where you do not wish to attract attention. I have emphasized this design for it gives you horizontal and vertical lines which create interest and fluidness.

Jewel becomes Jewel Shell by simply paring it to the bone! Refer to Figures 200 and 201. Use your adjusted Jewel pattern, and shape in a semi-bateau neckline from line 8 to line 8, or a bateau neckline from line 6 to line 6. (Necklines are detailed later in this chapter.) Visualize your Shell knitted in Muffy's Tiny Bell lace pattern combined with a Jewel Coat-dress. The armhole of the Shell is a rolled edge and the neckline is turned under and tapered to each shoulder seam. Different stitch patterns, when turned under, create decorative edging, if this is so, use tiny hidden stitches to firm the edge. Also make a large triangle or long scarf in the same stitch pattern; vary your accessories. Have fun!

A book could be written just on the innumerable changes to your Jewel pattern, and I am briefly expressing some thoughts that will stimulate and broaden your personal attitude towards knitting and crocheting.

Knitting and crocheting will help you to develop objectivity. Objectivity is the ability to look at one's self with complete honesty. As you develop the ability to really see yourself, scale, proportion, balance, and harmony will become obvious to you when you are judging the design that will be individually yours.

Make your gauge sample and do not stretch when measuring for gauge; allow for luxurious rippling. This rib is worked to the hipline and then decreased to the width of the hips plus ease. Place all decreases, evenly distributed, within the purl ribs.

141

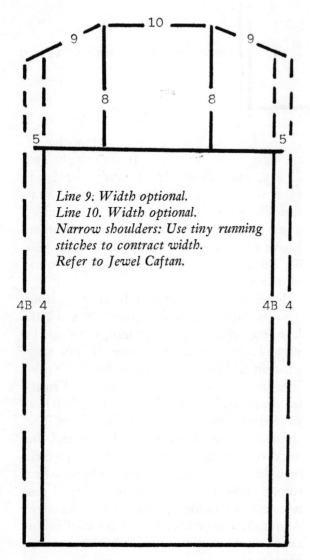

Line 9: Width optional.
Line 10. Width optional.
Narrow shoulders: Use tiny running
stitches to contract width.
Refer to Jewel Caftan.

Figure 200. Jewel Shell—Semi-Bateau neckline.

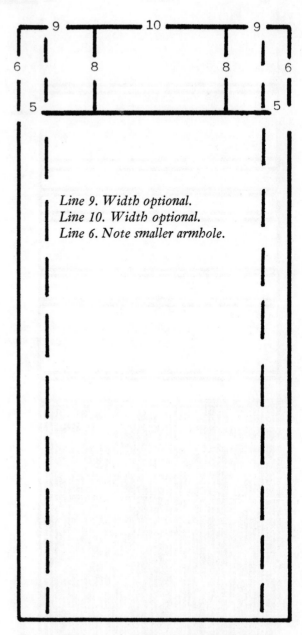

Line 9. Width optional.
Line 10. Width optional.
Line 6. Note smaller armhole.

Figure 201. Jewel Shell—Bateau Neckline.

Scale, proportion, and balance will be obvious to your eyes as you will immediately see what appeals to you and what jars your sensitivity. Fashions may change but style is timeless. Style is achieved by knowing what looks best on you. Develop this quality in yourself by really seeing the styles that are illustrated in the newspapers and magazines and shown in the stores. Look at them critically, just as if you were going to buy each and every one of them tomorrow. Would they be an addition to your wardrobe? Would they relate to your lifestyle, or would the purchases be reflecting the mood of the moment? Learn to distinguish the lines that continue to please you. Learn to understand what attracts the eye and how *you* wish people to see *you*.

When knitting and crocheting your designs you will be considering all of the elements mentioned. Scale refers to the proportion of the skirt to the top, or the pattern within the design. Think of the additional interest created simply by not dividing them equally in half; create interest through unequal divisions. Your Visual Pattern will aid you in planning the *proper proportions* because you are working with *your measurements.*

Study your figure, know your limitations, and accent your good features. If you desire to appear taller do not interrupt the flow of the eye as it skims over you. Know that an illusion of height is created by an uncomplicated look, using one color, making a V neckline, or lowering or raising the waistline. Emphasize your good points and diminsh all others!

You will enjoy cutting-up your Visual Pattern when you see how imaginative you can be. Allow your ideas to flow and capture them by drawing them on your pattern. Draw Midnight Jewel and Midnight Delight with the adjustments needed to make your individual patterns. Write your details on them.

CUTTING-UP

Dresses—Short

Dresses, short, also become tunics, long!

Refer to your measurements and use the measurement from above or below the knee to the underarm. Mark this on your Jewel pattern, draw a horizontal line, and CUT.

Slits

Slits may be 12″ long, to the upper thigh, to the lower or upper hips, or as high as 3″ below the underarm. Visualize this on your dress and understand how many different designs you have! Mark the depth of the slit on your pattern. Cut your pattern.

Round Needle Details: Cast on stitches to equal one-half your hip or bust measurement

plus ease (optional according to desired use) times body gauge on body gauge needle *twice.* Use two balls of yarn. If working a border for hem and slit edging while knitting, use a stitch pattern that will give you a firm edging and prevent curling. Knit your two pieces the length of your slits. Make sure that you are on the right (front) side so the sequence of the stitch pattern will not be interrupted when joining. Tie one ball in and cut, leaving a 4″ strand. Adjust the stitch pattern for the round needle as detailed in Chapter Nine. Continue the border across the top of the slits, the same width, for a finished, professional look. For other details; refer to Midnight Jewel.

Straight Needle Details: Cast on as detailed under Round Needle, but add stitches for seam allowance on completion of slits. Work seam stitches in the body stitch pattern but continue border pattern across the top of the slits to equal the width of the border.

Crocheted: Refer to Midnight Jewel—Crocheted. Do not add seam allowance until slits are completed.

This design may be worn as a dress or a tunic. Make it sleeveless or with short, wide sleeves and you have a super jumper or beach dress. Draw this with a V, square or scooped neckline and you have the pattern that you have been looking for.

Long-longs

Long-longs are short, short dresses (above the knees), or long sweaters; their versatility is in the way you wear them. If you plan to wear one as a dress but love the sweater look, consider making the ribbing on larger needles than the body gauge needles. This gives you the effect of ribbing without the contraction. Long-longs may also be made with slits. You can easily adjust your Jewel or Delight Visual Patterns.

Long Sweaters

Sweaters are usually long and narrow, but if you desire them wider, refer to Midnight

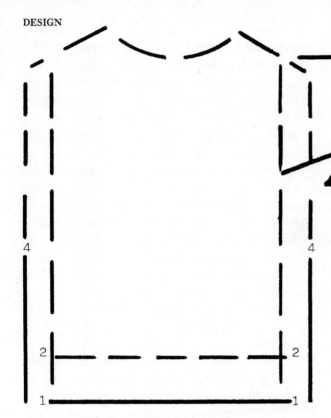

Figure 202. Long sweater.

Delight. Long sweaters may be worn any length, but an inch or two can make a tremendous difference in camouflaging wide hips. Study your figure in a full length mirror, try on different lengths, and look at yourself critically from many angles. The best length for you may vary from 5″ to 9″ below the waistline. Understand that the look will change when the same sweater is worn with a short skirt or long skirt or pants.

Details: Draw the basic Jewel, adjusting the width of the pattern for additional ease (approximately 2″ to 4″). See Figure 202. Measure from the desired point on the hips to the underarm; allow for blousing. Mark this on the pattern. Using this length draw a horizontal line, line 1. Draw another horizontal line, line 2, representing the depth of the border. Lines 4 represent the side folds or seams. (Observe how the additional ease affects the placement of the armhole and the length of the sleeves.) Cut the pattern.

144

Round Needle Details: Refer to Midnight Delight .

Straight Needle Details: Refer to Midnight Delight with seams.

Crocheted Details: Refer to Midnight Delight—Crocheted.

Neckline and sleeve styles are optional. These are detailed in this chapter. Each change creates another design and you are gradually learning how to adjust and make your individual Visual Patterns.

Short Sweaters

To create a short sweater, look again at Midnight Jewel, for the top is the basic shape for your dressy or suit sweaters.

Dressy Sweater Details: Draw the basic Jewel. Use the measurement from your waistline to your underarm, allowing for blousing and border. Mark this on your pattern and draw a horizontal line, #1. Draw another horizontal line, the border depth, above line 1, #2. Cut the pattern along line 1.

Round Needle Details:

Line 1. Cast on waist measurement X ribbing or border gauge on proper needle. Work depth or 3″.

Line 2. Change to body gauge needle and stitch pattern. Increase to bust measurement and ease times body gauge. Distribute increases evenly in one round. For other details, refer to Jewel.

Straight Needle Details:

Line 1. Cast on one-half the waist measurement times ribbing gauge on ribbing gauge needles. Work depth or 3″.

Jewel turtleneck (page 24)

Line 2. Change to body gauge needles. Increase to bust measurement plus seam allowance and ease times body gauge. Work in body stitch pattern. For other details, refer to Jewel or Delight with seams.

Crocheted:

Line 1. Chain the length needed for one-half the waist measurement plus seam allowance. Border may be worked on a smaller hook, using the Vertical Single Crochet.

Line 2. Change to body gauge hook and increase to equal bust measurement, ease and seam allowance times body gauge. Space increases evenly apart. Change to body stitch pattern.

Short-shorts

Short-shorts are sweaters that skim the waistline or reveal the midriff. Your Jewel is still the basic pattern, allow it to be your foundation. Measure, scantily, from the waist or above the waist to the underarm. Mark the Visual Pattern, draw the horizontal line, line 1, and cut.

Borders may be ribbed, crocheted, or gathered with elastic or a drawstring. Cord may be laced through eyelet openings, double crochet, or a casing. If you prefer a casing or hem, do not make a border. The thinnest backing for your casing is organza. Eyelets may be made (refer to Picquot Hem), or space the eyelets further apart by knitting one or two stitches between the yarn overs. Short-shorts may be based on the Jewel or Jewel Shell.

Boleros

A darling and daring look; its up to you! All that you have to do is make your Visual Pattern (Jewel is your base), crop it short, and shape in an armhole (optional). See Figure 203. Make your pattern twice since one will be cut down the exact center. You will then have the back and two fronts. Plan for the

edging or borders, give thought to a thick crocheted chain, a double crocheted strip, velvet ribbon, or fringe. There is no limit to the imaginative treatments possible, whether worked in or appliqued.

HEATHER CLASSICS

You now have your collection of sweater patterns and are on your way to sweater dressing—the classic look for day or night. Look at the Jewel pattern and the details that you have used. A round needle, measurements, gauge, yarn, and your own ingenuity are giving you pleasure beyond belief! Let us now combine a Dressy Sweater and Midnight Delight with the simplest of skirts. Let us use the bottom of Jewel, in the desired length, for this skirt is straight with easy gathers at the waist which are barely discernible when worn. Consider this in a length about 3″ above the anklebone and visualize it worn with a long-long for the ultimate in sophisticated understatement. Adjust the length; add a good 2″ to accommodate the hem and casing.

Heather Skirt Details. (Figure 204.)

Line 1. Cast on or chain Heather (pattern width doubled) measurement X body gauge on round needle, one size *larger* (if ribbing) than body gauge. *K2—P2* for 2″, or use border pattern for 2″.

Line 2. Change to body gauge size round needle and body stitch pattern. Suggested: plain knitting to . . .

Line 5B. Change to round needle, two sizes smaller, and repeat ribbing or border for 2″.

Line 5A. Bind off.

Heather Skirt Finishing Details

Hem is doubled under and sewn. Repeat at waist for 1″ casing for elastic.

Heather Under-Sweater is hip-length, ribbed or border stitch pattern throughout, with Jewel neckline 1″ lower; refer to Jewel.

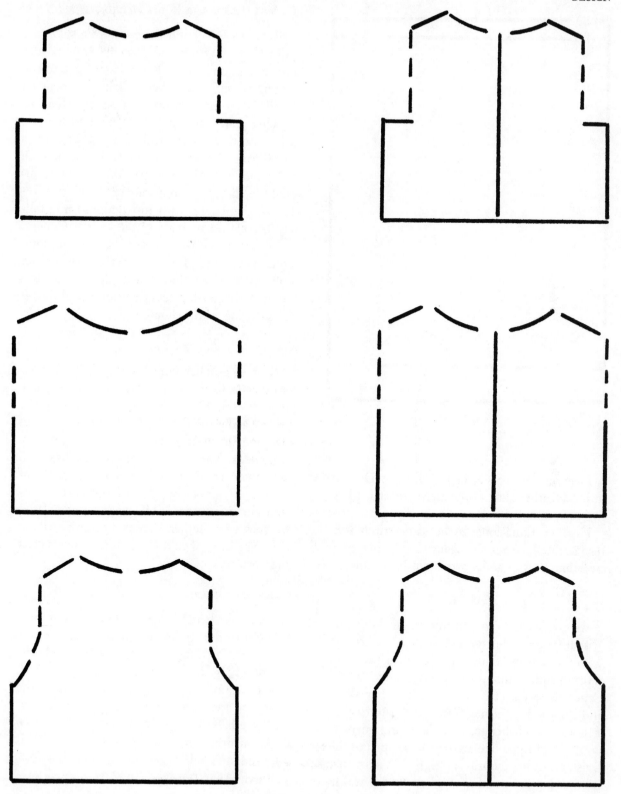

Figure 203. Boleros.

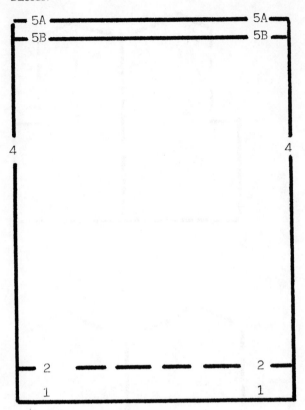

Figure 204. Heather Shirt.

Heather Over-Sweater is Midnight Delight in the Heather skirt body stitch pattern. (Try the yarn doubled.)

Heather Long-long is the same stitch pattern as the skirt. See the beauty in making your sweaters, dresses and skirts interchangeable!

CAPERS

As we have been cutting-up, making our Visual Patterns shorter and shorter, we are left with the remains. Do not cast them aside. I will refer to a piece that is below knee length as the Caper Skirt Pattern. (Figure 205.) The front and back are the same. Caper is a pattern that is going to challenge, stimulate, and surprise you! Would you like a skirt that is open to the waist, revealing contrasting tights? A skirt that is slit as high as the thigh and ties at the waist? Or would you like the swing of pleats?

Caper Open to the Waist Details

Refer to Jewel and the section on slits. Use your Caper Pattern and plan for your border at the hem and sides. There is no limit to the edging possibilities, whether fringe, crocheted braid, or an interesting stitch pattern. Knit or crochet your matching pieces; bind off loosely. The waistline is controlled by elastic or a drawstring. The two pieces may be joined with a 2″ seam or with hooks. If you use hooks, install the elastic without joining the pieces. Refer to Chapter Five for instructions on installing the elastic or making the casing. Conceal your hooks with crocheted buttons or pompons; have fun! The joy of this skirt is not only its flippiness but also its double use as a poncho. If needed, conceal additional hooks for securing on the shoulders.

Caper with Slits and Ties

Knit or crochet your Caper; refer to previous details. Cords may match or contrast; they may be attached at the waist or laced up the sides. Lacing the cord through eyelets requires planning on your Visual Pattern for uniform placement. Yarn over twice for eyelets, and remember to decrease for compensation of yarn over. Knot the ends of the cord or attach a luxurious tassel. The waistline and elastic are melded together. Think of how striking your Shell top would be with the same eyelet and cord treatment!

Caper with Pleats

Plan your hem border on your pattern; give thought to the stitch pattern as it must not be too thick. Nothing should interfere with the edgestitching of the pleats. See Figure 205. The pleat underlay pattern is the length of the skirt, and the width is determined by deducting one-half the waist measurement from Caper width. For instance, if Caper width is 20″ and one-half waist measurement is 14″, you would have an excess of 6″. Thus you have 3″ turning under at each side for the pleat, and

Figure 205. Caper.

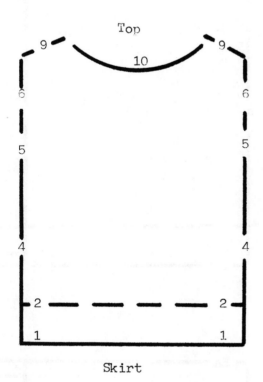

Top

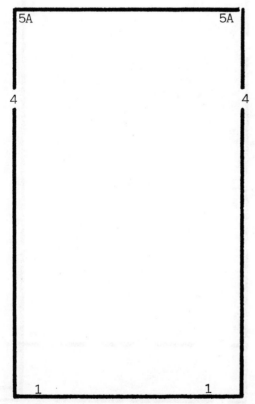

Skirt

5A Waistline

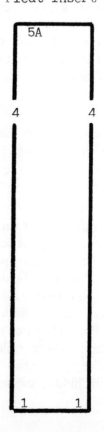

Pleat Insert

the need for a 6″ underlay. Knit or crochet Caper, twice, plus two underlays. The underlays are made in the same stitch pattern and yarn; for added fun use a contrasting color. The underlay is sewn in on the wrong side. The pleat is edgestitched, ½″ in, on the right side. (Refer to Chapter Six.) The pleat is then fastened at the waist or stitched down to the hipbones at a point where you wish. Use hidden stitching to close the pleat. Elastic at the waist is optional. If you wish the skirt to just settle at the waist, do not stitch the pleats down, simply secure each pleat with a concealed hook; you thus have the needed waist measurement.

Caper Top

Look at your Figure 205 again. The top is Jewel Shell, twice. Match your skirt and make your top simply caught at the underarm, allowing it to swing open and show the undersweater, lace it at the sides, or set in pleats. You now know how! There is no limit!

CAPER'S JEWEL

Caper has shown you the fun that you can have with a simple oblong pattern. Its basic strength is its measurements, since it is based on *your* Jewel. Observe the next Caper diagram, Figure 206, for there are two oblong shapes which differ in length and width. We are now going to make another set of Visual Patterns by simply adding to the width, a minimum of 6″ to 8″. The different lengths will be determined by your measurements and desires. I visualize this design with the top ending at the hips. Measure and add for hem and neckline casing (approximately 2½″). Create interest by planning an unequal division for the skirt; do not have it the same length as the top. The skirt could be one-third longer; add for hem allowance. Draw and cut the patterns.

Knit or crochet two matching pieces, thus making four pieces, two for the top and two for the skirt. (Round needles may be used; adjust pattern accordingly.) Muffy's Tiny Bell Lace pattern is divine when used upside down; if you wish a solid stitch pattern consider Petite. These four pieces, assembled, will become a precious jewel in your collection by following the next few simple steps.

Caper's Jewel Skirt

Pin the seams and hem, baste and sew. Attach 1″ width elastic to the waist; refer to Sewing Chapter.

Caper's Jewel Shell Top

Caper's Jewel Shell is gathered at the bateau neckline and at the bottom. Pin your seams, allowing for a small armhole and narrow shoulders. The armhole edge should not be dropped, and it should be small but comfortable. Baste and try on. Turn bateau neckline under 1″ all around for a casing. Pin and baste. Pin and baste a 1½″ hem. Baste a little rolled hem around the armholes; try on. Sew armhole hems permanently with hidden stitches. Sew

150

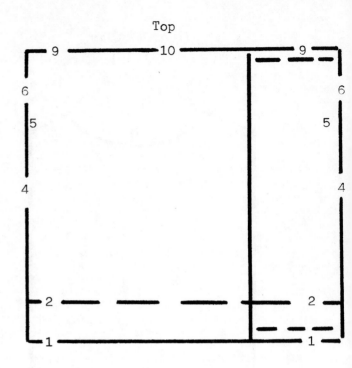

Top

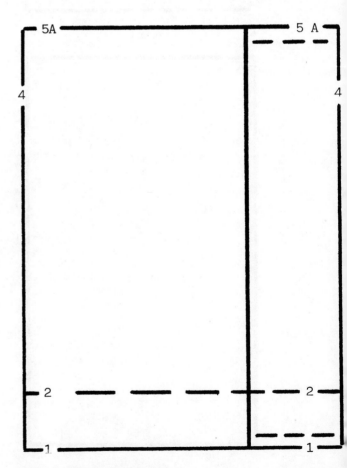

Skirt

Figure 206. Caper's Jewel.

seams as detailed in Chapter Five. Do not close casings until after the cord or elastic is drawn through. The neckline is gathered by using cord or ¼″ wide elastic. This length is measured straight across the neckline (see bateau necklines); double this and cut the elastic. The hem is gathered by cord or 1″ wide elastic. Refer to your hip measurement and cut the elastic 3″ shorter. You now have a superb top!

I bought yards and yards of velvet ribbon and made two floppy bows with long streamers. I placed the first bow on my shoulder with the streamers touching the hem. I placed the second bow on the same side, at the hem of the top, and its streamers flowed gracefully to the hem of the skirt. The same effect may be achieved with long cords.

You now have experienced gradual changes in your patterns. You have shortened them, cut them, and added to them. The next design is for a caftan, and you will see how your Jewel is used to broaden your understanding, thoughts, and approach to designing.

JEWEL SHELL CAFTAN (SEMI-BATEAU)

Prepare your brown paper for a pattern that will be double Jewel Shell width. Center your Jewel Shell pattern, as you are going to draw the additional width (one-half of Jewel Shell pattern) on each side of the Shell. Extend the shoulder slant at the same angle, thus creating a wide, sloping shoulder. Mark you pattern for deep armholes, see Figure 207. Front and back patterns are the same.

Jewel Caftan is knitted with or without seams and may be crocheted; refer to Jewel details.

Jewel Caftan Finishing Details #1

The shoulders may be gathered before seaming. Use one row of running stitches; pull to desired width. Baste together and try on. Make another row of running stitches, pull to firm gathering and width, and fasten securely. Try

on again. Carefully backstitch over the last row of gathering. The neckline may be turned under (bateau neckline) or a simple casing may be made for a cord.

Jewel Caftan Finishing Details #2

Plan on an armhole at least 12″ deep; your shoulder line continues down the arm. Make two patterns, pin and try on. This shape must flow as you will not gather the shoulders for this version. If you have the slightest doubt, use your Visual Pattern and cut a muslin pattern. When you have doubts, you should always take the time to make a muslin pattern. (Use an old sheet if you wish.) Cut, baste, and try on. Study the shape and make all adjustments. This is a must when making pants or any design that demands perfection.

Jewel Caftan Variation

Jewel Shell Caftan Visual Pattern becomes the *front* of this design. The *back* pattern is drawn the same as the front except for the neckline; shape in a deep scoop. Cut the pattern exactly down the center. Draw and cut another basic Jewel Shell the length of the caftan. Tape this in the center of your pattern and continue the deep scoop. See Figure 208A.

Jewel Caftan Variation Finishing Details

You have knitted or crocheted your front and back, referring to your Jewel. Shoulders are a smooth seam. The armhole is turned under and hemmed. The front bateau neckline is straight and tapers to the shoulders. The back neckline is fully gathered thus centering the draping of the caftan through the center back. Gathering would be made by making two rows of running stitches, pulling, and fastening securely. Pick up stitches, retaining the gathers, around the front and back necklines for a 1″ Stockinette Stitch band (Round needle; just knit). Bind off, double over, and hem. This makes a smooth piping. If you are crocheting, use the border stitch that you desire.

I will now interrupt our pattern making so

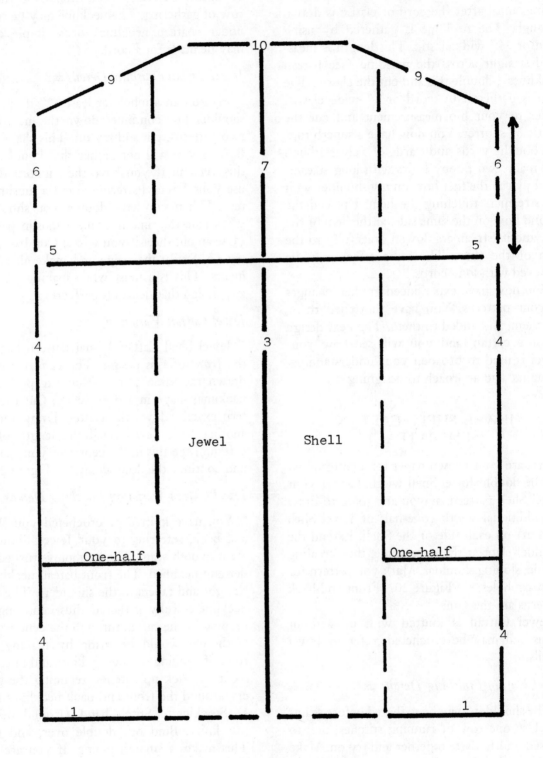

Figure 207. Jewel Shell Caftan—Semi-Bateau.

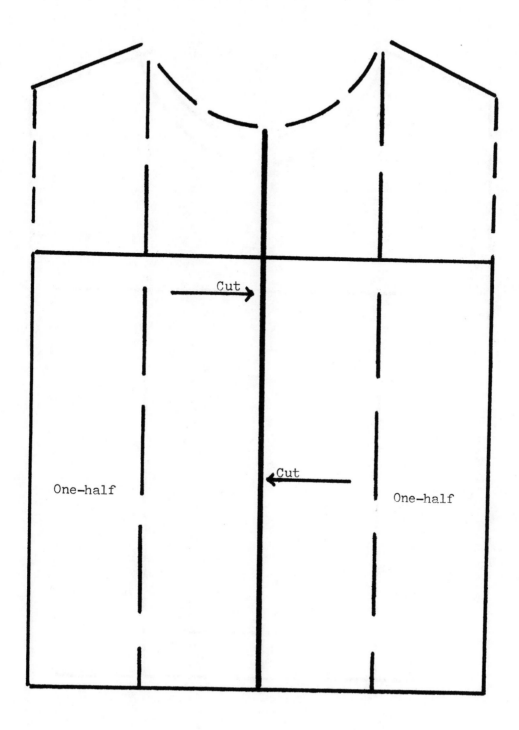

Cut

Cut

One-half

One-half

Figure 208. Jewel Shell Caftan Variation.

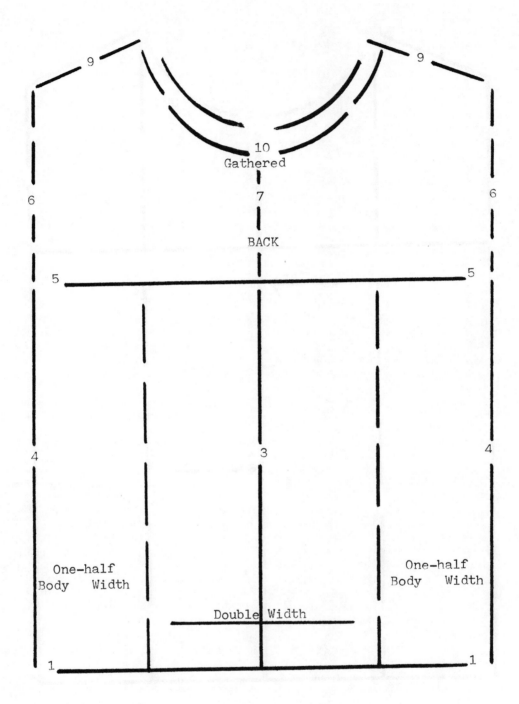

Figure 208A.

that we may discuss necklines, armholes, and sleeves. This will enable you to plan future Jewel designs.

NECKLINES

The same shape—round, V, or square—will look and create a different effect when made high or low. Square, round, V, bateau, semi-bateau, boat, crew, turtleneck, or a slash, front or back are neckline variations. A design may specify a neckline but that does not prohibit you from changing the style or placement. The following diagrams are drawn from your underarm line, line 5, to your neckline, line 10, and shoulders, lines 9. See Figures 209 and 210. As you have observed, the shaping of your neckline is dependent on the measurement from your underarm line to the beginning of the shaping, always considering the edging or border. Your measurement chart should have measurements for various styles and depths.

The shaping of your neckline is accomplished by binding off and decreasing, or just binding off or decreasing, depending on the style. Draw the neckline carefully on your Visual Pattern so that you can calculate the shaping accurately. The number of stitches to be bound off in a straight line is determined by the measurement and your gauge. The number of stitches to be decreased is dependent on the measurement from the end of line 7 to where line 8 meets line 9 (neck edge at the shoulder seam). Inches to be decreased may be transposed to stitches and rows by referring to your gauge. An average round (Jewel) neckline is decreased more rapidly than a deep round or V neckline.

Plan your stitch pattern for the border or edging, whether worked in or added later, so that the neckline will be flat and smooth with a finished look.

Round (Jewel) Neckline

This is the basic shape for boat, crew, turtleneck, or collared necklines. It is shaped by

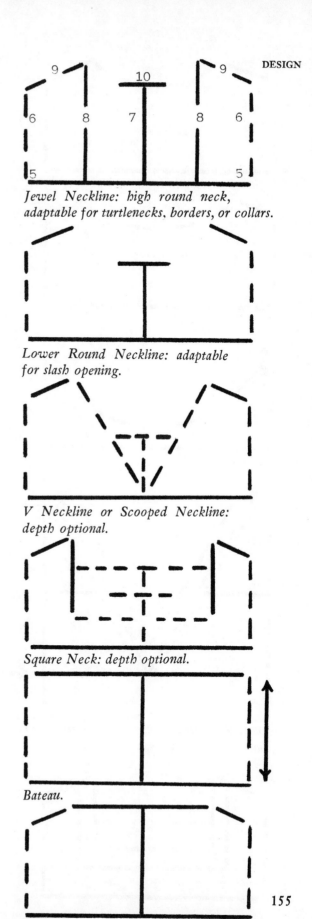

DESIGN

Jewel Neckline: high round neck, adaptable for turtlenecks, borders, or collars.

Lower Round Neckline: adaptable for slash opening.

V Neckline or Scooped Neckline: depth optional.

Square Neck: depth optional.

Bateau.

Semi-Bateau.

155

Figure 209. Neckline Shaping.

Figure 210. Jewel Neckline: high round.

Round, 1″ Lower.

Deep Round.

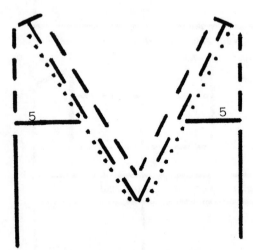

Deep V. Decreases placed ½″ from border, depth optional.

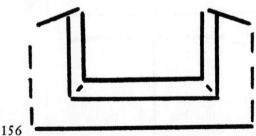

156

Deep Square.

binding off the center stitches at the base of the neck, lower than the collar-bones, or as deep as you wish for a scooped neckline. The shaping is continued by decreasing. This style is timeless and may be changed simply by adding a matching triangle or long scarf.

The Jewel neckline may be embellished with a loose, deep turtleneck or an attached hood.

Square Neckline

Draw the square neckline on your Visual Pattern exactly as you wish it to appear, and also draw the lines needed to depict the border or edging, and you will not be able to resist making it whether knitting or crocheting. This style is unique. Square necklines are made by binding off in a straight line and working straight up to the shoulder. Stitches are picked up for the border and counted for uniformity. Decreasing is done in each corner on each row or every other row. The corner is accented by a seam stitch (knit) with a decrease on either side or a triple decrease, slanted in the proper direction. Refer to decreases in Chapter Eight.

V Neckline

V necklines are dramatically simple. They may be made as deep as you wish and worn front or back. Draw the V on your Visual Pattern. If you are making a deep V, you will observe that the V formation may start below the armhole. Remember—the deeper the V, the more gradual the decreasing. Space the decreases evenly apart at the neck edge. The border or edging may be knitted or crocheted; care must be given to retaining the sharp V. This is accomplished by making a center seam stitch with decreases on each side; refer to Chapter Eight. The V neckline is also the base for a shawl collar.

Bateau Neckline

Look at Figure 209 and you will see that the Visual Pattern is drawn with a straight line across the shoulders and neckline; allowing for sufficient depth for the armholes. Bateau neck-lines are bound off in a straight line; if you are crocheting, fasten the last stitch. Measure for the desired shoulder width, pin and baste. Try on and sew when satisfied. Bateau neck-lines may be turned under and hemmed; this is optional.

Semi-bateau Neckline

Decide on the desired width and draw this on your Visual Pattern. Your basic Jewel pattern helps you to know the exact width remaining across your shoulders. Shoulders are bound off gradually (refer to Jewel), and the neckline stitches are bound off straight across. If you are crocheting, fasten the last stitch. The same method for shaping is used when crocheting.

Slashes

Slashes look best when coordinated with a Jewel neckline. Draw the slash the desired depth on your Visual Pattern, and observe whether it starts before the armhole is reached. A slash is made simply by separating the whole into two halves and tying in another ball of yarn; working the two pieces simultaneously. The garment may be worn with the slash in the front or back. Plan for the edging, whether worked in or added later, and select a stitch pattern so that the slash will lie flat without drooping. Note: If you wish a very fine edging, such as picquot or single crochet, but the slash droops, try the following remedy. Use organza or matching ribbon and tack in, on the wrong side, with tiny running stitches. This lining may be cut a little shorter and the slash melded in; steam gently.

Imaginative Variations

Interesting effects may be created by using the scooped, square, or U shaped neckline as the base for a full turtleneck (cowl) or shawl collar. Draw your Visual Pattern, experiment with different necklines, and visualize the result. Knit or crochet your garment with the

desired shape, sew the shoulder seams, and pick-up stitches as detailed in Chapter Eight. The turtleneck would be worked with the body gauge size needle or hook to the base of the neck and then the full turtleneck would be shaped as detailed under Midnight Delight.

Shawl Collars

Shawl collars are simple, effective, and easy to make, and luxurious in feeling as they cuddle about your neck. In essence, they are long oblong strips that encircle the neckline, gradually folding over, thus becoming the collar. The collar stitches are picked-up along the straight binding off (the base of the neckline) and 2 stitches beyond (seam allowance). These stitches are then worked in a non-curling stitch pattern for the length that will encircle the neckline; measure carefully as you work.

Bind off and pin the collar in place, tucking the end directly behind the picked-up stitches. Baste, and try the garment on. Sew carefully with matching mercerized cotton thread.

This seam is optional. If you wish you may omit the 2 stitches by working the last stitch into the neck edge. This is done by knitting to the last stitch on the right-hand needle and using the point to pull a loop through the very edge of the neck. The last stitch is then dropped over this loop; turn your work and repeat this for the length of your collar. Bind off and tuck end behind the front; sew carefully.

The shawl collar may also be made by picking-up the stitches around the neckline. The width of the collar would equal the base of the neckline. This width may be picked-up as you knit, or sewn on completion. Remember that one end is tucked behind the other.

Another variation is to work straight up. Think of a cardigan or sweater with a deep front slash; do not shape the front neckline. Bind off for narrow shoulders and work the remaining front stitches to the center back; allow for a seam. This approach may be used on any garment.

DESIGN

Collars

The beauty of knitted or crocheted collars is in the flexibility of their texture since the secret of any collar is that it must fit properly around the neckline. A little steaming goes a long way toward giving you a professional look. The neckline used determines how the collar will lie. If you want the collar to lie flat use a deep neckline. If you want a rolled collar use a Jewel neckline.

Refer to your gauge when picking-up stitches and work the desired shape. If you wish a tie collar, cast on sufficient stitches, then pick-up stitches around the neckline, and then cast on to equal the previously cast on stitches.

If you wish to back (line) your collar, make the same shape but work it slightly smaller. If you want, you can use a thin organza between the two collars. Sew carefully, easing the two collars together. Steam and crochet around the edges. If the texture is bulky, crochet around the edges.

ARMHOLE SHAPING

The depth of your armhole is determined by your personal preference and the selection of sleeve style. (Figure 211). Sleeveless armholes should be small, lie close to the upper arm, and fit smoothly without gapping. If you find that your armhole is too loose control the extra width by making tiny, hidden stitches with matching cotton thread. Pull thread to the desired width, fasten securely, and carefully steam.

Armholes for picked-up sleeves usually have a minimum of 1″ ease. An extreme dropped shoulder line (2″ to 3″ onto upper arm) changes the needed depth of the armhole. If you wish a narrow sleeve your actual armhole measurement plus seam allowance is sufficient. Armhole depth should conform to the width of the sleeve; this will be explained further under sleeves.

If you prefer a shaped armhole, draw the shape on your Visual Pattern. Compare this to an armhole in a garment that you have worn and found comfortable. If you do not have a garment to refer to, make a muslin pattern. When making the knitted or crocheted garment the armhole may be shaped by binding off approximately 1″ at the beginning of two rows (crocheted binding off is detailed in Chapter Eight under Crocheting.) Decreasing at the beginning and end of a row (or every other row) continues the shaping. This is done until the desired curve is attained. Various methods of decreasing may be used to achieve different effects. Decreases are detailed in Chapter Eight.

If you prefer a square armhole, draw the shape on your Visual Pattern. Plan on a deeper and more cut-out armhole. When knitting or crocheting, bind off the number of stitches needed to equal the measurement on the Visual Pattern. Work straight up to the shoulder. This armhole is complemented with a picked-up sleeve.

SLEEVES

The sleeves that I will detail are timeless classics and adaptable to your Jewel. Use them as you wish to enhance your design. Sleeves should conform to the shape of your arms without signs of strain and mold smoothly over your shoulders. The shoulder seam (centered) at the top of the shoulder joins the front and back and does much to strengthen the feel and appearance of the garment. The texture of knitted and crocheted clothes allows your arms to move freely and gracefully without constraint.

Check all of your arm measurements carefully and remember to add 1″ ease (minimum) through the upper arm and elbow. Measure your length carefully and allow for bending your elbow. Do not fail to compare your work to your Visual Pattern. If you have the slightest doubt, make a muslin pattern.

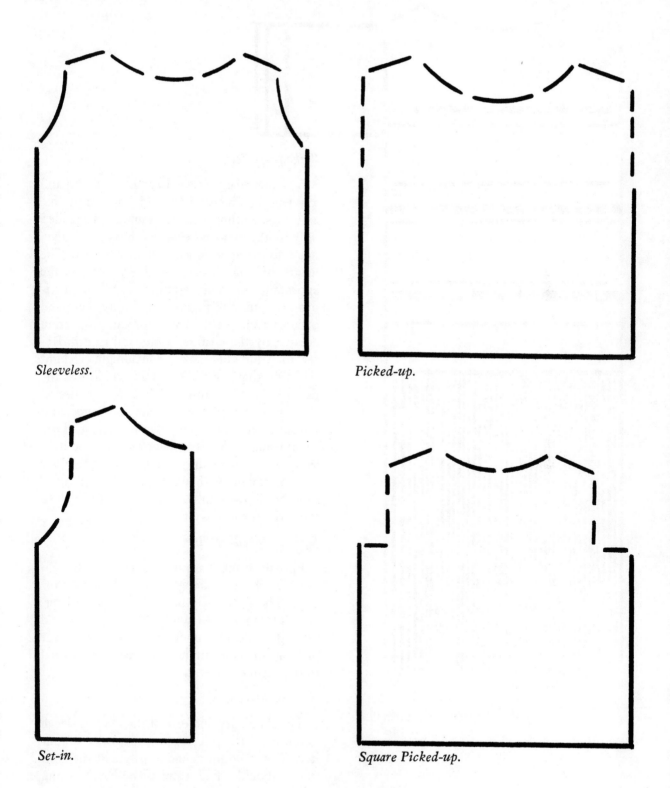

Sleeveless.

Picked-up.

Set-in.

Square Picked-up.

Figure 211. Armhole Shaping.

Figure 212. Sleeve Design.

Picked-up Sleeves

The picked-up sleeve may be any width and any length. The neatness of the picked-up line and the smoothness of the shoulders is equalled only by the kimona sleeve. Each style is a gem, not only in appearance, but in comfort. The length of your sleeves definitely changes the appearance of your design; refer to the previous diagrams and Figure 212. Study them and become aware of the harmony and proportion created by the change in line and length. Refer to Midnight Jewel or Midnight Delight when making your Visual Pattern. Adjust the details for the width and length you desire, always planning for ease, seam allowance, and border or edging. If you plan for a hem, allow for turning under. The hem may also be used as a casing for a drawstring. Visualize your sleeves straight without shaping, gathered below the elbow with contrasting cord or full to the wrist for a peasant sleeve.

Square Picked-up Sleeves

Pick-up stitches around the armhole but do not pick them up along the straight bound off edge. The sleeve may be made and sewn later. An alternative is to work the straight bound off edge as detailed under Shawl Collars. After picking-up these stitches the sleeve is worked to the desired shape and length.

Kimona Sleeves

The simplicity and ease of the kimona sleeve (Figure 213) is priceless; its versatility unlimited. The smoothness and elegance of the continued shoulder line, emphasized by the seam, make this style a great favorite. Draw your

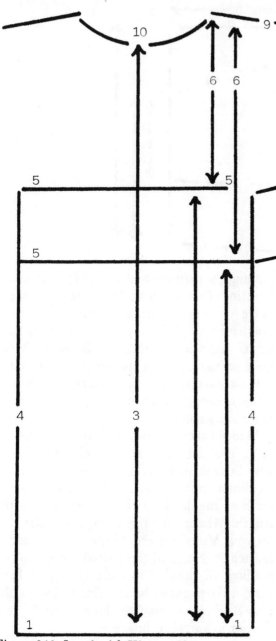

Figure 213. Jewel with Kimona Sleeve.

Jewel pattern and practice drawing sleeves in various lengths and widths. Observe in Figure 213 that the body and sleeves are one and that there is no armhole line, also observe the changes in the armhole depth and in the slant of the under-sleeve and shoulder line. Shape the continued shoulder line to the end of the sleeve. Look at Figure 214 and see how square

the sleeve and neckline can be shaped. They become one by simply binding off or ending the work in a straight line. Care must be given to calculate the exact length to the armhole. Your Visual Pattern eliminates any guesswork; your muslin pattern gives you the opportunity to experience the feel of the design.

I suggest working with round needles. It may be necessary to work with two; one for the front and sleeves and the other for the back and sleeves. This prevents stitches from falling off. Divide your stitches in half, if you do not have seams before starting the sleeves. Stitches are cast on or chained on each side, graduated or in a straight line, forming the under-sleeve edge (line 14); allow for border or hem. The sleeve is worked until you have the width plus ease and seam allowance. The minimum width is where the sleeve ends on your arm, plus ease and seam allowance. This *total* measurement is divided in *half* because the kimona sleeve has a seam from the neckline and centered down the shoulder and sleeve. You have *two* seams and must calculate seam allowance accordingly. Binding off is done gradually or in a straight line, depending on the shape and width of the sleeve and the desired shoulder line. Calculate this shaping on your Visual Pattern and transpose the inches to stitches.

A kimona sleeve, narrow or average, is formed by casting on or chaining gradually,

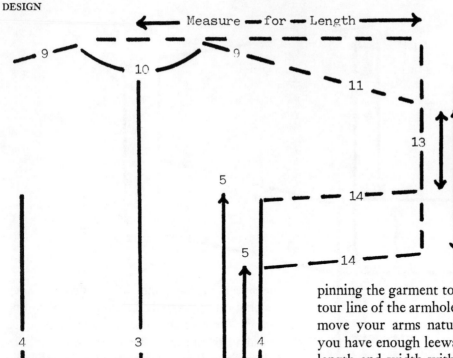

Figure 214. Kimona Sleeve. Measure for length.

approximately 1″ at a time, until you have the desired length. Work evenly for one-half the width plus ease and seam allowance and then bind off. Binding off may be done at the same rate as casting on (refer to your Visual Pattern) or according to the desired length and shoulder line. The number of stitches to bind off each time is determined by the additional length needed to complete the armhole. Refer to your gauge, the number of rows in one inch, and the length to be worked. For instance, if you need 2″ more and the count is 8 rows to 1″, you would count the stitches on the needle *to the armhole edge* and divide by eight. The result would be the number bound off each time.

Narrow kimona sleeves should have a separate diamond shaped gusset sewn in at the underarm; see Figure 215. The gusset is first drawn on paper, then cut in muslin, before knitting or crocheting it in the same stitch pattern. Correct measurements are derived by

pinning the garment to about 3″ from the contour line of the armhole. Try your garment on, move your arms naturally, and determine if you have enough leeway. Establish the needed length and width with seam allowance. Make your patterns, pin the muslin gusset in, and if it is satisfactory, knit or crochet it. This prevents unsightly folds and keeps the armhole taunt and smooth.

Wider kimona sleeves are formed by casting on or chaining more stitches, each time, with very little shaping to the sleeve; approximately 2″ minimum at a time. Observe Figure 214 and see how the depth of the armhole affects the length. Measure for this change and plan this on your Visual Pattern. Wide kimona sleeves, knitted or crocheted (crocheted casting on and binding off detailed in Chapter Eight) have very little shaping, barely discernible to the eye. Binding off may be done about 2″ at a time or in a straight line.

Puffed Sleeves

Puffed sleeves (Figure 216) are stunning in any length: short ones have an illusion of fantasy, elbow-length an illusion of sophistication, and full-length an illusion of femininity. The shape of the sleeve is drawn on your Visual Pattern by using the Jewel as your base. Measure for the desired length, allow for puff, and mark this on the pattern. Measure and

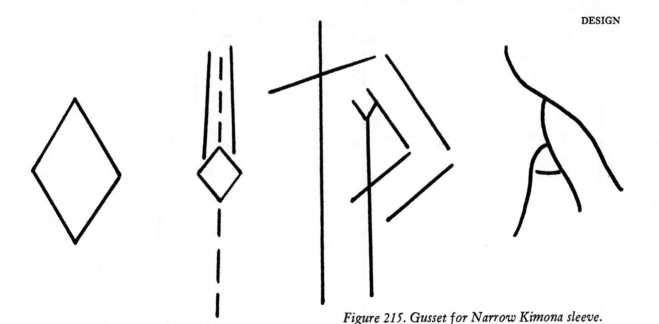

Figure 215. Gusset for Narrow Kimona sleeve.

mark for desired depth of border. The width may be Jewel sleeve doubled.

Line 13. Draw line one-half the border (cuff) width plus seam allowance.

Line 12. Draw line the same width as line 13, designating the depth of border.

Lines 11 and 14. Drawn and shaped the width of one-half the puff, plus seam allowance. (Seam allowance is optional as the puff may be worked on 16" round needle. Border could be worked on 4 double-pointed needles.)

Puff Width: The width of the sleeve is Jewel sleeve doubled and the pattern is drawn one-half the width.

Picked-up puffed sleeves; refer to Picked-up Sleeves.

If you wish a very full sleeve, whether knitting or crocheting, work one row evenly and on the next row increase into each stitch. Work the desired length, always adding an inch or two for the puffing. Decreasing is done in one row; it may be necessary to double decrease to reduce the width to the needed measurement. Work one row before starting the border, or two rows if you are going to pick-up stitches for an edging.

Peasant sleeves; refer to Puffed Sleeves. Work to the wrist.

Remember • Refer to your Visual Pattern, and if you have the slightest doubt make a muslin pattern.

• Always consider your stitch count and the multiple of the stitch pattern.

• Always try your sleeve on while working.

Note: The number of stitches to increase in the increase row is determined by your gauge and the desired width.

Unpressed Pleats at Border or Cuff

Sleeves are worked as previously detailed; bind off after attaining the desired length. Pin in ¾" pleats, evenly spaced to reduce to desired width, measure, and baste firmly. The first row of basting is placed against the binding off, while the second row is placed ¼" away. This sets the pleats in place. Pick-up the stitches for the border, carefully going through both thicknesses. When you have worked a few rows, pull the basting thread out. Do not use this method if you have worked with a bulky yarn or a thick stitch pattern. This detailing is superb on a shirt or cardigan design.

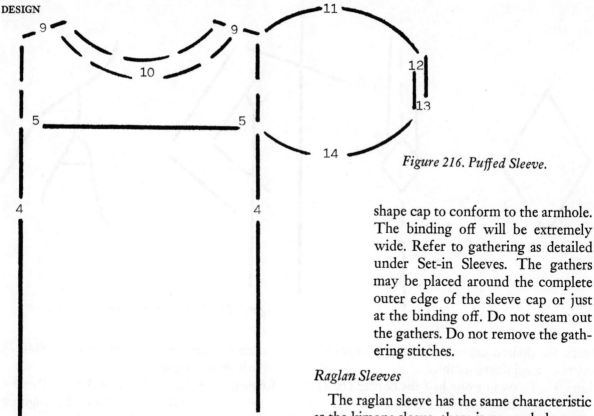

Figure 216. Puffed Sleeve.

shape cap to conform to the armhole. The binding off will be extremely wide. Refer to gathering as detailed under Set-in Sleeves. The gathers may be placed around the complete outer edge of the sleeve cap or just at the binding off. Do not steam out the gathers. Do not remove the gathering stitches.

Raglan Sleeves

The raglan sleeve has the same characteristic as the kimona sleeve; there is no armhole seam. The shaping of the shoulder and sleeve starts at the neckline, therefore the garment is made from the top. See Figures 217 and 218. The Visual Pattern has the same outline as Jewel or Delight; the change is in the armhole line.

Line 20. Measure your neck loosely. Cast on or chain. Work band or border.

Line 10. Change to body gauge 16″ round needle or crochet hook. Refer to Figure 217, and place pins at the four corners, as a guide for seam lines. Double increasing is used, every other round, making 8 increases to a round, until you reach the underarm, plus ease (line 5).

Note: Various increases are discussed in Chapter Eight. If you wish a solid seam, try the following double increase. The seam stitch (4 in all) is the pivotal point; mark it for accuracy. Knit into the back of the stitch in the row below; then the back of the pivotal stitch. The third stitch is made by using the left-hand needle point and inserting it into the pivotal

Set-in Puffed Sleeves

Refer to Set-in Sleeves for making your Visual Pattern.

Line 13. The width of arm plus seam allowance.

Line 12. Repeat line 13, spaced for border depth.

Lines 11 and 14. The width of the desired puff. (Double Jewel Sleeve width.)

Sleeve Cap: Shape in as on set-in sleeve but accommodate for the doubled width.

This sleeve is usually made from the cuff up, therefore:

Line 13. Cast on width times border gauge on proper needle. Work to . . .

Line 12. Change to body stitch pattern and needle, increasing to desired width (fuller puff may necessitate two rows of increasing.) Work the desired length, allowing for puff. Then

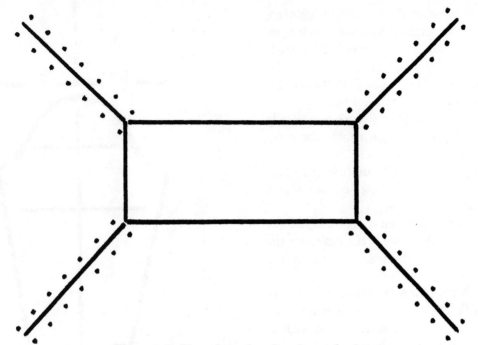

Figure 217. Top view of raglan sleeve shaping.

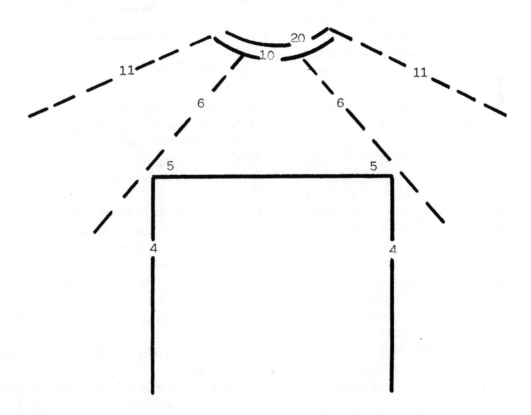

Figure 218. Jewel with raglan shaping.

stitch and drawing up the left strand; knit into the back of this strand. As your stitches increase, change to 24″ (longer, if needed) round needle, body gauge size.

Line   5. Try on. (Place one-half the stitches on another round needle.)

> Note: Raglan sleeves are usually used on casual garments; allow for comfortable armholes.
>
> Re-measure for accurate length of . . .

Line 14. and plan the shaping on your Visual Pattern.

> Note: Cast on a few stitches for seam allowance. If desired, the sleeves may be made on 16″ round needle.

These details are for a Jewel neckline. Other styles of necklines should be drawn on your Visual Pattern, and calculations worked in reverse. Open garments: Do not join.

Crocheted garments are shaped the same as knitted; with or without seam lines. The formula of increasing remains the same, 8 stitches every other row, but the distribution of the increases varies when omitting seams. The idea is to be scatter the increases, thus avoiding a definite line.

Note: It is optional whether sleeve stitches or body stitches are placed on a long strand of yarn first.

The previous details for shaping in shoulders and sleeves are applicable when making capes. Capes may require the use of more than two round needles, depending on the fullness. Capes are detailed later in this chapter.

Set-in Sleeves

Measure your arm as detailed in Figure 219. Prepare your brown paper as detailed in Chapter Four. Draw your Visual Pattern, referring to your measurements and design, shaping the sleeve cap to conform to your armhole. The diagram shows the shape of the cap, the line over the cap represents the top of your armhole.

Observe Figure 220 for Visual Pattern num-

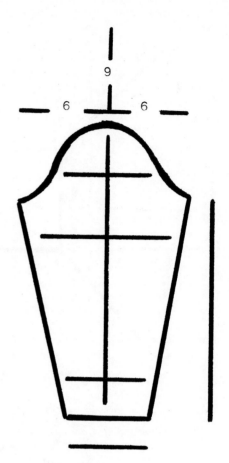

Figure 219. Measuring arm for sleeve.

bers. The following code numbers are listed in numerical order, not in drawing sequence:

Line   6. Shaping cap to conform to armhole.

Line 6B. Binding off.

Line 11. Center fold and center measuring line.

Line 12. Optional: Depth of border.

Line 13. Wrist width, plus ease and seam allowance. Ease suggestion: 1″ to 3″, depending on design.

Line 14. Under sleeve seam, also where shaping is done.

Line 17. Measuring line to start of shaping cap.

Line 18. Lower elbow width and measuring line.

Knitted or crocheted set-in sleeves require the same precision in shaping, fitting, and sewing as when working with fabrics. You must

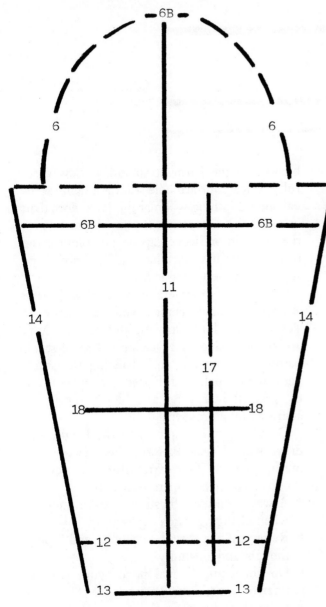

Figure 220. Visual Pattern for Set-in Sleeve.

Knit or crochet your sleeve starting at the bottom.

Line 13. Cast on or chain the needed width on border gauge needles or hook; measurement at beginning of sleeve, plus ease and seam allowance X border gauge.

Line 12. Change to body gauge needles or hook and stitch pattern. Increase to measurement at this point, plus ease and seam allowance X body gauge; consider stitch pattern multiple.

Line 14. Straight Sleeve: Work evenly.

Shaped Sleeve: Increase at the beginning and end of one row (spacing increase rows evenly apart) to equal measurement at line 18. Then calculate the number of increases needed to reach the desired width on completion of length as shown by line 17.

Line 11. Center measuring line. Always measure work flat.

Line 6. Binding off and shaping to conform to armhole. Bind off approximately 1″ at the beginning of two rows. Decreasing for shaping usually averages 2 stitches every other row.

Line 6B. Bind off.

Note: Plan to have sufficient width through the cap and bind off to conform to the armhole.

Carefully pin and baste the sleeve seams together. Place the right side of the sleeve against the right side of the garment, set the sleeve inside the armhole with the wrong side of the garment towards you, and gently meld it in. If one is wider than the other do not rush into the sewing.

Prepare the wider armhole edge or cap edge by making little running stitches all around the edge. Pull the thread to bring the armhole or cap to the desired width and fasten securely. You now have tiny puckers all around the outer edge; distribute these evenly. The center top of your sleeve cap must align with the shoulder seam. After pinning to make certain that the cap fits smoothly; remove the pins.

prepare your Visual Pattern and then make a muslin pattern. A set-in sleeve joins the garment with a seam that encircles the armhole. The secret of a good set-in sleeve is the coordination of the upper arm section, called the sleeve cap, and the armhole (armscye). The sleeve cap must be shaped properly and set in smoothly. The shape of the outer cap must conform with the armhole.

Figure 221. Tunic with contrasting stripe.

blend into the garment smoothly. Sew carefully, since your armhole seam is a definite focal point. Nothing will mar this look more than crooked or bulky seams. If you wish to control the armhole or sleeve cap do not remove the running stitches. Armhole seams should be steamed on the wrong side.

There are innumerable variations to the sleeves that I have detailed. You may wish your sleeves to be long, straight and cuffed. Cuffs are simply made by reversing the same stitch pattern and bending up, changing the stitch pattern, or crocheting. Flared sleeves are made by gradual increasing and blousing may be achieved by a drawstring.

Decide on the shaping and the length and draw your Visual Pattern; then make your muslin pattern. This extra effort will reward you over and over again. Remember:

• Always consider the stitch pattern multiple when changing stitch patterns.
• Refer to the Stitch chapter and apply thought and ingenuity!
• Do not skimp in making of your sleeves; refer to your Visual Pattern.
• Keep the edging simple; if your border or edging is appliqued, start and finish in an inconspicuous spot.

Each variation, whether in the sleeves or at the neckline, will create a different design. Each design then becomes the basis for many changes, whether in yarn, stitch pattern, or cutting up. The patterns that you have made, plus the section on necklines, armholes, and sleeves, will be the answer for your individual designs for many years to come. They prepare you for any trends and desires. Buy extra yarn

The sleeve cap or armhole will now be carefully steamed. The puckers will be shrunk in by using your sleeve pad, press cloth, and steam iron carefully. Insert the pad, place your press cloth and steam lightly. The extra fullness will gradually contract. Allow to dry thoroughly.

Pin carefully, starting at the underarm and working to the shoulder seam, turn, and repeat, working from underarm to shoulder seam. Baste and try on. Your sleeve should

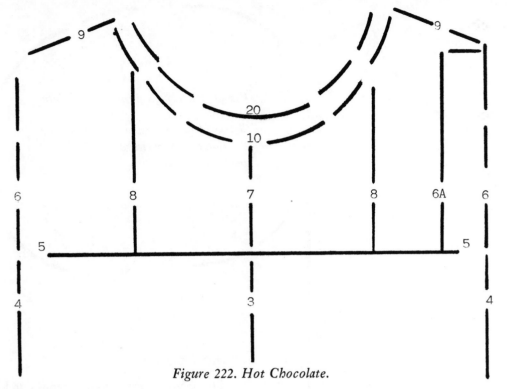

Figure 222. Hot Chocolate.

and plan for matching or contrasting accessories. Think of a tunic with a contrasting stripe, see Figure 221, with matching leggings or tights and contrasting scarf and hat. Visualize your long-longs being worn with matching knee socks.

HOT CHOCOLATE

This is your Jewel but the low, scooped neckline and the full puffed sleeves take full advantage of the previous details. (Figures 216 and 222.) The neckline is finished with a 2″ ribbed hem and the sleeves with a 1″ ribbed hem. See how easy it is! Draw your Jewel Visual Pattern.

Line 7. Allow for a deep scoop and the 2″ border; refer to your measurements.
Line 10. Shape the scoop.
Line 20. Shape the border allowance.
Sleeves: Refer to Puffed Sleeves.
Length: Below the elbow.

The sweater which tops this dress is Chocolate Delight, Figure 223. This design is drawn on Midnight Delight with a 2″ lower neckline.

This makes a narrower shoulder-line but the neckline ribbing will complement the shoulder. I suggest doubling your yarn, thus emphasizing the combination of dress and sweater. The full puffed sleeves are about 2″ above the wrist-bones. Repeat the ribbed hems at the neckline, waist, and wrists. The ribbing from the dress fills the neckline of the sweater; this is a super look! Hot Chocolate also has a terrific coat, detailed under Tiger Eye.

AZTEC JEWEL

Whether cutting-up or adding, Midnight Jewel and Midnight Delight are your basic patterns for you have proven that their original shape is faultless and workable; they are the strength of our collection. It is one thing to design, it is another to create workable designs.

Aztec Jewel becomes many designs as you are now going to make the base for bridal or party dresses, shirts, tunics, loungewear, and easy fitting coats. This is accomplished by cutting your Jewel at line 5. The upper por-

169

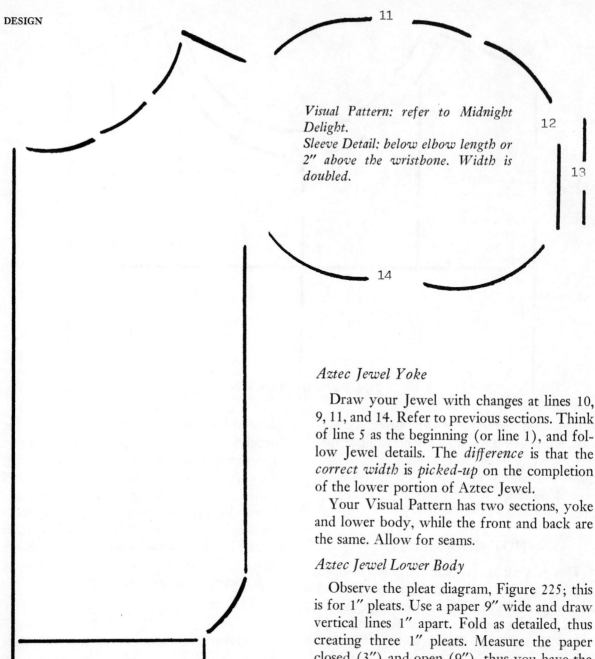

Figure 223. Chocolate Delight.

Visual Pattern: refer to Midnight Delight.
Sleeve Detail: below elbow length or 2″ above the wristbone. Width is doubled.

Aztec Jewel Yoke

Draw your Jewel with changes at lines 10, 9, 11, and 14. Refer to previous sections. Think of line 5 as the beginning (or line 1), and follow Jewel details. The *difference* is that the *correct width* is *picked-up* on the completion of the lower portion of Aztec Jewel.

Your Visual Pattern has two sections, yoke and lower body, while the front and back are the same. Allow for seams.

Aztec Jewel Lower Body

Observe the pleat diagram, Figure 225; this is for 1″ pleats. Use a paper 9″ wide and draw vertical lines 1″ apart. Fold as detailed, thus creating three 1″ pleats. Measure the paper closed (3″) and open (9″), thus you have the need for an additional 6″. (Pleat Rule: 3 X Width). Aztec Jewel is planned with three pleats at each side (see Figure 224), and you will therefore draw your pattern with an additional 12″ in width.

Line 5. Unpressed pleats are set-in (after binding off) before picking-up yoke stitches. Measure and form pleats, pin, and baste carefully. Sew firmly along binding off.

tion of your pattern is your yoke; in subsequent designs or patterns this yoke line will be differently placed. Observe Figure 224 and notice the square neckline, narrower shoulders and puffed sleeves.

170

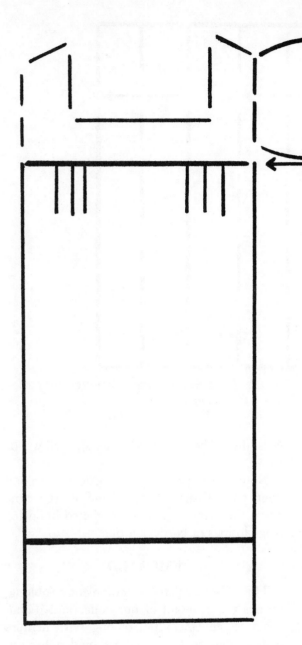

Figure 224. Aztec Jewel.

Cut

Line 10. Draw a scooped neckline, retaining the narrow shoulders.

Line 6. Allow for deeper armhole, the depth of the yoke.

Lines 11 and 14. Kimona sleeves with very little shaping.

Details: Refer to Aztec Jewel

Line 5 and 14. Cast on or chain a minimum of 3″ at a time.

Line 5. Decrease line (12″ to be reduced). Distribute decreases evenly to equal Yoke Pattern, line 5.

Line 10. Bind off for neckline shaping.

Lines 9 and 11. Sleeves bound off in a straight line; shoulders may be barely slanted.

Finishing Details: Refer to Aztec Jewel

This design may be worn with a cord under the bust and wound again around the upper waist.

TOPAZ

A striking variation of Gracefully Yours; the change is in the provocative curve and slits. (See Figure 227.) The depth of the curve can be as long as you wish. The slits can be extended to the underarm; think how fascinating this would look over a body stocking or pants.

Line 1. Start of curve; width equal to Jewel. Increasing at the beginning and end of one row or every other row is determined by desired depth of curve. Increase until

Line 2. Width should equal Gracefully Yours.

GRACEFULLY YOURS

This is superbly different, yet it is based on Aztec Jewel; the change in neckline and sleeves is optional. The variation is mainly at line 5. Instead of unpressed pleats, there is one row of decreasing for a gathered bodice. The armhole is deeper, in line with the yoke, and kimona sleeves are suggested. (See Figure 226.)

171

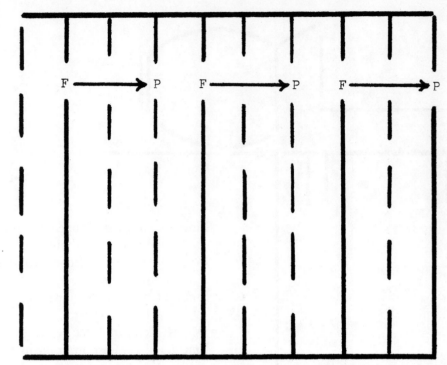

Figure 225. Aztec Jewel—1″ Pleats.

9″

F = Fold over, creating rolled edge and 1″ pleat.
P = Placement line.

Lines 4. Mark for depth of slits; refer to Slits. Other details: refer to Gracefully Yours. Front and back are the same.

Hem Finishing: Keep it simple. Single or Reverse Single Crochet.

Curve will be shaped in when pressing.

Gracefully Yours and Topaz become the Super Shirt! Simply by opening the front (where you wish) and shortening your design.

VIVACIOUS

Your Visual Pattern is Gracefully Yours! Think of the fun that you have been having, how moving a line can create an entirely new design! (Figure 228.)

Line 5. Drop this about 2″ to 3″ lower for gathering row. (Becomes line 5A.)

Line 5. Draw your underarm line for the desired armhole depth. This is determined by the sleeve style. If sleeveless; plan on a small armhole or be daring and have it slit to line 5A.

Note: Line 5A will be used to designate waistline, whether *at* the waist, below, or above.

Note: Coat patterns are made by making your two Visual Patterns and cutting one down the center. Plan on crocheted braid for frog closings or cords that tie.

EMERALD

This Visual Pattern, completely oblong, creates the Emerald of our collection! Think about it: an emerald is oblong with definite lines carved to bring out its hidden beauty. Emerald is shaped completely oblong with lines of pleats from neckline to hem. (Figure 229.) Select a fine yarn and knit Emerald on a small size, 29″ round needle, #2 recommended.

Measurements Needed:

Width: Line 6 to line 6 across the shoulders and neck; measure loosely. Refer to Bateau Neckline. (Your pattern, pleated, resembles Jewel Shell, Bateau.)

Length: Your preference.

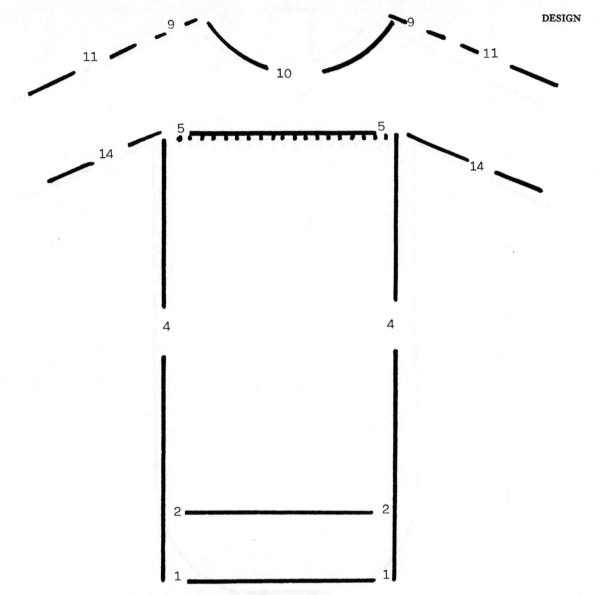

Figure 226. Gracefully Yours.

Pleats: 1″ wide. Refer to Aztec Jewel Pleat Plan and your body gauge.

Pattern: Sl 1 st every other row (pleat edge), K ⅞″ to inner fold, P2 or 3 sts (inner fold line), K2″ for pleat and underlay. Transpose this to stitches; refer to Chapter Nine.

Emerald Width: Double the width measurement, multiply by 3, and add 2″ ease.

Emerald Visual Pattern Width: One-half the above total; your pattern is a flat view, one-half. Draw Jewel Shell Bateau.

Line 1. Cast on Emerald, doubled, x body gauge on body gauge round needle. Mark the end of the round. (Dreamers, mark the slipped stitches.) Work to . . .

Line 5. Jewel Shell allows for a small armhole; try on. For other details, refer to Jewel Shell Bateau.

Emerald Finishing Details:

Hem turned under, about ½″; sew carefully.

Pleats edgestitched at slipped stitch line, refer to Chapter Five. Edgestitch through hem.

Set 1″ pleats in, across the top, basting care-

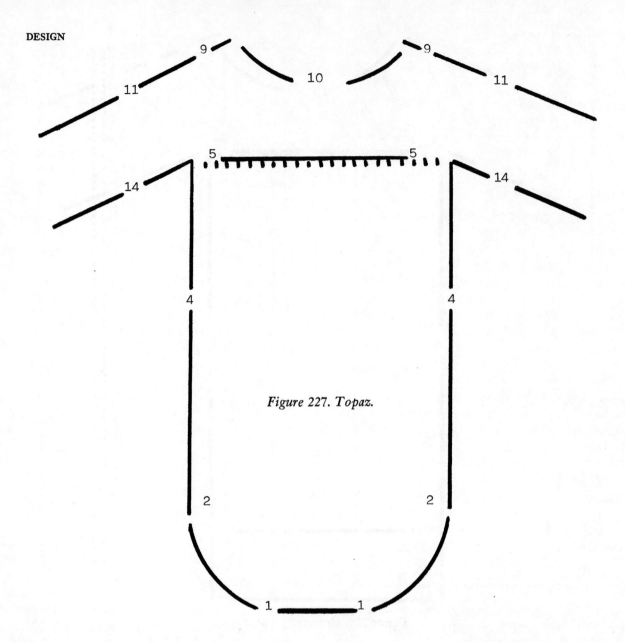

Figure 227. Topaz.

fully along the bound off edge. Sew permanently.

Narrow shoulders pinned together and basted; try on. Sew.

Neckline turned under about ¼″ and sewn.

Armhole edges turned under to match neckline. Sew.

Emerald Cardigan or Coat

Polish your jewel off with a striking match! Draw another Emerald Visual Pattern, the desired length, and open it down the center.

Line 1. Cast your stitches on a round needle; refer to Emerald.

Do not join. Adjust your stitch pattern.

All other details are the same.

Sleeves: Create the same stitch pattern effect by:

Knitting the width of the pleat, slipping a stitch, and repeating this across the row. Purl the reverse side. Edgestitching the slipped stitch line is optional.

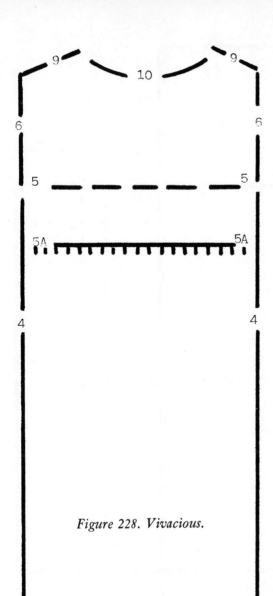

Figure 228. Vivacious.

Figure 229. Emerald.

Suggested: Pick-up the stitches for straight, narrow sleeves with matching hems.

Note: Visual Pattern is made the full width by taping the fronts to the sides of the back.

Emerald—Cabachon

A skirt that you will cherish!

Measurements Needed: Waist or Hips (if you plan to stitch pleats down to the hips).

Width: Measurement x 3, add 1½″ for width taken up by pleat thickness.

Length: Your preference.

Pleats: Refer to Emerald. If you desire wider pleats (2″), double the formula; refer to Chapter Nine. Always plan pleats on paper using the body gauge.

Details: Refer to Emerald.

Optional: Opening for zipper or just hooking at the waist. I suggest 2 short openings; plan the length and adjust the stitch pattern.

Finishing Details: Refer to Emerald

Hem: Refer to Emerald

Waistline: Refer to Chapter Five.

Note: Remember to mark the end of a round, the slipped stitches, and to work one round evenly between the slipped stitch round.

Think of the joy that you have been experi-

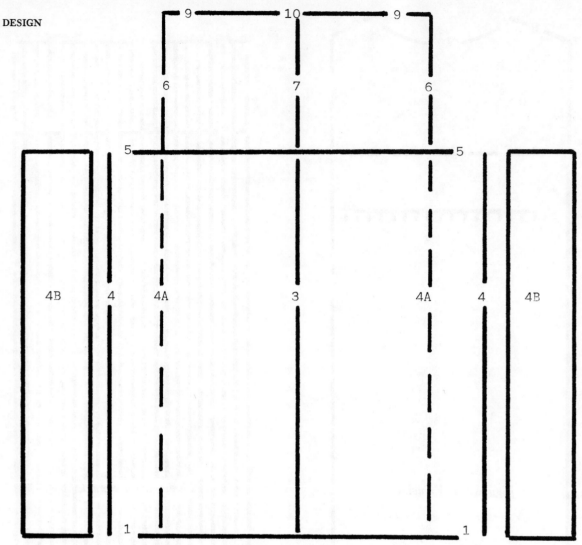

Figure 230. Swirl—1.

encing while learning to change designs to enhance your figure and fulfill your needs for
your lifestyle. You have learned that the same
design will look different when you change the
color, the yarn, or the stitch pattern. You have
also learned that knitted and crocheted clothes
have characteristics all their own. There is
absolutely no need to imitate fabric detailing
or to fuss over zippers, seams, buttons, or buttonholes unless you so desire.

SWIRL

It is at this point that I wish to detail a
dynamic fun coat or dress; its ease and comfort cannot be eclipsed! This beautiful, timeless
classic drops over your head and swirls about
you in any length you select. It has a wide
bateau neckline, extremely dropped shoulders
with wide elbow-length sleeves, and deep set-
in pleats at each side. Knitting or crocheting
with a single strand of yarn gives you the dress
and doubling your yarn gives you a terrific
coat!

Before drawing your Visual Pattern you
should understand this very simple design. The
basic shape is oblong; think of your Jewel
Shell, Bateau. Visualize this with extra ease and
pleat allowance. The underlays are worked
separately. Observe Swirl 1 (Figure 230) and

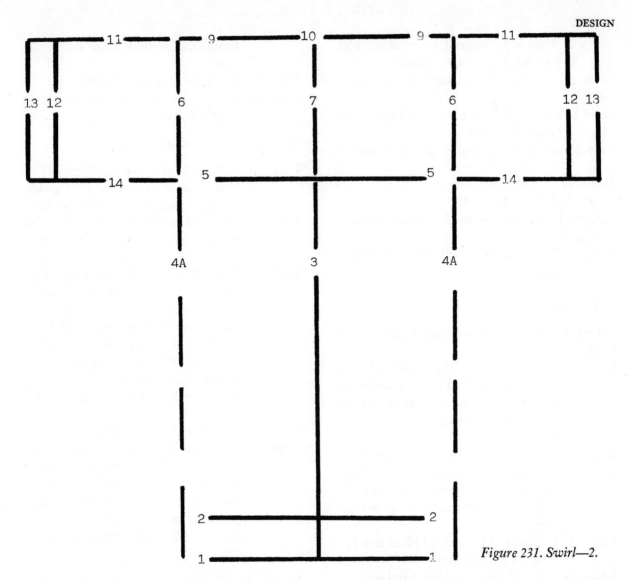

Figure 231. Swirl—2.

notice the added width from lines 4A to 4; this is the pleat fold-over (3″, with seam allowance 3½″). Line 4A is the foldline (pleat edge). The underlay, 4B, is the widths of the fold-overs (7″) with seam allowance. This underlay is made the length from line 1 to line 5 (hem to underarm).

Observe Swirl 2 (Figure 231) and notice the basic shape and how it is exaggerated. Your Visual Pattern is drawn on paper wide enough to add additional ease, pleats, seam allowance, and elbow-length sleeves to each side. The measurements you use may be added to your Jewel Shell, Bateau. The Visual Pattern is the same for front and back; therefore your pattern consists of the body and the underlay (4B).

Measurements Needed:

Line 3. Length with hem allowance (2½″) to underarm (line 5).

Line 7. Length from underarm to center back-neck. Front and back are the same.

Line 6. This matches line 7. Armhole depth is a minimum of 2″ deeper than Jewel. Remember, the deeper armhole affects the length from line 1 to line 5.

Line 1. Add ease to Jewel width (4″ to 8″) plus pleats and seam allowance (7″).

177

Ease is determined by whether you are making a dress or coat.

Lines 11 and 14. Elbow length plus optional hem allowance (2″).

Lines 12 and 13. The same width as line 6, plus seam allowance.

Line 12. Length to hem edge or start of border.

Line 13. Complete length.

Swirl Underlay—Insert 4B

Length: From line 1 to line 5, plus seam allowance at the *top*.

Width: 7″; this equals the fold-overs and seam allowance.

Swirl Visual Pattern

Prepare your paper as detailed in Chapter Four.

Line 3. Draw a vertical line, centered, the complete length; mark for accurate placement of line 2 (hem or border depth), line 5 (length to underarm), and add line 7.

Line 1. Draw a horizontal line; refer to Measurements Needed, line 1. Mark for accurate placement of lines 4A (3½″ pleat fold-over). Refer to Figure 230.

Line 2. Optional. The same width as line 1.

Line 5. The same width as line 1.

Lines 4A. Vertical lines from line 1 to line 5.

Lines 4. Vertical lines from line 1 to line 5.

Line 6. Continuation of lines 4A, the depth of armhole. Refer to Measurements Needed.

Line 7. Continuation of line 3. Equals the depth of line 6.

Lines 9 and 10. Horizontal line from lines 6 to 6.

Sleeves

Line 11. Continue from line 9 to the desired length. Refer to Measurements Needed.

Line 12. The same width as line 6 plus seam

allowance at hem edge or border start.

Line 13. Complete length and width.

Line 14. Same as line 11; there is no shaping to this sleeve.

Swirl Details: Front and Back

Line 1. Cast on or chain to equal Swirl Pattern; refer to Jewel and your gauge. Use appropriate needles or hook.

Line 2. Depth of border or hem. Change to body stitch pattern and needles; work to . . .

Line 5. Bind off pleat fold-over (3½″ each side). Refer to line 4A. If you desire a square armhole or Kimona Sleeves, you must bind off pleat fold-over and then shape the desired armhole or sleeve; refer to the respective sections in this chapter.

Line 6. Work armhole depth; refer to Visual Pattern.

Line 7. The same depth as line 6.

Lines 9 and 10. Bind off straight across. Pin carefully, allowing for wide bateau and low dropped shoulders. Try on. Baste and sew shoulders. Turn neckline edge under 1″, gradually tapering towards the shoulders, baste and sew.

Sleeves: Picked-Up

Line 6. Refer to Midnight Jewel.

Line 14. There is no shaping to this sleeve.

Line 12. Start of border stitch pattern or hem; use appropriate needles.

Line 13. Bind off.

Swirl Underlays: Two matching pieces

Insert 4B. Work in matching stitch pattern. Contrasting yarn may be used. Refer to your Visual Pattern.

Swirl Sewing Details

Carefully pin and baste the underlays to the front and back. Try on and make certain that seams are straight and smooth. Sew the seams of the pleats and sleeves; attach them together neatly and securely at the underarm. All hems should be sewn before edgestitching. Edgestitching is done ½″ in from the pleat edge; refer .to Chapter Five. The pleats are closed from the underarm for 2″ with concealed stitches. Carefully sew the top of the pleat (wrong side) and tack to the underarm.

Note: If you wish, the front may be made in two pieces. Make your Visual Pattern twice and cut one pattern down the center.

Attach a matching scarf and casually tie your coat at the neckline.

LUSCIOUS

A three-piece set, soft and easy. (See Figure 232.) The skirt is based on Jewel. The undersweater is the top of Jewel. The over-sweater is an exaggerated top, again based on Jewel, with a bateau neckline and wide, elbow-length Kimona Sleeves.

Note: Use your Jewel Pattern. Remember that it is a flat view, one-half your body width.
Skirt Measurements Needed:

Line   3.   Desired length plus hem (optional) and casing allowance, approximately 5″. If you wish a border, plan for it on your Visual Pattern and omit the hem allowance.

Luscious Skirt Visual Pattern

Front Panel: Prepare your paper for a doubled width. Draw the Luscious pattern full width (meaning double Jewel) plus seam allowance. Length is as previously measured.

Back Panel: The width is one-third of the front panel, plus seam allowance. (For a fuller skirt, use one-half the width.) Length is the same as the front panel.

Luscious Skirt Without Seams: The Visual Pattern would be made one-half the width of the total of your front and back panel measurements.

Under-Sweater

Use the top of your Jewel pattern; refer to Dressy Sweaters. The neckline is Jewel with a narrow turtleneck. Draw three irregularly placed stripes under the bust (optional).
Over-Sweater Measurements Needed:

Line   3.   Desired length from hip-bone to the underarm (line 5), considering the sleeve style and hem allowance. Hem or border treatment should be the same as on skirt.

Line   7.   Measure from line 5 to center back neck. Front and back are the same.

Line   6.   Depth of armhole should correspond with line 7.

Lines   11 and 14. Measure for elbow-length sleeve.

Lines   12 and 13. Observe Figures 232. Width of line 6 plus seam allowance. (Remember that there are *two* seams.)

Line   1.   Jewel width plus 4″ to 6″ ease.

Luscious Over-Sweater Visual Pattern

The front and back the same. Refer to Figure 232. The Jewel is the base pattern.

Lines 3 and 7. Draw center line, marking for accurate placement of lines 2 and 5.

Line   1.   Draw horizontal line; referring to Measurements Needed.

Line   2.   The same as line 1, allowing for hem or border.

Line   5.   The same as line 1.

Lines   4.   Vertical lines from line 1 to line 5.

Line   6.   Continue lines 4, refer to Measurements Needed.

Lines 9 and 10. The same as line 1.

Lines   11 and 14. Refer to Measurements Needed.

Line   12. The same width as line 6, plus seam allowance.

Line   13. Complete length and width; refer to Measurements Needed.

Luscious Skirt Details

Front Panel:
Line 1 to line 5B. Refer to Jewel.

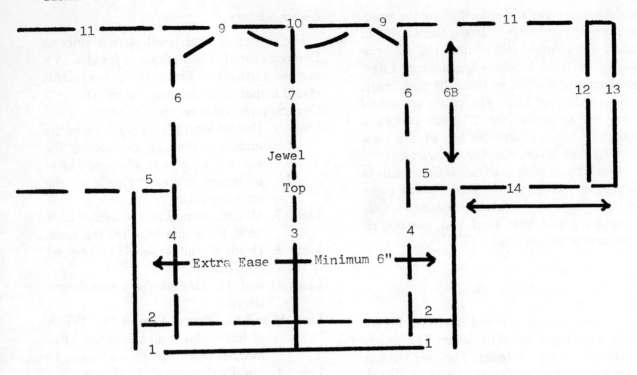

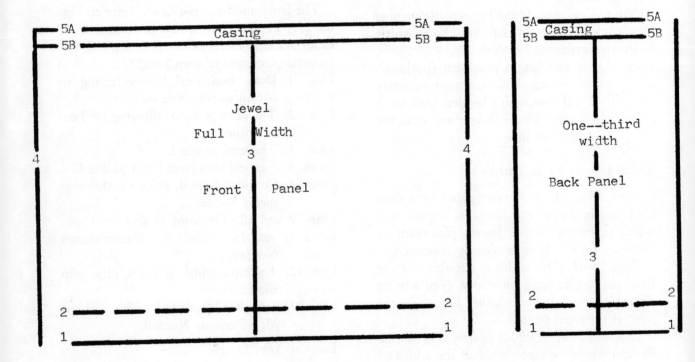

Figure 232. Luscious.

Swirl (page 176)

Line 5B. Change to smaller needles and work in ribbing pattern for 2″ casing.

Line 5A. Bind Off.

Back Panel: Refer to Front Visual Pattern and directions.

Luscious Skirt Finishing

Sew seams, hem, and casing, as detailed in Chapter Five. 1″ wide elastic or drawstring may be used.

Luscious Skirt on Round Needle

Line 1. Refer to Luscious Visual Pattern Without Seams. Cast on or chain to equal this width, doubled. Refer to Jewel and Luscious to . . .

Line 5B. Change to ribbing gauge size needle and rib for 2″.

Line 5A. Bind Off. Sew, as previously detailed.

Luscious Under-Sweater Details

Refer to Jewel Dressy Sweater and your Visual Pattern.

Line 10. Pick-up stitches for narrow turtleneck; rib for 6″.

Luscious Over-Sweater: Front and Back

Line 1. Cast on or chain to equal Luscious pattern. Work hem or border to . . .

Line 2. Change needle and pattern stitch. Work to . . .

Line 5. Start Kimona Sleeves (line 14). Cast on or chain 3″ minimum at a time, or all the stitches needed; refer to your Visual Pattern and the Sleeve Section.

Line 6. Depth of armhole. Sleeve must conform to Visual Pattern, measure carefully.

Line 14. Length cast on to equal length plus hem allowance.

Lines 12 and 13. This width is worked to conform to armhole depth, plus seam allowance, and Visual Pattern.

Lines 9, 10, and 11. Measure and compare before binding off in a straight line.

Luscious Over-Sweater Finishing Details

Sew seams and hem. Bateau neckline.

Note: Skirt and Over-Sweater should match in hem or border treatment.

Wear the Under-Sweater tucked inside the skirt; accent the gathers. The turtleneck and long sleeves look stunning peeking out from the Over-Sweater.

Open Front Over-Sweater with Chanel-type Opening

Make two matching patterns; cut one down the center. For buttons and buttonholes, add 1½″ to each side of the center front; refer to Jewel Coat-dress.

ROSY GLOW

Rosy Glow is everything its name promises! An entirely new look is achieved by Rosy Glow's A-line skirt combined with an under-sweater, with or without a narrow turtleneck (Dressy Jewel), and an over-sweater (Luscious). An A shaped skirt should have the most gradual shaping. The line should flow from the waist down, the eye should travel smoothly, without a jarring note. Look at Figure 233 and notice the gradual tapering and understand that length must be considered. The bottom width of your skirt is determined by the length and your hip measurement; observe Figure 233.

Measurements Needed:

Line 5A. Width of waist.

Line 5B. Width of hips.

Line 3. Full length, length from waist to hips (this may vary between 7″ and 9″), and length from hip to hem.

Rosy Glow Proportions: Lines 1 and 2

Knee Length: Hip measurement, ease 1″ or 2″, and 10″.

Mid-calf Length: Hip measurement, ease 1″ or 2″, and 12″.

Ankle-Length: Hip measurement, ease 1″ or 2″, and 15″.

Note: Slimmer A is made by adding ease plus only 10″ to hip measurement, regardless of length.

Rosy Glow Visual Pattern—No Seams

Prepare your paper as detailed under Midnight Jewel; your center and horizontal lines are most important!

Line 3. Draw a vertical line, centered, the desired length. Mark for depth of border or hem allowance and the correct placement of line 5B.

Line 1. Draw a horizontal line, one-half of your Rosy Glow measurement.

Line 2. Depth of border or hem allowance, the same width as line 1.

Line 5B. Draw a horizontal line one-half of Rosy Glow measurement.

Line 5A. Draw a horizontal line one-half of Rosy Glow measurement.

Lines 4. Draw side lines from line 1 to line 5B, then from line 5B to line 5A. Do not worry if the slant changes.

Note: This pattern is for a round needle; there is no seam allowance. Rosy Glow with seams will be detailed later.

Rosy Glow Shaping (Figure 234)

1. Measure for the additional length to be worked from line 2 to line 5B. Optional: Know the number of rows to 1″, since this may aid you in calculating the spacing of the decrease rows.

2. Measure for the difference in width; sub-

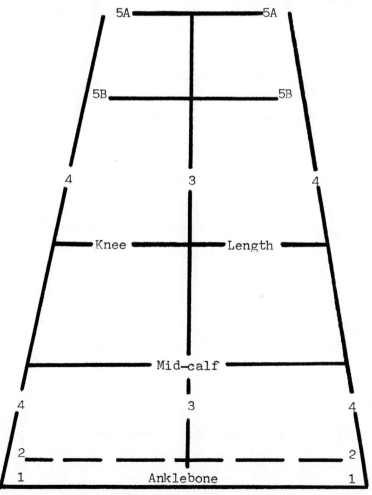

Figure 233. Rosy Glow. A-shape without seams, round needle.

tract the width at line 5B from the width at line 2. The result is the inches to be reduced.

3. Know your gauge. For instance, if your gauge were 8 stitches to 1″ and you had 10″ to reduce, the result would be 80 stitches to decrease. The decision on how many stitches to decrease in one row depends on the length to be worked.

4. For example, if you have an additional 10″ to work, your decrease rows (8 to a row) would be spaced 1″ apart. If you have an additional 20″ to work, your decrease rows would be spaced 2″ apart.

5. Decreases must be spaced evenly apart in the row. If there were 80 stitches on the needle and you wished to decrease 8 stitches, you would knit 9 and 10 together. Decreases would be 8 stitches apart; this number changes with each decrease row. This is important if you wish to leave symmetrical placing.

6. Additional calculating should be done for the decreasing from line 5B to line 5A. It may be necessary to increase the number of decreases in the decrease row; refer to your Visual Pattern and calculate carefully. Use the same formula.

IMPORTANT! Alternate slant of decrease rows is discussed in Chapter Eight. This keeps your skirt from twisting or hanging on the bias.

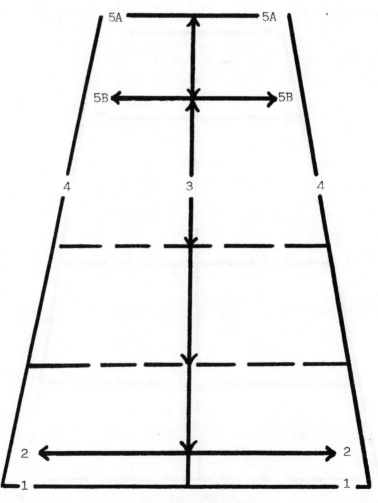

Figure 234. Rosy Glow shaping.

Rosy Glow Details for Knitting or Crocheting in the Round

Line   1. Cast on or chain Rosy Glow pattern (doubled) x body gauge on body gauge needle. Remember that your pattern is a flat view, one-half. Hem: Use needle one size smaller. Border: Use stitch pattern.

Line   2. Hem: Change to body gauge size needle. Border: Change to body stitch pattern. Refer to Rosy Glow Shaping, to . . .

Line 5B. Calculate shaping to . . .

Line 5A. Optional: 1″ Border repeat at the waist. Bind off.

Rosy Glow Skirt Finishing

1″ Wide elastic is installed at the waist, the hem is sewn.

Rosy Glow With Seams (Figures 235 and 236)

Refer to Rosy Glow, no seams, for measurements and add seam allowance.

Prepare your paper as previously detailed, observe the diagrams, and note the seam placement. The seams are not just a means of joining two pieces; they are a focal point and aid in creating a thinner illusion. The front panel is two-thirds of your total measurements, plus ease and seam allowance. The back panel is one-third of your measurement with ease and seam allowance.

Rosy Glow Visual Pattern: Front Panel

Line   3. Draw a vertical line, centered, the desired length. Mark for depth of border or hem allowance and the correct placement of line 5B.

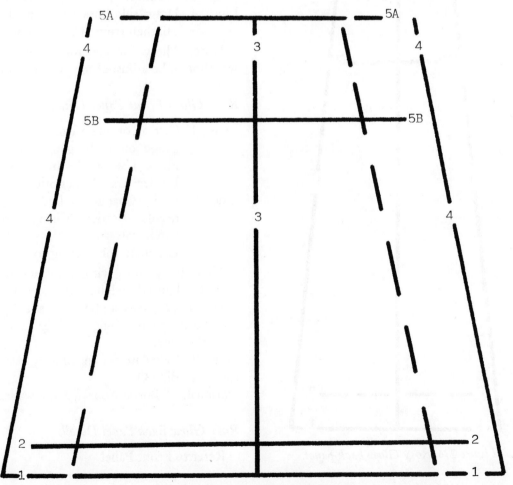

Figure 235. Rosy Glow front panel.

Line 1. Draw a horizontal line two-thirds the skirt hem width plus ease (1″ or 2″) and seam allowance; refer to Rosy Glow measurements.

Line 2. Depth of hem allowance or border; the same width as line 1.

Line 5B. Draw a horizontal line two-thirds of hip measurement plus ease and seam allowance.

Line 5A. Draw a horizontal line two-thirds of waist measurement plus ease and seam allowance.

Lines 4. Draw slanted lines from line 1 to line 5B, then from line 5B to line 5A. Do not worry if the slant changes. Remember that the front panel of Rosy Glow is two-thirds of your total

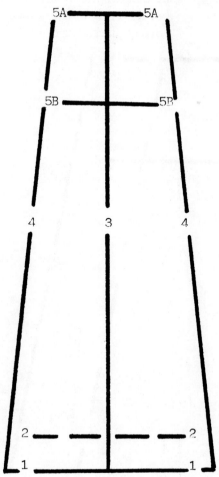

Figure 236. Rosy Glow back panel.

186

measurement because of the overlaps.

Rosy Glow: Back Panel Visual Pattern

One-third of the total width plus ease 1″ and seam allowance.

Line 3. Draw a vertical line, centered, to match the front panel.

Line 1. Draw a horizontal line one-third the skirt hem width. (One-half of Rosy Glow front panel.)

Line 2. Match the depth drawn on the front panel. Match the width of line 1.

Line 5B. Draw a horizontal line one-third of hip measurement plus ease and seam allowance.

Line 5A. Draw a horizontal line one-third the waist width plus ease and seam allowance.

Lines 4. Draw side lines from line 1 to line 5B, then from line 5B to line 5A.

Note: Allow for generous seams. Ease at waistline to be adjusted for your comfort.

Rosy Glow Front Panel Details

Line 1. Cast on or chain Rosy Glow x body gauge on body gauge size needle. Hem: Use needles one size smaller. Border: Use Border Stitch Pattern.

Line 2. Hem: Change to body gauge size needle. Border: Change to body stitch pattern.
Calculate for shaping to . . .

Note: Rosy Glow with Seams, whether crocheted or knitted, will have the decreases at the sides. Bulky yarns and thick stitch patterns may be decreased along the edge and ½″ in from the edge.

Line 5B. Calculate for shaping to . . .

Line 5A. Bind Off.

Optional: 1″ Border repeat at the waist.

Rosy Glow Back Panel Details

Refer to Front Panel

Luscious (page 179)

Rosy Glow Skirt Finishing

Short zippers at seams are optional. Elastic is inserted.

RUBY

A precious look in any length: a dress that skims over the body, with a brief over-sweater. The dress is an extension of Rosy Glow Skirt (without seams) into the Jewel. The neckline is a high V and the sleeves may be long and narrow. This is optional, for the very same shape would look lovely sleeveless. The over-sweater is an abbreviated Luscious with a lower V neckline, thus repeating the neckline ribbing and showing the ribbing at the midriff of the dress. The Ruby Visual Pattern is made by combining a Rosy Glow seamless skirt with a Jewel top. The Ruby over-sweater is made by drawing Luscious shorter, narrower, and with a V neckline. (See Figures 237 and 238.)

Measurements Needed:

Refer to Rosy Glow, Jewel and Luscious. Ruby Dress: Refer to Jewel, Rosy Glow and Minx.

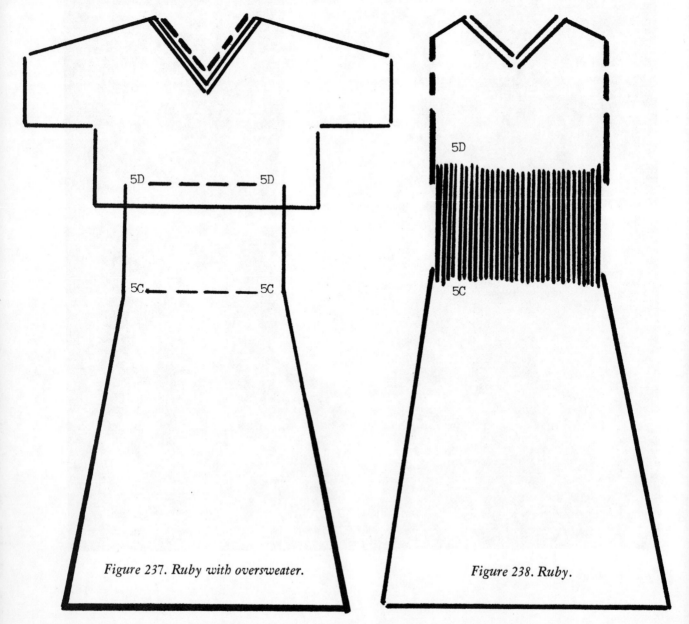

Figure 237. Ruby with oversweater.

Figure 238. Ruby.

Line 5C. Length from hem to start of ribbed midriff.

Line 5D. Length from line 5C (depth of ribbing).

Line 7. Depth of V neckline.

BRISK AUTUMN

I never cease to be amazed at the innumerable changes possible to a basic pattern and the variations in wearing a design. Brisk Autumn is Rosy Glow Skirt, interchangeable with a tunic (a long Luscious) or a hooded coat (Jewel Coat-dress). Visualize this outfit double crocheted in a thick mohair or tweed yarn. The skirt can be worn with a pretty shirt or a knitted Jewel top. Make a matching scarf and hat, tie a perky bow, and treat yourself to more than one top. The Luscious Tunic can be as loose and low on the hips as you desire.

Brisk Autumn Coat with Hood

This coat is a Jewel Coat-dress without buttons. The hood is a continuation of the neckline. It is made luxuriously deep. This makes it fun if you wish to wear Brisk Autumn skirt with a hooded sweater. The finishing is 1" turned *over*, not under, all around; this is a nice surprise. Your Visual Pattern is based on Jewel Coat-dress with additional ease, deeper armholes, and a change in neckline shaping. Your Visual Pattern is most important!

Brisk Autumn: Back

Line 1. Refer to Jewel Coat-dress and add 4" ease to the existing pattern. (Remember that your Jewel Coat-dress pattern also has ease, but do *not* deduct this.)
Other details the same to . . .

Line 5. Draw the underarm line a minimum of 2" lower.

Line 6. Armhole is 2" deeper to conform with lowered underarm on line 5.

Lines 8 and 9. Refer to Jewel Coat-dress.

Line 10. Draw line straight across to lines 8.

Brisk Autumn Coat: Fronts

Line 1. Divide Brisk Autumn Back width in half and add 2". Fronts should be liberal; match fronts to back, to . . .

Line 10. There is no neckline shaping; draw a straight line, 8 to 8.

Lines 11 to 14. Refer to Jewel Coat-dress. Recommended: Draw straight sleeves. The width is determined by the depth of the armhole, line 6. Allow for a 1" cuff.

Brisk Autumn Coat Details: Back

Refer to Jewel Coat-dress
Line 10. Place stitches on a long strand of yarn (reserving stitches for hood) or you may bind off and pick-up stitches later. Note: if crocheting; fasten off.

Brisk Autumn Coat Details: Front

Refer to Jewel Coat-dress
Line 10. Refer to Back. Note: Stitches must be bound off if crocheting.

Brisk Autumn Finishing Details

Shoulders are sewn together before making sleeves or hood. Hoods are detailed in the next Chapter.

Note: Do not sew seams to the very hem or edge; allow for turning *over* 1". Sew the needed amount on the right side. Include the hood when turning 1" over.

CAPE COD MINX

There is nothing that equals the feeling of a full skirt and elegant matching sweater. Once you make and wear this set you will want it in all textures and colors! This set is seasonless and timeless. The over-sweater is long and full and will become the most important garment in your wardrobe, eliminating the need for the coat that is "just right." The under-sweater is based on Dressy Jewel and the over-sweater is a long Midnight Delight. The Minx skirt is prophetic and will look new for years to come. (See Figures 239 and 240.)

Measurements Needed:

Line   3. Length from hem to waist, length from hem to lower hip (line 5B), and length from lower hip to waist (line 5A).

Line 5A. Measure waist, holding tapemeasure loosely.

Line 5B. Measure hips, holding the tapemeasure *tightly*.

Cape Cod Minx Skirt Visual Pattern

  Prepare your paper.

Line   3. Draw a vertical line, centered, the desired length. Mark for the depth of border or additional hem allowance and the correct placement of line 5B.

Line   1. Draw a horizontal line the full hip measurement (5B).

Line   2. Depth of border or hem allowance, the same as line 1.

Line 5B. Draw a horizontal line the same width as line 1.

Line 5A. Draw a horizontal line one-half the waist measurement (5A).

Lines 4. Draw side lines from line 1 to line 5B. The next set of side lines are the width apart of line 5A. See Figure 239.

Lines 5C and 5D. Spaced evenly apart in hip yoke. The width of line 5A. See Figure 239.

Minx Skirt Details: Round Needle

Line   1. Cast on or chain the doubled width of Cape Code Minx Pattern X body

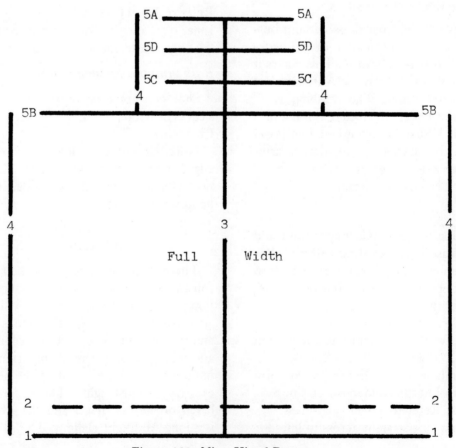

Figure 239. Minx Visual Pattern.

gauge on body gauge size needle. Hem: Work on needle one size smaller than body gauge. Border: Work in border stitch pattern. I recommend repeat of yoke ribbing on needle one size larger.

Line 2. Hem: Change to body gauge size needle. Border: Change to body gauge size needle and stitch pattern. Work to . . .

Line 5B. Skirt is reduced to one-half its width by working every 2 stitches together, Figure 240. Next Round: Pattern Ribbing *K2—P2*.

Line 5C. Continue ribbing on round needle one size smaller.

Line 5D. Continue ribbing on needle two sizes smaller than body gauge.

Line 5A. Bind Off.

Skirt Finishing

Install elastic, 1″ wide.

Note: Minx Visual Pattern would need yoke adjustment for crocheting. Skirt could be made with seams and pattern would be the same for front and back.

Line 5B. Reduce to one-half the width and use Yoke Stitch Pattern. The yoke

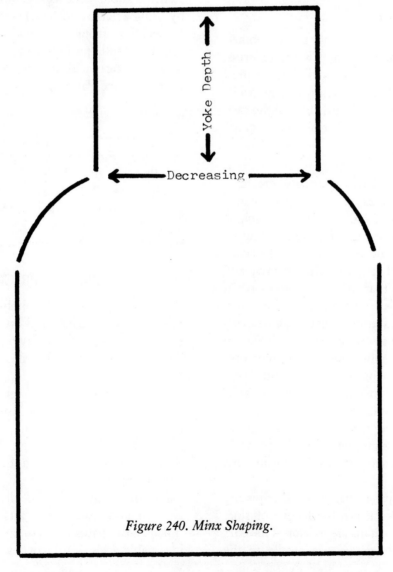

Figure 240. Minx Shaping.

would be decreased on lines 5C and 5D, plus changing hooks (refer to lines 5C and 5D) to reach one-half waist width. Remember — when working yoke allow for seams.

TIGER EYE

The Reverse Stockinette Stitch and a slipped stitch ribbing make this delightful variation of Minx. A matching ribbed Dressy Jewel, a Reverse Stockinette Stitch Delight with a low, scooped neckline plus the bonus of Chocolate Delight prove the beauty of inter-related garments.

Hot Chocolate Coat

This coat is used in many ways, combined with Tiger Eye or the Hot Chocolate dress. It is the Jewel Coat-dress with long puffed sleeves and ribbed borders all around the neckline, front borders, and hems. Its straight easy look depends on loose measuring over a dress.

ONYX

Candlelight and bare shoulders create a glamourous aura and cast a unique spell, changing one's personality, and adding that touch of mystery that sparks an evening. Onyx, knit of delicate yarn, will be the seductive classic of your wardrobe. Make a matching shawl and it will be a gown that you will always reach for. This design is based on the Minx skirt. The ribbed yoke, extended, becomes a strapless top. The full skirt is mid-calf or 2″ above the anklebone. The combination of the measurement over the bust (line 5), ribbing, and elastic will hold the dress in place. Added insurance can be obtained by combining the yarn with matching elasticized thread. For the woman who loves this design but hesitates to wear strapless dresses, I suggest matching thin cord straps.

Make your Onyx Visual Pattern, adjusting your Minx Visual Pattern for length of skirt and bodice. Other details are similar. The skirt is worked on body gauge size needle to the

ribbing, and the ribbing is as previously detailed to the under-bust. Change to body gauge needle (or a size smaller) for the bust, minus the upper 2″. The upper 2″ may be combined with matching elastic thread and worked on a needle two sizes smaller.

SAPPHIRE

Every woman has the urge to collect jewels and every woman has her favorite. No collection is complete without Sapphire; a dress to dance in (Figure 241). Visualize Minx with its ribbed yoke low over the hips, and then swirling about your legs. Continue at the waist by using a narrowed Jewel pattern with a deep V neckline, front and back. An added touch could be full, puffed sleeves. Combine your Visual Pattern with a thin blue yarn and My Favorite Lace Pattern.

Sapphire Variation

If you prefer a two-piece lace dress consider modifying the skirt. Use your Minx skirt Visual Pattern, and change the yoke depth by placing line 5B 2″ below the waist. This creates an entirely new design. Do not hesitate to change a line! Use Jewel, loose and straight to the ribbing, for your classic top.

SPICED APRICOT

Spiced Apricot is definitely a conversation piece, for its sparkles and attracts! It consists of knickers topped with two superb sweaters. The under-sweater is based on Jewel, a short-blousy top with straight, long blousy sleeves. The over-sweater is based on Delight, a long-long, 3″ shorter than the knickers. Knit the ribbing at the bottom on needles one size smaller than the body gauge. This will make a slight blousiness and add to the fun!

Pants in any shape and any length have become an integral part of all our wardrobes. Knitted and crocheted pants are classic and timeless; the pants that you make should be an invaluable asset. My favorites are knickers and

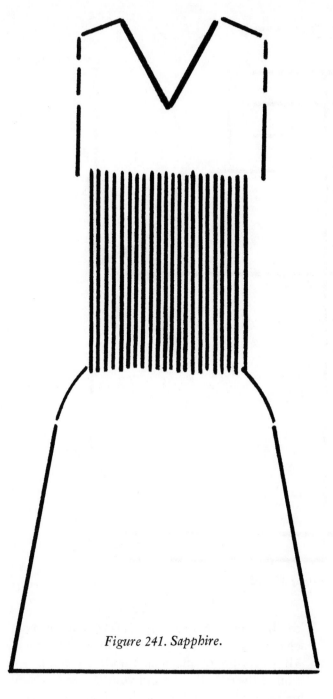

Figure 241. Sapphire.

serve how they fit at the waist, through the hips and crotch, especially when sitting, and around the upper thighs. If you are satisfied with all these details I would suggest that you use the pants as your guide when making your Visual Pattern. Measure them carefully, allowing for wide seams and a deeper crotch. If they are worn, take them apart, ignore all darts and draw the shape a hair larger. Think about the design, for many details that are used with fabric are not necessary when knitting or crocheting. Do not imitate, be innovative, use your ingenuity and the dexterity of your fingers. Care should be given to the Visual Pattern and time should be spent on a muslin pattern.

Assuming that you have no guide for your Visual Pattern, the first step is your measurements.

Measurements Needed:

Observe Figure 242.

Line 3. Lengths are measured down your *side*. Length from waist to cuff or border, from waist to full hip (line 5B), and from waist to crotch (line 5).

Line 5A. Measure your waist where you wish your pants to settle, either at the waist or within 2″ below.

Line 5B. Measure fullest hip, usually 7″ to 9″ below the waist.

Line 5. Note: As the underarm line is of the utmost importance (line 5) I have designated the crotch depth with the same number. Take this measurement sitting down in a hard chair. Measure down your side (holding the tapemeasure firmly) from your waist to the seat of the chair, and add a minimum of 1″ ease.

Lines 1 and 2. Circumference of leg at desired length.

Line 5E. Circumference of the upper thigh; measure loosely. Ease at this point varies according to style.

I have simplified my design and approach;

harem pants. Understanding your figure, its good and bad points, plus understanding what makes good fitting pants, will enable you to knit or crochet the pants that you desire.

Ease is most important. The most perfect figure can be ruined by wearing pants that are too tight. Put on your favorite pants and ob-

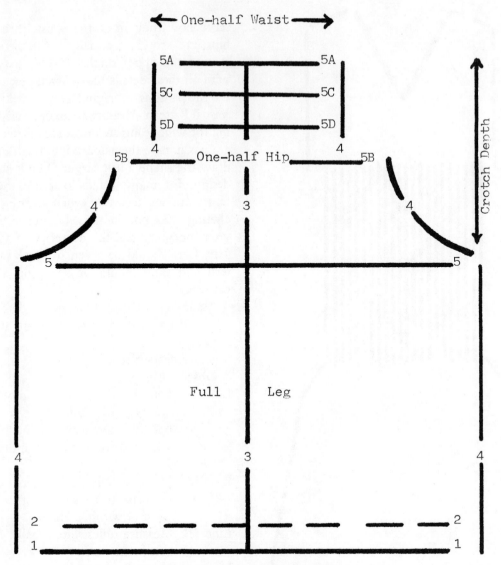

Figure 242. Spiced Apricot Visual Pattern.

think about it and modify it for your needs. Observe Figure 242. The pattern consists of two pieces, each side and leg, as there is a seam down the center front and back. Therefore, line 3 is the exact center of the pattern, but is your *side* line. There are no side seams. The center line of the front and back is continued down the inside of the leg. There are no zippers and the front and back are the same, thus the wearing may be reversed. This helps the pants to stay in shape. Observe Figure 242 again: there are lines across the hips from 5A

to 5B. These lines (5C and 5D) denote needle changes and help to create a flexible yoke. Line 5B is very important since it notes the completion of the ribbed yoke and your full hip measurement plus ease. Ease at this point may vary depending on the style. Line 5B is where increasing should be done for full knickers or harem pants. The added fullness could be equal to one-third your measurement.

Next, notice the curve. It is simply the shape of a reversed armhole, made by increasing and casting on. You have control of the width of the leg by increasing at line 5B and at the seam edge. Leg shaping, whether increasing or decreasing, should be placed at the seam edge.

Spiced Apricot Knickers Visual Pattern

This is most important. It will be your base for the pants you desire—*make your muslin pattern.* An accurate length for your knickers may be obtained by wearing pants, tucking the legs into woolen socks, and judging the degree of blousiness needed. Mark with a pin or two and then measure the pant leg on a flat surface. Prepare your paper. This pattern is not drawn with the actual, finished width of lines 1 and 2.

Line   3. Draw a vertical line, centered, the desired length. Mark for accurate placement of lines 5B, 5, and 2.

Line 5A. Draw a horizontal line one-half the waist measurement plus ease and seam allowance.

Line 5B. Draw a horizontal line one-half the hip measurement plus ease and seam allowance.

Line 5C. Draw a horizontal line 2″ below line 5A (waist) the same width as line 5A.

Line 5D. Draw a horizontal line 2″ below line 5C, the same width as line 5C.

Line   5. Draw a horizontal line one-half the hip measurement plus ease according to desired fullness (consider circumference of upper thigh) and seam allowance. Minimum suggested ease is 5″. (Optional, refer to your measurements.)

Line   2. Draw a horizontal line, at start of border the same width as line 5.

Line   1. Refer to line 2.

Lines 4. Vertical lines from line 1 to 5. Shaped lines from line 5 to 5B and then from 5B to 5A.

Spiced Apricot Knickers Details

Knickers start at the waist and should be measured *on* as much as possible.

Line 5A. Cast on or chain stitches to equal Spiced Apricot by multiplying measurement x ribbing gauge. Suggestion: use needles 2 sizes smaller than body gauge Pattern *K2—P2*.

Line 5C. Continue pattern on needles one size larger.

Line 5D. Continue pattern on needles one size larger (body gauge size).

Line 5B. Distribute increases evenly in one row to have needed width plus ease and seam allowance. Change to body stitch pattern. Calculate for start of increasing for crotch.
(This may vary from 1″ on from this point.) Increase and shape crotch; compare with Visual Pattern. Shaping and casting on is determined by the additional width needed at line 5.

Line   5. Work the desired length. If extra width is needed through the upper thighs, increase at the seam edges. Allow for blousing in the worked length. Length should be below the knees or to the desired point.

Line   2. Knicker length. (If you desire to use this pattern for harem length, the detailing follows.) Decrease, spacing decreases evenly, in one row to desired width. Start ribbing for border, change to Ribbing Gauge size needles.

Line   1. Bind Off. MAKE MATCHING SIDE.

Knickers Finishing

Sew Seams. Install 1″ wide elastic.

Harem Details

Ankle length, allow for blousing.

Line 5B. The crucial point. Increase to luxurious fullness, in either every second or third stitch; refer to body gauge. Other details as under Knickers.

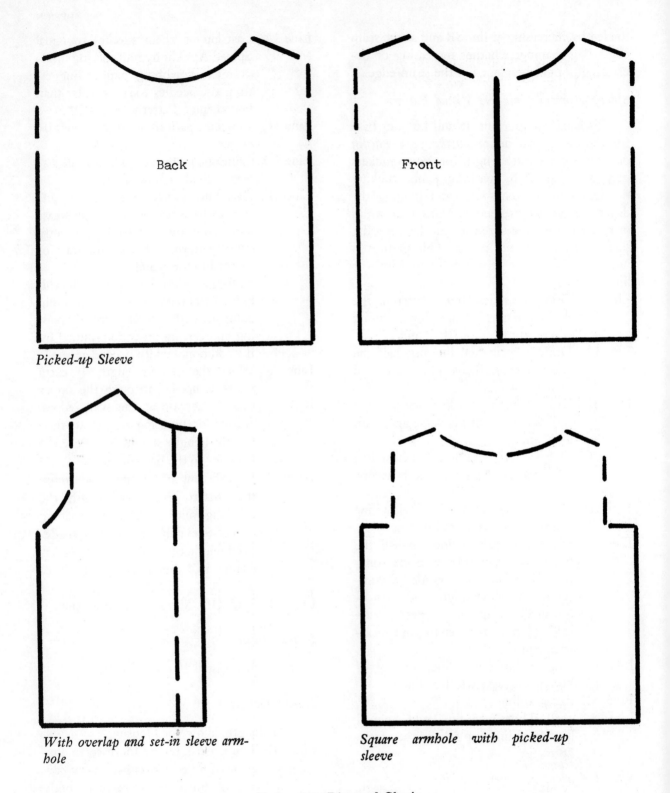

Back

Front

Picked-up Sleeve

With overlap and set-in sleeve arm-hole

Square armhole with picked-up sleeve

Figure 243. Diamond Classic.

Pants Details

Leg Ease of 3″ minimum, optional.

If you wish, use the above ribbing details to line 5B. This ribbing may be worked shorter and the body stitch pattern may start at line 5C. Calculate at this point for the needed increases. Other details are the same; the length and width of the leg is optional. A zipper may be placed in the center seam.

DIAMOND CLASSIC

As Diamonds are a girl's best friend so is the Diamond Classic. Crocheted, knitted, or both combined, this is the suit at its best. The jacket is a basic unbuttoned cardigan, simple and trim to the upper hips. The skirt may be pleated, A-shaped, or wrap-around, and is coordinated with a Jewel Shell, sweater, or blouse.

Whether you choose to button the jacket or wear it open is not important. What is important is that this classic will give you inspiration. This jacket is usually made without buttons, and just meets at the center front. Think of the many borders and edgings that may be used. Secure it with your favorite pin, tie it with contrasting cord, or wear it open. Your Jewel or V neckline enables you to accessorize it as you wish.

Diamond Classic Jacket

Your Visual Pattern is based on the top of Jewel Coat-dress. Decide on the style of the sleeve, armhole, and neckline before making your Visual Pattern.

Measurements Needed: (See Figure 243)
Line 3. Length from underarm to the upper hips.
Line 6. Depth of armhole.
Line 7. Depth of front and back neckline from line 5 (underarm).
Lines 11 and 14. Length of sleeve.

Diamond Classic Jacket Visual Pattern

Prepare your paper and draw your pattern. Refer to Jewel Coat-dress. Make the back and front, dividing the front in half. If you desire more ease in the front, draw it accordingly and then cut it down the center. For a buttoned jacket, refer to Jewel Coat-dress. Shape the armhole for the selected sleeve; refer to armholes and sleeves. Draw the sleeves with sufficient ease and seam allowance. (If you wish the borders of the under-sweater to peek out; measure and draw the sleeves that much shorter.)

Diamond Classic Under-sweater

This is Dressy Jewel with or without sleeves; the neckline is your choice. You may decide to make Jewel with a matching tie or scarf or with a turtleneck. I suggest making more than one sweater for this outfit.

Diamond Classic Skirt (See Figure 244)

The style of your skirt is your personal preference; consider your figure and the look you desire. The following skirt is a timeless classic in any length. I visualize it below your knees and edged to match the jacket. The secrets to a good wrap-around skirt are the overlap, underlap, and ease. If you observe Figure 244 you will see a full-fashioned seam (symmetrical placement of decreases) on each side and a row of decreases at the waist. This row of decreases insures that your skirt will hang properly, it allows for sufficient ease through the seat, hips, and overlap.

Measurements Needed:
Line 3. Length of skirt.
Line 5B. Full hip measurement and depth from line 5B to 5A.
Line 5A. Waist measurement plus 1″ ease. Work with this total when calculating.
Note: A well-balanced skirt averages 10″ wider at the hips than the waist and 10″ wider at the hem than at the hips.

Diamond Classic Wrap-around Skirt

This pattern is going to require a wide piece of paper, therefore, you will be taping pieces (measure for adequate length) together before drawing. The width should be full hip measurement, plus 4″ ease, *doubled*. This will give you sufficient width for accurate drawing of your Visual Pattern. Prepare your center line as detailed in Chapter Four. See Figure 245, steps one and two. You must have the exact center (line 3) as this pattern will be drawn in sections. Step 1 is the drawing of the back and Step 2 is the adding of the fronts to the sides of your back pattern. Your actual waist measurement will not be drawn on this pattern. This pattern is drawn for the actual shape (for comparing your work) before the decrease row at the waist.

Step One: Back

Line 3. Draw a vertical line, centered, the exact length of the skirt. Mark for the depth of border (line 2, optional) and the correct placement of line 5B. This varies between 7″ and 9″ from the hips to the waist.

Line 1. Draw a horizontal line the width of one-half your hip measurement plus 7″ (5″ for additional balance width and 2″ for ease).

Line 5B. Draw a horizontal line the width of one-half your hip measurement plus 2″ ease.

Lines 4. These lines are most important; retain their angle as you draw lines from line 1 to 5B and continue the slant for the needed length (to waist 5A). See Figure 245.

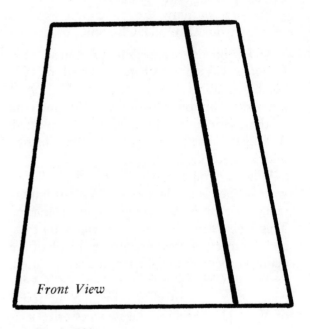

Front View

Figure 244. Diamond Classic Skirt.

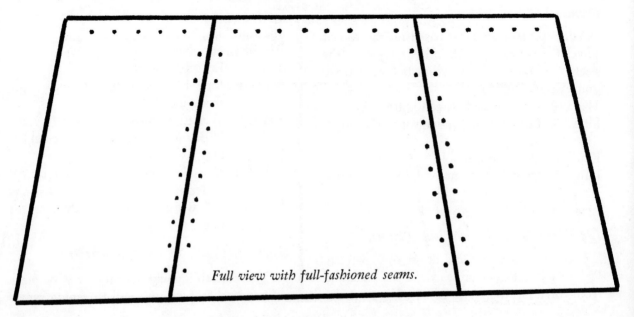

Full view with full-fashioned seams.

Line 5A. Will measure wider than your actual waist measurement. This will be detailed later.

Line 2. Optional. This line is drawn the same width as line 1.

Note: Border at the waist is not drawn on this pattern.

Step Two: Fronts

Before you draw the fronts onto your pattern, I would like to discuss the placement of the overlap. Each side is one-half the waist measurement plus 1″ ease. It is necessary to deduct one-fourth of this measurement or the overlap would reach the side seam. Refer to your measurements and see if this is exactly where you would like the overlap to fasten at the waist. Therefore, deduct this one-quarter from the measurement used to draw line 1 for the back.

Line 1. Back measurement, minus the one-quarter.

Line 5B. Deduct the one-quarter from the measurement.

Lines 4. Refer to back.

Line 5A. Complete the width of this line; see Figure 245.

Diamond Classic Wrap-around Skirt Details

Observe the diagrams and notice that the side seams are clearly marked (sides of back pattern). These lines (4A) are your guide for placement of decreases to form full-fashioned seams. See Figure 246 and refer to Chapter Eight. (If you do not wish seams, disperse decreasing.) The shaping of this skirt is very

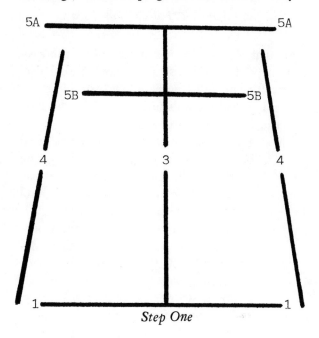

Step One

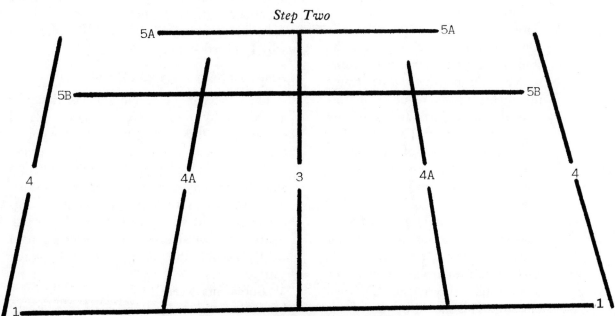

Figure 245. Diamond Classic Skirt.

199

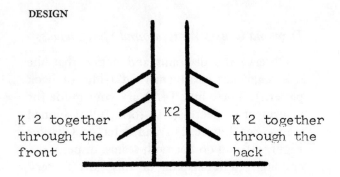

Figure 246. Full-fashioned seam.

K 2 together through the front

K2

K 2 together through the back

gradual for you do not want to lose the easy A shape. Retain the shape of your Visual Pattern for the full length of the skirt. The decrease row at the waistline will reduce the skirt to the desired measurement.

Line 1. Cast on or chain to equal Diamond Classic, refer to gauge and use gauge size needle. Start border stitch pattern (optional). Suggested : Round needle used as if it were straight.

Line 2. End of border. Retain width of border along the front edges. Start decreasing at the seams, and space decrease rows a minimum of ¼″ apart; do not decrease too rapidly. You *must* form a seam line and a gradual A shape. Continue this to the waist.

Line 5A. Care must be taken in your decrease row. Measure the back (between the seams) and your actual back measurement. Deduct this and determine the inches to be reduced. Transpose this to stitches and distribute the decreases evenly. This will insure the proper placement of the seams.

Fronts are decreased to one-half the waist measurement *minus* the one-quarter. This decreasing will create an easy, barely gathered look. Do not steam this out! If you do not want a border, change the needle size to two sizes smaller, work in the body stitch pattern for ¾″, then bind off. This should be turned un-

der and sewn. 1″ wide elastic or grosgrain ribbon may be used for inside belting; sew in concealed hooks to fasten the underlap and overlap.

Optional: Waistband is made in the stitch pattern, after the decrease row, on needles two sizes smaller.

AMETHYST TWEED

Knitting worsted at its best! Used imaginatively for a walking suit, casual and sparkling by day, glamorously elegant at night. While working in my studio, feeling the autumn breezes as they came through the windows and observing the brilliant hues of the dogwoods, tupelos, and pampas grass, I subconsciously designed an outfit that I have always desired. Tweeds in rainbow hues were all about me, enticing me to leave the typewriter. I finally compromised by writing during the day and knitting the outfit that I am going to share with you at night.

Amethyst skirt, sweater and cape were so luscious in a purple tweed that I also designed short, straight pants and a superb over-sweater. The frosting to Amethyst Tweed is a pair of gauntlets, scarf, and cloche. As you read the descriptions and detailing you will understand why I knitted away!

Amethyst Skirt (Figures 247 and 248)

The understated ease and grace of this skirt is created by four unpressed pleats, placed evenly apart, thus making it possible for you to vary the effect. The hem is a ribbed border, *K1—P1*, doubled under; this rolls gracefully and adds a barely discernible shape to the skirt. The lushness of the brilliant tweed was intensified by the stitch pattern that I selected. Amethyst Tweed came to life when I used #10½ needles and the Reverse Petite stitch pattern.

Measurements Needed:

Line 3. Suggested length: waist to mid-calf.

Line 2. Border depth: 2″

Line 5A. Waist plus 2″ ease (ease must allow for thickness of unpressed pleats) plus . . .

Pleat Allowance: 5″ for each pleat. There are four pleats, so this totals 20″.

Amethyst Skirt Visual Pattern

Prepare your paper by taping two pieces together for sufficient width. Note: This pattern does not show the waist border. Your pattern is one-half the width for comparison while working.

Line 3. Length and mark for accurate placement of line 2.

Line 1. Draw a horizontal line one-half the width of waist, plus ease and pleat allowance.

Line 2. Draw a horizontal line the same width.

Line 5A. Draw a horizontal line the same width.

Lines 4. Draw vertical lines representing side folds or seams.

Note: Seam allowance must be added when needed.

Amethyst Skirt Details

Line 1. Cast on or chain, refer to body gauge to equal Amethyst pattern doubled. If crocheting or knitting with seams, equal the width of pattern. Needle size is dependent on yarn and stitch pattern; if you plan to rib hem, use the size needle that will not contract the ribbing. (I used #7 29″ round needle with tweed worsted.) Work to . . .

Line 2. Change to body gauge round needle and stitch pattern. Ribbing is worked on an even multiple. Reverse Petite, on a round needle, must be worked with an odd number. I suggest using Row 2 of Petite. This is most important when using tweeds or bulk yarns. (I used #10½ 29″ round needle with tweed worsted.) Work to . . .

Line 5A. Bind off.

Amethyst Skirt Finishing Details

Press carefully. Double the hem under and sew loosely. *Unpressed Pleats:* Divide the skirt

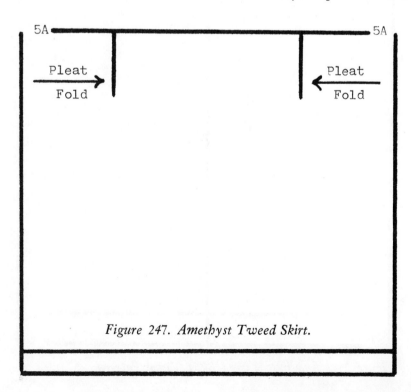

Figure 247. Amethyst Tweed Skirt.

in *exact* quarters, measure carefully, and fold 2½″ over at each quarter point, thus making four unpressed pleats. Pin carefully at the bound off edge and try on. Observe how the skirt may be worn front or back, or with sides to the front? Baste and sew securely along the bound off edge. If you have seams (press them on the wrong side), conceal the seams in the inner-fold of the unpressed pleats. *Skirt Waistband:* Use ribbing gauge round needle (#4) and pick-up stitches to equal waist measurement. It may be necessary to use a crochet hook at the pleating; you must go through the triple thicknesses. Ribbing is worked 2″ (match hem) and doubled under to form a casing. Draw 1″ wide elastic through. Elastic should be measured easily; do not make it too tight as it will affect the hang of your skirt. Do not press the pleats.

Amethyst Jewel Sweater (Figure 249)

The Amethyst skirt combined with this sweater is the answer to any occasion. The square neckline, the subtle fullness in the scanty, long sleeves and the blousing at the upper hips assures you of feeling casually elegant. The doubled ribbing is repeated at the hem, cuffs, and neckline.

Measurements Needed:

Line 3. Length from upper hip to underarm; allow for blousing.

Line 7. Back, length from underarm to 2″ below the neck. Front, length from underarm to 3″ (optional) below the collarbone, including border allowance.

Line 6. Length from underarm to shoulder with ease and seam allowance (line 5 to line 9).

Line 1. Snug upper-hip measurement. (Do not use waist measurement as sweater blouses over the fullness of the skirt.)

Line 2A. Loose bust measurement plus 4″ ease, minimum.

Lines 11 and 14. Sleeve length to 3″ above the wristbone; allow for blousing.

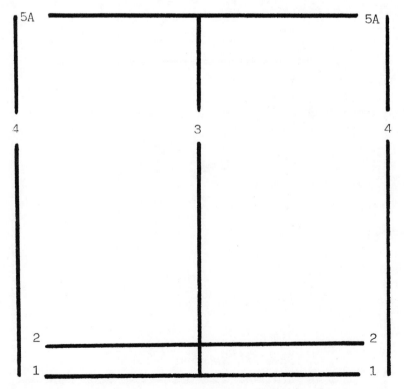

Figure 248. Amethyst Tweed Skirt Visual Pattern.

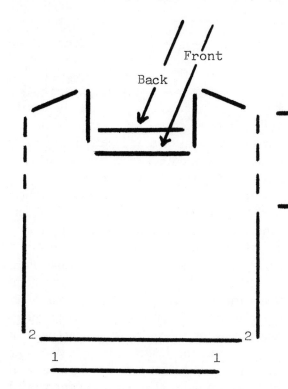

Figure 249. Amethyst Jewel.

Line 12. Length to 3″ above the wristbone. Width is two-thirds of line 6 doubled.

Line 13. Length to 1″ above the wristbone (cuff doubled) and the same width as line 12.

Note: Seam allowance must be added when needed.

Amethyst Jewel Sweater Visual Pattern

This pattern may be based on your Jewel or Delight pattern; refer to the previous measurements. Draw your patterns, front and back, with the square neckline, plus the 1″ border. Sleeves are drawn straight to the wristband.

Amethyst Jewel Details

Note: Suggested needle sizes relate to yarn and stitch pattern previously described.

Line 1. Cast on (refer to ribbing gauge) or chain to equal Amethyst pattern. Use straight ribbing gauge needles (#4) *K1—P1* to . . .

Line 2. IMPORTANT! Gradual transition from small needles to large, therefore, use #7 or #8 needle for increase row.

Space increases evenly apart to equal line 2A. On the next row, use 10½ needle and start the stitch pattern. Straight Needles: Reverse Petite. Round Needle: Refer to Amethyst Skirt. Other Details: Refer to Jewel and respective sections in this chapter.

Line 12. Gradual transition from large needles to small before decreasing is done on the next two rows; work pattern on #6 needles. This will prevent holes from forming when decreasing. The next row is worked on ribbing gauge size needle, continue Petite. Decreasing should be done on the right (Reverse Petite) side. You will decrease every other stitch, *K1—P2 tog*, thus reducing the width one-third (line 12). Ribbing 2″ to . . .

Line 13. Bind off.

Amethyst Delight

This is a luscious sweater with a deep cowl or shawl collar. The cowl is deep enough to be worn as a hood. The armholes are deeply squared, approximately 10″, and the front square neckline is deeper, see Figure 250. Refer to Delight and sections in this chapter for an incomparable sweater.

Amethyst Short Pants

Spiced Apricot Knickers Visual Pattern is used. Do not blouse at the knees, as these pants have a straight shape. Repeat stitch pattern and ribbing border. Work desired length.

Amethyst Cloche

Headband is a 3″ ribbing and the crown is Reverse Petite. Refer to Chapter Eleven.

Amethyst Scarf

The desired length, Reverse Petite, and ribbed borders or luxurious fringe.

Amethyst Gauntlets for Fun!

Refer to Chapter Eleven.

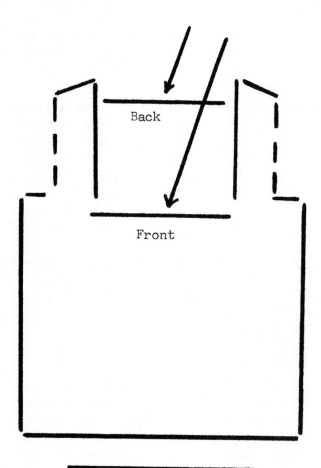

Back

Front

Figure 250. Amethyst Delight.

ABOUT CAPES

The pleasure, the luxurious, sensuous feeling that one enjoys when wearing a cape makes the knitting or crocheting completely worthwhile! Be lavish in your thinking and do not consider the yarn or time involved; just think about the joy and satisfaction that you will derive from having what *you* want!

You may have the best pattern and the most detailed instructions, but if you do not understand the why's and wherefore's it is unlikely that you would be completely satisfied.

You must constantly try your cape on as the texture and your body must be in complete harmony. Have confidence in your "eye" and you will be able to make constant judgments as to the fullness, correct placement of arm-slits, and the length. Plan on two long round needles, the same size, using them as if they were straight. (Do not join your work.)

Whether knitting or crocheting, the start would be based on a loose neck measurement, and the increasing formula would be eight stitches in one row, every other row, until your cape measures 6″ to 8″ (this depends on desired fullness) or the equivalent of a deep armhole, approximately 10″. Increasing may be done symmetrically, forming seams lines, or scattered. I prefer the latter and plan my increases to be as invisible as possible. As I proceed I mark each increase (or set of increases) with a small pin and am constantly aware of dispersing the placement. As you proceed you will appreciate owning a few round needles (same size) for they will enable you to distribute the stitches evenly, to work comfortably, to observe any flaw, and to carefully press your work. Pressing will be done in stages as this is the only way to have a true picture.

Reading this you are probably saying to yourself, "How easy! Why haven't I made a cape before?" It is at this point that I wish you to stop and think, as the best pattern or the most detailed instructions do not reflect *your body*. This simple approach has to be modified if you are small breasted as this affects the front length. Your body measures differently from the center neck-bone down than it does from the shoulder neck-edge to the same point as your arm. If there is a marked difference in this measurement I suggest short rows through the shoulders and then continuing all around.

After knitting or crocheting and pressing the first 10″ I would like you to study the folds, the fullness, and determine if you will continue increasing at the same rate, or diminish the increasing to every fourth row for the next four to six inches.

Determining the placement of the arm-slits is done on your muslin pattern when your cape measures approximately 10″ in length. Many proficient knitters are hesitant as to the proper placement, but by distributing your stitches on four round needles you will be able to make an accurate judgment. You will find that about two-thirds of the stitches become the back and that one-half of the remaining one-third becomes each front side. Do not skimp on the fronts; allow them to have soft folds. Each front should be on a separate needle; study your cape in relationship to the inside bend of your elbow. Determine if you desire an average (approximately 8″) or a deep arm-slit. Arm-slits are optional, but most functional, when making a full-length cape. The depth of the slit is determined by your full arm measurement, fully clad, and the ease desired, divided in half. An arm-slit is simply made by tying in another ball of yarn and continuing the row. Arm-slits necessitate three balls of yarn to complete a row. Understand that a minimum 2″ facing (casting on) is done on the fronts (slits) and the border is made on the back of the slits. Think about this: your arms come through and are against the front and your back is obvious to the eye.

You have now pressed the cape, decided on the placement and depth of the slits, and are able to judge the fullness. It is at this point that you will see that you have to gradually space your increase row further and further apart.

Do not abruptly cease increasing. Use the following approach: space the increase row eight rows apart for the next few inches, (assuming that you have been spacing them four rows apart), then twelve rows apart for another few inches, and then gradually increase with inches apart. Continue increase rows to the very hem.

If you are wondering why I have not emphasized comparing your work to your Visual Pattern or muslin pattern, it is simply because they may be your guides but they do not have the same texture and *weight* as your cape. The *constant trying on* of your own cape insures your success!

Decide on your border or edging before you start; considering your yarn and the use of the cape. As you work you will be joining in new balls of yarn. Do this carefully, and conceal the ends as you work. After drawing them through a few stitches with your crochet hook, carefully cut the end. Your cape should be just as magnificent on the wrong side. Do not hesitate to reverse it for a different look! There is nothing to stop you from applying trim to the wrong side!

We have discussed a full, rounded cape but that may not be the style you desire. It is very possible that you may wish a cape that gathers at the neck. This is very easy to achieve. A stunning cape may be attached to a long scarf! Decide on your full width (a minimum of three times your hip measurement), and work the desired length. Make your scarf. Gather the cape to the width you wish about your neck and sew securely; attach this to your scarf. Double your scarf over to conceal the stitches. An alternate approach is to cast on your loose neck measurement and to increase rapidly to the desired width in the next few rows.

A third approach to cape styling is to make a yoke and then to increase to the desired fullness in one row. The yoke would be made by increasing eight stitches every other row, until you have the desired depth and width; refer to previous details and Raglan Sleeves.

A collar or hood may be attached and the fastening of the cape may be concealed or be a definite focal point.

AMETHYST TWEED CAPE

One word describes this cape: fabulous! This cape is one tremendous curve, it swings about you and you may wrap it or put your arms through the slits. The ribbing completely encircles the cape.

Amethyst Tweed Cape Visual Pattern (Figure 251)

Double the width of your paper; the left edge is your center, line 3. You are going to draw a one-half view, using the measurements stated. Your first adjustment would then be in the width of the neckline; if you draw it wider, the one-half additional width would be added to your drawing (line 10). The second adjustment would be in length; draw your desired length (line 3). The third adjustment is the depth of the curve; it should be placed to conform to your length. However, your muslin pattern should be made full width.

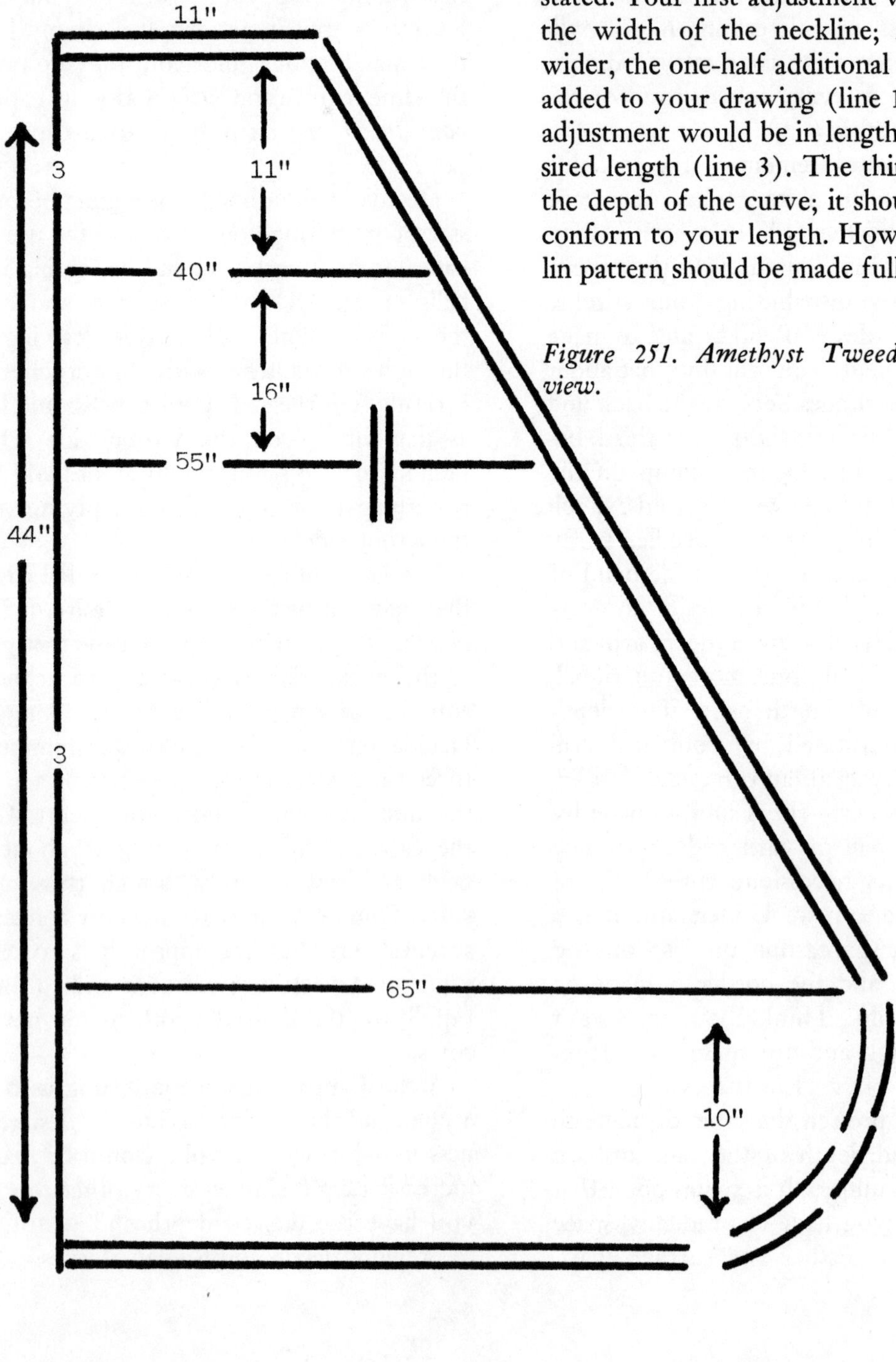

Figure 251. Amethyst Tweed Cape, one-half view.

Amethyst Tweed Cape Details

A smooth border is accomplished by using smaller double-pointed needles. I used #5 needles. (Size is dependent on yarn and the average size used.) This avoids any rippling. The *hem* is worked on one size *larger*, (referring to the tweed and Reverse Petite Stitch Pattern, I used #7 round needles.)

In making the Amethyst Tweed Cape, you must complete and press the neckline before determining exact placement of arm-slits.

Arm-slits

Fronts: Cast on stitches equivalent to 2″ and work in Reverse Petite or body stitch pattern for length of the slits.

Back Borders: Cast on stitches to equal doubling under (optional, not required if you are not doubling the border). Work the border width on the same size double-pointed needles as for the front borders; repeat border stitch pattern. (Border consists of stitches cast on and the number needed into the cape body.) Work the first and last few stitches on the back in the ribbing pattern for the width of the border.

On completion of the slits bind off the cast on stitches, omit the extra balls of yarn, and continue working the complete rows. My cape is mid-calf length; when I reached my knees I proceeded to decrease one stitch immediately after the border to create a curved edge to the hem. This emphasizes the roundness of the cape. (Optional)

IMPORTANT: Capes should swing with the illusion of a little more length through the back.

Neckline Finishing

This should be done when your cape measures 10″. Stitches are picked-up, corners are marked, and the neckline is ribbed with a square shaping. This ribbing should also be doubled under.

Cape Finishing

Neatly tack facing of arm-slits, double the ribbed edge of the slits, front borders, and hem. Sew carefully. Attach a concealed hook and make a matching eye using mercerized cotton tripled.

Note: Always use double-pointed needles (proper size for borders.) If you are a loose knitter use needles two sizes smaller than average.

Tip: Always run tiny stitches, using mercerized cotton, through borders ribbed along the fronts. This gives you an additional firmness without affecting the design. Retain the roundness.

Tip: When shaping curves while pressing, use common pins, a damp cloth, and steam. Shape gradually, allow drying time between pressings, and mold the curve.

DEEP PURPLE

Purple is a color that is most intriguing and mysterious, sparkling with clarity by day and mysteriously subtle at night. For years I looked high and low for just the right shade. I tried various blends and hues entwined but never found the jewel tone that I desired. Finally, I found it right under my nose, in my needlepoint basket, truly proving that one must not limit the search.

I plan to double the yarn and make a cape extravagantly edged with 3″ tassels. I will make dozens of them and place them 3″ above the hemline. My skirt will flare from my waist and be edged to match the cape. My sweater will be a tawny beige Tussah silk, loose and soft, with a scooped neckline. The sleeves will puff at the wrists and be piped with a loose wristband. Thanks to Jewel, this is so easy to achieve!

Deep Purple Skirt (Figure 252)

Measurements Needed:
Line 5A. Waist measurement plus ease.

Line 5B. Hip measurement plus ease.
Line   3. Length with border or hem.

Deep Purple Skirt

Line   1. Hem is three times the waist measurement. Optional: If flaring from the hips; use the hip measurement X three.

A flared skirt should be full and taper smoothly to the waist; the shaping should be uninterrupted as with Rosy Glow. Decreases will alternate as detailed under Rosy Glow. Decreases may be planned to be evenly spaced apart from the hem to the waist or, if you desire, from the hem to the hips, and then from the hips to the waist. This is very simple to achieve for you now know all the basics; success is yours!

Deep Purple Skirt Visual Pattern

Make your Visual Pattern, one-half view, plan the border or hem, and decide if you will add a waistband. Optional: Extra width to the waist. Refer to Diamond Classic, and decrease the extra width to waist measurement in one row.

ROYAL PLUM PEASANT SKIRT

A super skirt, shirred through the waist to the hips, just by tying your cords. (See Figure 253)

Measurements Needed:

Line 5A. Waist measurement plus ease (minimum 10″).

Line 5B. Hip Measurement plus ease (minimum 10″).

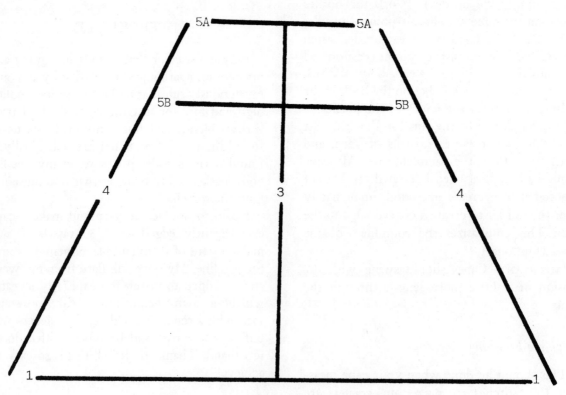

Figure 252. Deep Purple Skirt Visual Pattern.

Line 3. Length.

Decision: If more fullness is desired add 5″ to specified ease. Decide on border or hem. Suggested: Picquot Edging.

Royal Plum Peasant Skirt Details

Thin casings may be attached on the wrong side or . . .

Line 5B. Hip—a row of evenly spaced eyelets.

Line 5C. Mid hip—a row of evenly spaced eyelets.

Line 5A. Waist—a row of evenly spaced eyelets.

I suggest this skirt as an alternate to the Deep Purple Skirt. Refer to Deep Purple using the above measurements, or use the Amethyst Skirt Visual Pattern if you wish extreme fullness.

Finishing Touches: Crochet matching cords and attach full tassels.

Detailing the last three designs has been a joy, for I fully realize and appreciate the tremendous strides that you and I have made together. Truly, there is no greater joy than creating and sharing! With music, when one has the listener there is completeness; so it is with designing.

Figure 253. Royal Plum Peasant Skirt Visual Pattern.

CHAPTER ELEVEN

Accessories

Accessories! The opportunity to express imagination, versatility, and creativity. Creating your own original designs instills confidence and gives you the poise and assurance that shows you off to advantage.

For years women wanted to feel comfortable, look glamourous, and not be extravagant. Seldom did these goals go together. However, you can achieve this today with your handmade knits and crochets.

Handmade knitted or crocheted hats, scarves, belts, gloves, mittens, socks, and purses are the finishing touches that make for uniqueness and style. They are within the reach of your fingertips and can easily be made from an extra ball or two of yarn that you have discarded. Learn the extravagantly practical gesture—*always* buy extra yarn.

Match or contrast but make an accessory that will be an exclamation point! Experience a feeling of sophistication when wearing a deep cloche that is reminiscent of the twenties and drape your scarf, allowing it to trail, adding mystery and glamour. Knit or crochet brightly colored gloves or mittens, attach them to a thick, braided cord and wind them around your neck. Allow them to be your jewelry.

Think of lush, angora mittens as a purse, tuck in your lipstick, comb, and hankie! Have fun! Do the unexpected, but do not do the unexpected with everything. Allow *one* accessory to be your accent; allow nothing to overpower you!

A simple crocheted cord may be tied at your waist, under your bust, or low on your hips to create a new silhouette. It may be made in a tone to blend with your dress or shimmer from the glow of silver or gold metallic yarn. Make and hang a pouch or pocket on this cord. The very same dress, bloused above the knees and worn with spiral-patterned knee socks, will set the mood for a fun afternoon. Do away with pondering about length; wear the length that you desire for your mood of the moment. Allow no one to dictate style to you.

Match or contrast, but make a scarf with luxurious fringe. Sash your long, narrow scarf dashingly around your dress or coat, and if you wish, have a matching scarf about your head and shoulders. Sew pockets on your scarf; make a colorful half of a mitten or glove and applique it. Scarves in every conceivable shape and size may be used in a multitude of ways;

scarves oblong, triangular, or square. (The larger the square the better.)

Measure from shoulders to toes, and make a highlight of your wardrobe, a luxuriously fringed body-size wrapper! Wrap it about you from head to toe. Own the most elegant wrapper on this continent! Timeless and always stylish, whether worn casually with pants or provocatively with a dress. Shape and size are everything. Know the shape, size, length, and width, and how it will drape about you. Make your Visual Pattern and muslin pattern. Square is square, but think how many different sizes there are! And why make something and then not have it do! Get out your paper and yardstick; add to the width of the paper, do not limit your size. Look at the square and imagine it folded. Is it the right size? Make your muslin pattern, drape it, and study it. Eliminate any guesswork. Determine your yarn, stitch pattern, gauge, and trim, since with a little thought you will have perfection.

Top your outfit off! Make skull caps, cloches, bonnets, berets, and hoods. Skull caps that sit on top of your head, cloches that pull over your ears, bonnets that tie under your chin, berets that frame your face and soft, luxurious hoods to shelter you from the cold wind. All of these may easily be yours. For a dollar or two, you can make the hat that has been out of reach.

Learn to understand shape, texture, and the effect that you wish to achieve. Do you desire something luxuriously soft? If so, work with lush yarn. Do you desire a firm crown or brim? If so, work with yarn of consistency combined with a firm stitch pattern and smaller needles or hook. Tight knitting or crocheting, by itself, becomes firm and hard. Also consider using your yarn doubled. Once you understand shape, texture, and the desired result the choice of stitch pattern is easy.

Measurements Needed: (Figure 254)

Headsize: Your headband is your head circumference at the desired place. Fasten your

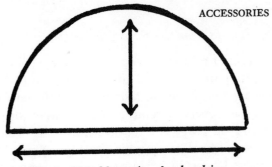

Figure 254. Measuring for headsize.

tapemeasure for accurate width. Write this down. Keep the tapemeasure on for . . .

Depth: With another tapemeasure, measure to the top of your head, allowing for your hairstyle.

Note: Measure for depth, while working, by placing the circle on your head and measuring to headband.

CONVERSATION ON HATS

The shallow crown becomes the skull cap; the deeper crown becomes the cloche. Have confidence, understand the shape that you are striving for; it is all at your fingertips! Do not be afraid to rip! If this is your first attempt at crocheting a hat; start from the top. Once you know how to crochet a flat circle you have opened the door to a complete collection. The size of the circle controls the style and size of the hat. The small circle (approximately 5″ to 6″) is the base for the skull cap, cloche, or bonnet. The larger circle becomes the beret. The larger the circle, the fuller the beret.

Note: Headband size remains constant.

The basic formula for crocheting or knitting the circle is: 6 increases to a round, 12 increases to every other round, or 19 to every third round. (The extra increase allows for the thickness of yarn that has accumulated in three rows.) Mark the beginning or end of each round. Exact instructions are impossible, since yarn and hook must be considered. Rippling is created by increasing too often in one round. Saucerlike shaping is the result of not increasing enough in one round. Learn by doing; allow your eyes to aid you.

Skull Caps from the Top: Crocheted

Refer to Crown gauge and chain about 5 loops. Join. Crochet 8 to 10 stitches into the center, not the loops, thus enclosing the chain. Increase every second or third stitch for a round or two. This is determined by your yarn and hook; keep your circle flat. You will gradually start to increase 6 stitches to a round; refer to the circle formula. When the circle size is reached; crochet evenly. This depth is accurately measured by trying on as you crochet. You will see exactly where you are. (With experience you will achieve the same understanding when making the hat from the headband.) Your cap will start to look like a saucer and then like an enlarged sock! You can trim with ribbon, beads, fringe, or knit a wide, ribbed band; there is no limit.

Skull Caps from the Headband: Crocheted

Refer to the required gauge (use Crown gauge if you are starting with the body.) Crochet the chain the needed length, join, and work evenly for the depth; try on. Reverse the circle formula (decreasing instead of increasing) for the top of the cap.

Skull Caps from the Top: Knitted
(Figure 255)

Four double-pointed needles, crown size, are used. Cast on 6 to 8 stitches and increase;

Figure 255. Skull caps from the top.

refer to circle formula. Increases may be dispersed or placed symmetrically; always consider the stitch pattern. Knit the circle and then knit evenly to the headband. (Headbands will be discussed later.)

Skull Caps from the Headband: Knitted

Refer to Headband gauge, stitch pattern, and proper size needle. (A 16″ round needle may be used until the decreasing requires double-pointed needles.) Cast on the required number of stitches and knit the headband. Change to crown needle, stitch pattern, and adjust the number of stitches for the measurement required. Work evenly, try on for accurate depth, and then make circle (reversing the formula). End your work by threading your yarn through a large-eyed sewing needle and drawing through the last few stitches. Fasten on the wrong side.

Cloche

A timeless classic! It is the basic skull cap made as deep as you desire and most striking when accented with a deep cuff. There is no limit to the imaginative treatments possible with this shape. Visualize it with matching or contrasting fringe; picture what this will do for your eyes!

Headband

This measurement is determined by the treatment. If you want it directly around your head, then that is the measurement. If you want it over the thickness of your crown, measure and allow for this. Headbands may be knitted or crocheted. A needle or hook two sizes smaller than crown size is usually used. The headband may be started by casting on, chaining, or picking-up stitches. Depth may range from 1″ to 5″. Ribbon or elastic may be used on the wrong side. A deep, ribbed, knitted cuff looks great on a crocheted crown and vice versa.

Ribbed cuffs become ribbed bands. You do

not have to attach a headband to a crown. Knit your ribbed headband about 3" to 4" wide in colorful tweeds for daytime and in metallic yarns for evening wear. They are delightful in cottons and linens for warm weather!

Make the same ribbed cuff, a few inches wider, and you have a waistband. Think of this worn with your Jewel and you have the look of tomorrow! Vary the depth from 4" to 7", and wear it with your shirts and full skirts. There is no limit to the colors, yarns, and stripes; a complete change with each wearing!

Bonnets

Knit or crochet your circle and then mark off the center back 3" with pins. Work rows back and forth to the pins; do not work the center back. Work the section for about 4" and try on. Edging may be knitted or crocheted; attach a matching chin strap. For a dramatic look, double crochet with silver or gold metallic yarn. Make the bonnet on the skimpy side, and encrust it with pearls, amber beads, or stones of your choice.

Berets (Figure 256)

Refer to Skull Caps from the top and circle formula, knitted or crocheted, as the beret is a larger circle and may be made as full as you wish. The beret may be gradually shaped by decreasing to the headband; this is the return. Or by decreasing in one row or two before the headband. Consider the depth of the return and the number of stitches to be decreased to calculate the number of decreases in each row. Decrease to headband size before changing needles and starting the headband.

Berets from the Headband

Refer to headband gauge and measurements. Cast on or chain the needed amount and join. Make your headband, change to crown gauge needle or hook and stitch pattern, and adjust the number of stitches for desired measurement. Increases are spaced evenly apart according to your calculations for the inches to be worked. When the return is completed, work in reverse, gradually decreasing to the center top. Fasten off as previously detailed.

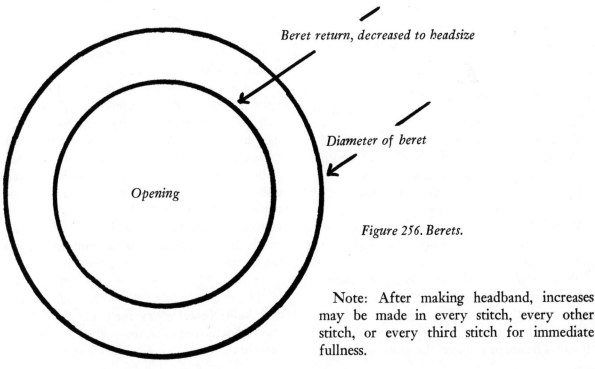

Beret return, decreased to headsize

Diameter of beret

Opening

Figure 256. Berets.

Note: After making headband, increases may be made in every stitch, every other stitch, or every third stitch for immediate fullness.

213

Hoods (Figure 257)

Measurements Needed:

Width: Loose neck measurement and tight neck measurement.

Depth: Depth of cowl to tight portion and neck area to chin.

Head: Refer to Hoods, attached.

What a joy—ribbed hoods, adaptable to any hairstyle, suitable for any occasion. A hood that molds over the shoulders, cuddles about the neck, and frames the face. The start is as full and deep as a cowl or loose turtleneck (ribbed on body gauge size needle), the neck is contracted (ribbed on smaller needle), and the crown is then shaped (back to body gauge size needle). Work to the chin and then bind off the center front for 4″, and shape each side by decreasing for approximately 2″ (shaped to mid-ear). Try on! Consider your hairstyle, and measure for the start of shaping at the center back. Decreasing is then done, in a seam line or at the seam edge.

Note: This hood may be made on a 16″ round needle or straight needles. If you are working with straight needles, the seam is at the center back. The depth of the shaping at the back is determined by the needed depth. Bind off and sew the seam. Edging around the face may be single crocheted.

Attached Hoods (Figure 257)

Measurements Needed:

Back Depth: From the center back at the neckline, to the top of the head. Add depth allowance for hairstyle and seam allowance.

Front Depth: From center front at the neckline, to the top of the forehead.

Width: From front of your ear, across the back, to the front of your other ear, with ease and seam allowance.

Shape your Visual Pattern using these measurements, and then draw a 2″ extra ease allowance around this shape. Think about this shape —is it full enough for you, the yarn, and the effect? The shape remains the same, although

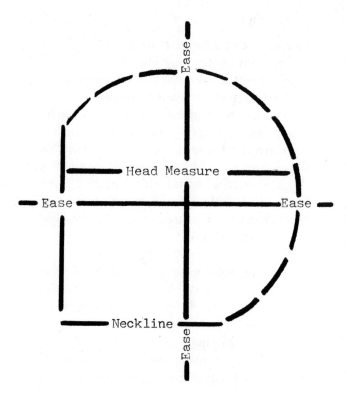

Figure 257. Attached hoods.

the size may be expanded in proportion. Study your Visual Pattern, consider all factors, and when you are satisfied, draw your pattern twice. Cut and pin together, and try on. Make a muslin pattern and, after making all adjustments, proceed.

Pick-up stitches around the neckline, plan your increase row for an even distribution of increases, and proceed to shape the hood. Shaping may be done by scattering increases through the crown or by making seam lines. Follow your Visual Pattern. Consider placing a stripe in a spot that is whimsical—around the neckline, down the back, vertically or horizontally—your pattern will help you to decide! Allow the designer in you to express imagination!

Ribbed Tubes

A valuable accessory for neckline or head; the full width of a turtleneck of an adequate length.

214

Mittens (Figure 258)

Measure carefully and make your gauge samples; know your gauge for wristband and mitten. Measure your hand, referring to Figure 258. I suggest a ribbing pattern for the beginner. The following directions are for the average size.

Cast 60 stitches onto #1 or #2 double-pointed needles. Divide by placing 20 stitches onto three needles; join. Cuff is *K2—P2* for about 3″ (optional). Change to #3 or #4 needles and work evenly for four or five rounds.

Right-Hand Thumb Gusset:
Round One
Needle #1—K1, increase in next stitch, K2, increase in next stitch. Complete round in ribbing pattern.
Round Two
Work evenly.
Round Three

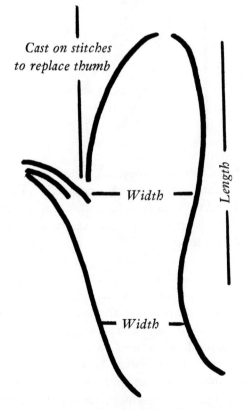

Figure 258. Mittens.

Needle #1—K1, increase, work 4 stitches, increase, work to end of round.
Round Four
Work evenly.
Round Five
Needle #1—K1, increase, work 6 stitches, increase, work to end of round.

Continue in this manner, increasing every other round, until there are 18 stitches for the thumb. (This is an example.) The size of your thumb averages one-third of your mitten.

On your next round, your thumb starts to be formed by: K1, slipping 18 stitches onto a pin or thread, turning, and adding 4 stitches to the K1. These added stitches, the 4 cast on, replace the thumb. Turn and work evenly to the desired length, minus 1″ or 6 rounds, for shaping the end of your mitten.

Mitten Shaping: Decreases are a multiple of 6. Decrease every other round. If your yarn is fine; decrease every third round. There are 5 rounds of decreasing; place them symmetrically. Weave or bind off and sew.

Thumb: You will now complete your thumb by slipping the 18 stitches onto 2 double-pointed needles and picking-up 4 stitches on the third double-pointed needle. Distribute stitches evenly among the three needles. Work the thumb length, minus 6 rounds. The tip of the thumb is formed by decreasing with a multiple of 4. Yarn is threaded and drawn through remaining stitches and fastened on the wrong side. Both mittens are worked the same if there is no stitch pattern. If you have a pattern; shape the left-hand thumb.

Left-hand Thumb: This is made by working to within the last 5 stitches of the round. The difference is that the thumb is made at the *end* of the round.

Gloves (Figure 259)

Gloves are fun! Use the odd ball of yarn that you have tucked away to advantage. The cost of handmade gloves in a store is astronomical!

215

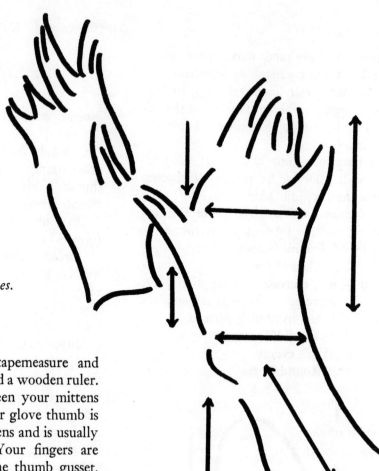

Figure 259. Measuring for gloves.

Measure widths with a tapemeasure and lengths with a tapemeasure and a wooden ruler.

The only difference between your mittens and gloves is the fingers. Your glove thumb is fashioned the same as on mittens and is usually started 1″ from the wrist. Your fingers are usually started 1¼″ above the thumb gusset. (At this point, I suggest the completion of your thumb.)

Gloves should be worked with fine yarn and small size needles. A gauge of 8 stitches to 1″ makes the best looking gloves. I will now give directions for the average size. Cast on 60 stitches, join, and *K2—P2* for wristband. Change to #2 needles for hands and knit; work evenly for a good inch. Try on; do not skimp! Form gusset as detailed under mittens until you have 16 to 18 stitches. Work one round evenly; place stitches onto a differently colored strand of yarn. (Safety pins can also be used.) Turn your work so that you are able to cast onto the K1 (at the beginning of Needle #1) 4 stitches. Turn, and continue knitting the 60 stitches that are divided among three needles. Fingers start about 1¼″ above the thumb gusset. Always work the thumb to completion. You will avoid any error in placing

your index (second) finger. You are now certain to start your fingers accurately. Fold stitches evenly in half. The exact side, center of the outside index finger, is exactly over the right increase of the thumb gusset (right hand). Fold for left hand is exactly over the left increase of the thumb gusset. If necessary, your index and third finger may be a little larger. For instance, 60 stitches, divided in half, become 30 stitches for front and back. Fingers would be divided: index 9, third 7, fourth 7 and little finger 7. This totals 30 stitches for one side and 60 stitches for both sides. For your finger gusset, cast on 2 stitches between the front and back. It may be necessary to pick up an extra stitch on each side of

216

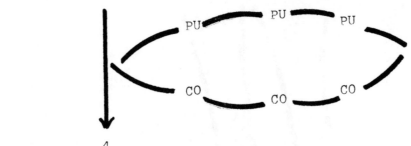

Figure 260. Gloves. Avoid holes by picking up a stitch in each corner. Decrease in next round, directly over increase, if not needed. Two stitches are always picked up where two stitches were previously cast on.

the cast on stitches. (Do this to avoid holes or loose stitches.) If you do not need the extra stitches, decrease exactly over them on the next round. (Figure 260.) IMPORTANT! Avoid holes when starting fingers: pick-up loose horizontal strand and work together with the stitch. Keep your finger joinings neat and tight. You will understand this when working on your fingers. Yarn must be tied in, carefully, with each finger. Work the desired length, allowing for the fingertip. Fingertips are shaped according to the shape of your fingers. Read thumb shaping; start with *K2, K2 together* and repeat, or start with *K1, K2 together* until there are 2 stitches left; fasten as previously detailed.

Second Finger from Thumb: (Figure 260.) Take an even amount of stitches from front and back as previously detailed. Finger gusset will now be formed. Pick-up two stitches exactly over cast on stitches of index finger, work stitches, and then cast on two stitches to bridge the gap between the front and back. Work this finger at least one-quarter of an inch longer, allowing for tip. Check your own finger measurements; try on.

Third Finger: Place stitches on needles, pick-up and cast on stitches for gussets as previously detailed, and work the same length as index finger. Refer to your measurements.

Little Finger: Place remaining stitches on needles, pick-up two stitches between fingers, and shape. Make the length, allowing for the tip.

Gloves may be made smaller by using smaller needles, larger by using larger needles. The basic concept is always the same. Pay attention to the length of your fingers, the width of your hands, and the gauges. If you desire snug gloves, use a ribbed pattern.

Understanding the construction of gloves and referring to a comfortable pair that you own are a great help. Crocheting gloves is no problem if you do not use too thick a yarn. Patience is synonymous with success.

Gauntlets

Gauntlets are stunning wrist-warmers, from 2″ under your sleeves to your knuckles. Make them ribbed or use narrow cables; use contracting stitch pattern.
Measurements Needed:
Length from knuckles to 3″ above the wrist-bone.
Width 3″ above the wristbone, wrist, and knuckles.
Gauntlet Details:
Use two sizes of double-pointed needles. The larger size is used at the beginning and end, the smaller size through the wrist. Mul-

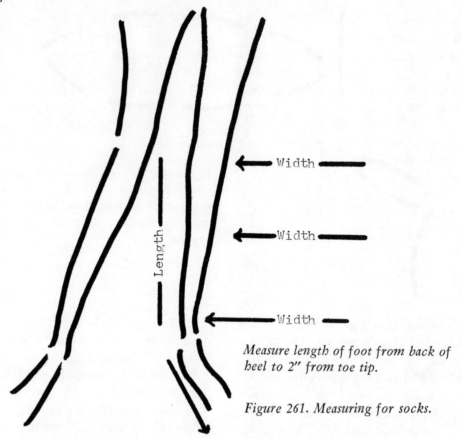

Measure length of foot from back of heel to 2″ from toe tip.

Figure 261. Measuring for socks.

tiply width X ribbing gauge; cast stitches onto larger size needles. Knit to wrist, change to smaller needles for about 2″ and then back to larger needles for needed length. Allow for contraction of ribbing. Bind off. Note: If change of needle size is not required; compromise by using the size between. Remember! Try gauntlets on as you knit!

Whimsical Touches

Miniatures have always been a collector's delight. Make your miniatures, crocheted or knitted, of berets, mittens, gloves, socks, and purses and hang them from your cords. Allow them to dangle at your waist, around your neck or at your wrists!

Knee Socks (Figure 261)

Knee socks in spiral ribbing without heels, in thin cables, and in colorful ribbing patterns are a valuable asset to one's wardrobe. Have fun

with socks, match them, stripe them, and utilize every scrap of yarn! Wash them properly, care for them, and they will last. Measure your leg, make your gauge samples and knit away!

The simplest way to have socks that fit is to own three sets of needles, graduated in size. Use the largest size for the thickest portions of your leg, the smallest for the cuff, and the middle size as you diminish the width towards the ankle. (The ankle area may require the smallest size and the instep the largest.) The number of stitches to cast on is derived by multiplying width X cuff gauge. I recommend a *K1—P1* ribbing. Use a larger needle to cast the stitches on, divide them evenly among three needles, and join. After making the cuff use a spiral ribbing stitch pattern; refer to Chapter Nine. Toes are shaped as with mittens. Another pair could be ribbed throughout *K2—P2*.

Humorous toes are shaped with one big toe

218

separation, contrasting the color of the big toe, or making separate toes as with gloves!

There is no limit to your stitch patterns and color combinations; any pattern is adaptable. There are several basic heel techniques and I suggest that you use the one that you are familiar with. If you are working with a soft yarn, strengthen it by doubling your yarn or combining it with mercerized cotton thread. Heels are often worked in the Stockinette Stitch, the pattern stitch, or a slipped pattern stitch. The width of the heel averages out to 40% or 2/5ths of your total stitches. Your back seam is the center of your heel. (Always mark with a pin.) I am going to detail two simple heels.

1. If you have 32 heel stitches and 40 instep stitches, do not work instep stitches until heel is completed. Place the stitches on a double-pointed needle or yarn.

    Row 1. Purl side facing you. Slip 1, purl across.

    Row 2. *Slip 1, K1*. Repeat from * across. Work these two rows for 2" to 2½".

    Turn: Knit half the stitches, plus 2 across = 16 stitches (this is an example), then K2 together, K1 and *turn*.

    Row 1. Slip 1, P5, P2 together, P1, turn.

    Row 2. Slip 1, K6, K2 together, K1, turn.

    Row 3. Slip 1, P7, P2 together, P1, turn.

    Rows 4, 5, etc. Continue in this manner, always having 1 stitch more before decreasing, and working the stitches on each side of the hole together. (You will easily understand this when the work is in your hands.)

Gusset: There are now 16 stitches (example) on your needle. K8 and then take:

Needle #1. K8 and pick-up stitches (14) along side of heel, 22 stitches on #1.

Needle #2. All instep stitches; continue pattern.

Needle #3. Pick-up stitches along the other side of the heel (14) and remaining (8) stitches. Note: The number of stitches picked-up along the side of a heel is determined by the length of the heel and the gauge.

Instep Shaping—First Round:

Needle #1. Knit.

Needle #2. Work instep in stitch pattern.

Needle #3. Knit.

Second Round:

Needle #1. Knit to last 3 stitches; K2 together, K1.

Needle #2. Work instep in stitch pattern.

Needle #3. K1, slip 1, K1, psso, Knit to end.

Repeat these two rounds until you have the same number of stitches as around the ankle. If the foot is wider, do not decrease to this amount, allow a few more stitches for the instep. Work this the length of the foot, minus 2" for the toe.

Toe—First Round:

Needle #1. Knit to last 3 stitches, K2 together, K1.

Needle #2. K1, slip 1, K1 psso, Knit to the last 3 stitches, K2 together, K1.

Needle #3. K1, slip 1, K1, psso, knit to the end.

Second Round:

Knit.

Repeat these two rounds until about 8 stitches are left. Leave a long strand for weaving. (Detailed in Chapter Eight.)

2. This heel has no gusset. Have your instep stitches either on a double-pointed needle or thread. Your heel stitches equal 40% or 50% of the total number of stitches. Have the purl side (wrong side) of the work facing you.

    1. You should always slip the first stitch of each row, whether knitting or purling.

    2. You should work 1 stitch less, each row, until the center 8 stitches are reached. End with a purl row. For instance: Heel = 28 stitches.

       Purl Side: Slip 1, P26, 1 stitch unworked, turn.

       Knit Side: Slip 1, K25, turn.

Purl Side: Slip 1, P24, turn.

Knit Side: Slip 1, K23, turn. Continue in this manner until center is 8 stitches with 10 stitches each side.

Note: This equals the 28 stitches. Your heel will have 8 center stitches with an even amount of stitches on each side. This is determined by the number of stitches you have for the heel. End with a purl row.

3. K8 stitches. Pick-up strand between the 8th and 9th stitch. Place this strand into the left needle and work it with the 9th stitch, thus reinforcing your 9th stitch. Turn.

4. Purl the 9 stitches. Pick-up strand between the 9th and 10th stitch. Place this strand onto the left needle. Work this with the 10th stitch. Turn.

5. Keep repeating this, always having one more stitch in each row, until you have worked all the heel stitches. End with a purl row.

6. You are now ready to resume work on all three needles. Work to toe. Directions detailed under Heel #1.

Alternate Toe: Count your stitches; reduce them to a count that is divisible by 7.

1. *K5, K2 tog.*. Repeat from * for entire round.
2. Knit. All even rounds are knit. (Determined by yarn.)
3. *K4, K2 tog.*. Repeat from *.
4. *K3, K2 tog.*. Repeat from *.

Continue in this manner until you have a few stitches left; break your yarn, run through the remaining stitches, and secure. Toes: The above methods or those detailed with mittens and gloves may be used.

Directions for socks cannot work without gauge, yarn, and needles being considered. If you are working with a fine yarn; you may have to work two even rows between the decrease rows when shaping toes. (This does not apply to separate toes.)

Socks may also be shaped by decreasing. Refer to Figure 261 and your measurements. Mark the back center stitch for the seam and place decreases on each side. (Use slant decreases; refer to Chapter Eight.) An alternative method is to decrease within the stitch pattern. Plan your decreases according to the inches to be reduced and worked.

Envelopes

Look at your stationery; think how functional it is. Neat, trim, and effective. What is better? Think of all the different sizes and shapes of envelopes and how versatile they are. Consider a long one, folded over, to become an attractive clutch. Roll out your brown wrapping paper and draw different shapes and sizes. Cut them out and fold them. Hold them. What feels the best in your hand? What shape would you like hanging from your belt? Imagine the shape, knitted or crocheted in metallic yarns, ribbons, or tweeds. Your Visual Pattern, gauge, and choice of stitch pattern are all that you need!

Purses

Pockets become hanging purses, whether flat or pouched, cans of any shape may be covered, and large shapes may be utilized to become the unique accessory within your pocketbook! Browse for antique frames, collect odd beads, and finger yarns, whether silken or of a burlap texture. Be adventurous, and you will be amazed at the new ideas that come to mind. Write down any idea, since the smallest thought may spark your creativity.

Creating your own accessories and setting the mood that you desire, allows you to express your everchanging personality.

Index

Accent stitches, 131–137
Alternate Weave, 114
Alternating Faggot, 118
Amethyst Tweed, 200–204
Amethyst Tweed Cape, 206–207
Armhole shaping, 158
Assembling crocheted garments, 95
Aztec Jewel, 169–170

Baby Left Twist, 108–109
Baby Right Twist, 109
Baby Twist Fabric, 109
Baby Twists in Both Directions, 109
Basket Weave, Double, 126–128
Basket Weave, Single, 122–124
Beads, 88–89
Bias Edging—Single Crochet, 137
Bias Strip Edging—Stockinette Stitch, 132–133
Binding off (crocheting), 92
Binding off (knitting), 81
Braid, 133
Brioche Stitch, 105
Brisk Autumn, 189
Broken Ribbing, 102
Buttonholes, 67, 86–87, 94
Buttons, 67, 94

Cable stitches, 110–111
Cable Strip, 133
Cape Code Minx, 189–192
Capers, 148–149
Caper's Jewel, 150–152
Capes, 204–206
Casting on (crocheting), 92
Casting on (knitting), 76–77
Chain stitch, 90
Chain stitch accent, 134
Cluster Border, 136
Clusters, 128–129

Cluster Triple, 136–137
Combined yarns, 83, 93
Continental Ribbing, 102
Cords, 95
Corner, crocheted mitred, 94
Crocheted stitches, 99–100, 121–137, 134–137
Crocheted garments, assembling, 95
Crocheting techniques, 89–94
Crossed Knitting, 97, 102

Decreasing stitches (crocheting), 92
Decreasing stitches (knitting), 78–79
Deep Purple, 207–208
Delicate Lace stitches, 125–126
Diamond Classic, 197–200
Diamond Lace, 120–121
Diamond Smocking, 117
Double crochet stitches, 91, 125–130, 134
Double Diagonal, 129
Double Shell, 130
Double Twist Rib, 109–110
Dropped stitch, 81

Edgings (crocheted), 93
Edgings (knitted), 87
Emerald, 172–176
Eyelet Rib, 120

Fasten off (crocheting), 93
Finesse, 106–107
Flat Ribbed Fabric, 113–114
Fragile stitch, 118
Francesca stitch, 129
Francoise's Twist, 108
Fringe, 87–88

Garter stitch, 97, 100
Gathers, 107–108
Gauntlets, 217–218

Gloves, 215–217
Gracefully Yours, 171

Half-double crochet stitch, 91, 125
Hats, 211–213
Heather Classics, 146–148
Hemming stitch (sewing), 68
Hems, 85
Hoods, 214
Horizontal Ridges, 106
Hot Chocolate, 169

Imperfections in yarn, 83
Increasing stitches (crocheting), 92
Increasing stitches (knitting), 77–78

Jewel Coat-dress, 57–63
Jewel Shell Caftan (Semibateau), 152–155
Joining yarn, 82–83, 93

Knee Socks, 218–220
Knitted Pleats, 108
Knitted stitches, 97–99, 100–121, 132–133
Knitting techniques, 77–89
Knitwise, 79
Knots in yarn, 83, 93

Laburnum Stitch, 120
Lace Faggot, 117–118
Lace patterns, 99
Ladybug stitch, 105
Leaf-like Couplet, 122
Length of pattern, changing, 143–146
Lingerie straps, 85
Lining, 67–68
Little Couplet, 122
Loops, crocheted, 131
Loop Trim, 135
Luscious, 179–182
Luscious Loops, 116–117

Midnight Delight, 42–57
Midnight Jewel, 24–40
Mildred's Couplet, 115–116
Mittens, 215
Moss Stitch, 102
Mother's Favorite, 105–106
Muffy's Tiny Bell Lace, 118–119
My Favorite Lace, 119–120

Necklines, 155–158
Needles, knitting, 84–85

Ombred yarns, 83–84
Onyx, 192

Pearl Drops stitch, 114–115
Petite stitch, 112
Picking up stitches, 80–81

Picquot Edgings, 135
Picquot Fabric, 124
Picquot Hem, 132
Pistachio Whip, 57
Plaiting, 85
PomPons, 88
Purling, 77
Purlwise, 79
Purses, 220

Quaint Lace, 120

Reverse Petite stitch, 113
Reverse Stockinette stitch, 97, 100–101
Ribbing, 97, 102, 104
Ribbon, 84
Ribbon edging, 66–67
Ripping out stitches, 81–82
Ripples, 115
Rosy Glow, 182–188
Round, crocheting a, 92, 94
Royal Plum Peasant Skirt, 208–209
Ruby, 188–189
Running stitch (sewing), 68

Sapphire, 192
Scallops, 136
Shell edging stitches, 134–135
Shimmering Autumn Leaf stitch, 126
Shoulder shaping, 93
Simplicity stitch, 125
Single crochet stitches, 90–91, 121–124
Skirt waistbands, 66
Sleeves, 35–36, 158–169
Slip knot, 89–90
Slipped Ribbing Fabric, 113
Slipped stitches, 79
Slipped Stitch Ribbing, 102
Slipped Stone, 114
Slip stitch, 92
Space-dyed yarns, 84
Spiced Apricot, 192–197
Spiral Ribbing, 104
Stockinette stitch, 97, 100
Stripes, 45
Swirl, 176–179

Tassels, 88
Teardrops, 104
Tiger Eye, 192
Tiny Favorite, 119
Topaz, 171–172
Triple crochet stitches, 91–92, 130–131, 135
Triple Diagonal stitch, 130–131
Triple Shell, 130
Turning post, 90
Twisted stitch patterns, 108–110
Twisted stitch variation of stockinette stitch, 97, 102

Van Dyke Lace, 121
Vertical Ribbing, 106
V Fabric, 124
Visual pattern key and symbols, 21
Vivacious, 172

Waistbands, 95
Washing, 74–75

Weaving stitches together, 85–86
Woven Couplet, 116
Woven stitches, 111–112

Yarn over, 79–80

Zippers, 66

Francesca Parkinson lives in North Falmouth on Cape Cod, in a house which she and her husband remodeled from a tumbledown wreck in the midst of a briar patch into a charming home in a beautiful natural setting. (All of the photographs in this book were taken on the grounds and in the home of the Parkinsons.) The interior of the house is enhanced by needlepoint, petit-point, and bargello works that she produces when she is not gardening, knitting, crocheting, sewing, or writing. Her husband, Bobby, is a talented amateur photographer and an art collector, and one of her two sons is an oceanographer at nearby Woods Hole, and the other an investment counselor. She is founder and president of the New England Backgammon Club and plays internationally.